THE ADVENTURES OF
Pioneer Women

The Adventures of Pioneer Women in New Zealand is a selection of stories and anecdotes which reveals a challenging and often dangerous way of life on the frontiers of old New Zealand. Here are women writing of the voyage to New Zealand, making do in early settlements, and as pioneers in the bush or in the mountains of both islands.

These stories include women of many backgrounds, sometimes alone, often with families and responsibilities to discharge in primitive conditions. Their adventures include floods and snow storms; crossing wild rivers and untracked mountain passes; settling in wild places and making sea journeys; living through the New Zealand wars. There are tales of heroism and natural disaster, of conflict and friendship.

Many of these stories are published here for the first time, culled from old diaries and reminiscences. Others come from popular early writers like Lady Barker and Mrs Godley. These stories, largely told in the first person by the women themselves, will warm the hearts of many New Zealanders, proud of their ancestors and the spirit with which they built their new homes and lives.

SARAH ELL who compiled this collection is descended from several pioneer families who settled in Nelson, Marlborough and Canterbury from 1842. She trained as a journalist with the *Auckland Star* and now works in publishing.

Selected by SARAH ELL

Published by THE BUSH PRESS

THE ADVENTURES OF

Pioneer Women

IN NEW ZEALAND

from their letters, diaries and reminiscences

This edition published 1992 by
THE BUSH PRESS OF AUCKLAND

(c) Introduction , notes and selection
    Copyright, Sarah Ell, 1992
    Copyright, G.C. Ell, 1992
(c) Photographs copyright, as recorded.
(c) Bush Press Communications Ltd, 1992

Printed in Hong Kong through
Bookprint Consultants Ltd,
Wellington, New Zealand

Published by THE BUSH PRESS,
4 Bayview Road, Takapuna, Auckland
Bush Press Communications Ltd
P.O.Box 33-029, Takapuna,
Auckland 9, New Zealand

ISBN 0-908608-61-6 (Limpbound)

Title pages: Viewing Whakarewarewa, Rotorua, Alexander Turnbull Library

Farm at Matamau, 1880s.
E.R. Williams Collection, Alexander Turnbull Library.

Contents

Acknowledgements

The compilation of a book like this places its editors under many obligations, in particular to the descendants, publishers and trustees of those whose stories are told. The publishers and compiler wish to thank those whose assistance and permissions make this collection possible.

In particular, we thank the Alexander Turnbull Library of the National Library of New Zealand for the considerable contribution from the Manuscripts and Archives section. A substantial part of this book has been drawn from manuscript records held in their care. Thanks are due for permission to reprint excerpts from the diaries, letters and reminiscences of Eleanor Adams, Jane Maria Atkinson, Elizabeth Pringle Caldwell, Caroline Chevalier, Elizabeth Colenso, Rhoda Carleton Coote, Jane Findlayson, Sarah Harris, Elizabeth Holman, Sarah Louisa Mathew, Maria Morris, Amy Paterson, Eliza Rachel Jean Stack, Mary and Ellen Taylor, Catherine Henrietta Elliot Valpy and Marianne Williams. The complete citation of these documents is given at the end of this book under 'Sources of the Adventures'.

We thank the following publishers and copyright holders for permission to reprint material, again cited in full in 'Sources of the Adventures':

Penguin Books (N.Z.) Ltd for material formerly published by Whitcombe and Tombs and Whitcoulls, and extracted from *Tales of the Golden West* by 'Waratah', Whitcombe and Tombs 1906; *Tales of Pioneer Women* edited by A.E. Woodhouse, published by Whitcombe and Tombs Ltd, 1940; *Letters from New Zealand by Charlotte Godley*, edited by J. R. Godley, Whitcombe and Tombs 1950; and *Lights and Shadows of Colonial Life* by Sarah Amelia Courage, Whitcoulls 1976.

Longman Paul Ltd for permission to excerpt from *My First Eighty Years* by Helen Wilson, Pauls Book Arcade 1950.

Independent Newspapers (Auckland) Ltd for the interview with Caroline Ngoungou originally published in *The Sun* Auckland, 27 July 1929.

The source of photographs is acknowledged alongside each picture. The Pictorial Reference Service of the Alexander Turnbull Library led us quickly to useful images of pioneer women. The Canterbury Museum and the Hocken Library were also helpful. The National Museum and Art Gallery is the source of the cover photograph. The compilers thank the Librarian at Independent Newspapers (Auckland) Ltd for permission to copy an historic photograph, and David Lowe of Auckland for further pictorial material. Many pictures come from the compilers' family library of nineteenth century material, originally made available by Mrs Cynthia Ell of Christchurch.

Our work in locating references and original records, encountered during the research phase, was made much simpler by the Alexander Turnbull Library's bibliographic publications *Women's Words* and *Victoria's Furthest Daughters* which descriptively catalogue much of the unpublished and published heritage of writing by pioneer women.

A number of public and institutional libraries were helpful in locating material, in particular the Auckland Institute and Museum, Auckland City Art Gallery, Auckland Public Libraries and Takapuna Public Library, the Canterbury Museum, and the Hocken Library at Otago University.

In the selection and compilation of these tales we received considerable help from Ruth Ell and Fiona Ell who joined in the task of reading in search of interesting adventures.

S.K.E. and G.C.E.   TAKAPUNA 1992

A NOTE ON THE EDITING

Much of the text of this book has been taken directly from transcripts of pioneer diaries, letters and reminiscences. Where spelling has been distractingly erratic or misleading the obvious corrections have been made to the manuscripts, much as the editors of the previously published work must have done with that material before publication. The style of expression, however, has been left in its original form, without benefit of editing for clarity, and consequently the text sometimes reflects idiosyncratic fashion while retaining the charm of the original.

Generally, Maori words in the text have been allowed to stand in their contemporary form but with the occasional addition of modern placenames and spellings in parenthesis where this helps to place the story less ambiguously.

Two of the authors were given to writing without punctuation, so a minimum of Capitals and Stops has been introduced to make the reading simpler. Such changes are noted in the introductions.

Distances and areas are given in their original Imperial form, with a mile equal to 1.6 kms and an acre being 0.4 of a hectare.

INTRODUCTION

About These Adventures

The pioneer women of this book tell their own stories. Their tales are culled from old books and manuscripts. The idea behind the selection is to show the range and variety of pioneer experience and give some idea of the adventurous spirit that required.

The common thread is that of people in an unfamiliar country coming to terms with new circumstances and generally making another life. There is high adventure, such as being captured by the Maori or withstanding a great storm. There is also adventure of a more domestic kind, adventures of the mind and spirit, such as in the realisation that the English past is no longer helpful and that a new way is needed by settlers who wish to succeed. Thus there are the women who must throw away their caste assumptions and enthusiastically enter into trade, and those who adopt roles traditionally reserved for men. From these experiences comes a picture of the kind of spirit required of the first European settlers and how they began to forge the traditions which we value as New Zealanders today.

The book is organised into five departments, giving varying dimensions of the colonial experience and containing differing pioneer responses. Pick and choose from each as you please, for each episode is self-contained, or savour each contrasting aspect through the progress of the nineteenth century. 'First Contacts' serves as an introductory experience; acknowledging strangers in a strange land. 'The Voyage Out' contains accounts of the longest of emigrant journeys from Britain, 25,000 kilometres by sailing ship, a life testing adventure in itself, to which all classes were exposed. 'Pioneering Life' presents a broad perspective of life in various settlements about New Zealand, with pioneer women coming to terms with new land and new roles. 'Explorations' probes into the interior of New Zealand with pioneer women who enjoyed the challenge of travel and discovering Maori society; 'Conflict with the Maori' deals with that uncomfortable, oft-hidden part of our history, when settler and Maori fought Maori for the title to land: here are some women's adventures in a land at war. 'Natural Disasters' realises the worst fears of people living in the 'shaky isles' as pioneer women experience the extremeties of nature. In counterpoint to the theme of this collection, 'Different Paths' contrasts four vastly different lives and experiences born of pioneer conditions.

This collection presents material largely to entertain and inform; for readers to make their own conclusions. Hopefully, the stories here will reawaken memories of family traditions and perhaps lead to their wider circulation. If it were not for the wealth of personal material lodged by New Zealand families in libraries of record much of our heritage might have remained only in official versions; surviving only as Government records, or as second-hand reports and their analyses by academics. Here, people speak for themselves.

Selection has involved choosing the more interesting, better told tales and giving them just sufficient introduction for the reader to place them geographically and in a context of each authors' experience. The reader can extend a particular interest by going to the sections 'Sources of the Adventures', 'List of Authors' and 'Related Reading' which lead to a broader knowledge of each writer's background and other writing. Many of these women wrote fascinatingly about other aspects of pioneer life; this brief was to publish the accounts of women facing a peculiar challenge of pioneering in New Zealand. Such writings would, hopefully, illuminate the spirit of the pioneers and enrich an appreciation of their contribution, at a time when it can be fashionable to deprecate their values.

Often the recollections are uncomfortable. Not simply because some deal with the sensitive areas of race relations and the assumptions of our ancestors over the land and its ownership. In fact, it is refreshing to find that many of the pioneers were as uneasy about the motives of authority and others in taking land from the Maori as modern historians. Rather, the diaries and letters, often reveal a hard-headedness, a hard-heartedness even, which fits uneasily with the present conscience. The quality of nineteenth-century life on the frontiers of New Zealand demanded an unsentimental outlook among the successful pioneers, whatever romantic values our vision now ascribes to the Victorians.

In trying to reflect the range of class and circumstances of immigrants, there are some difficulties representing the so-called working classes in their own words. While literacy among our pioneer generations is said to have been higher than in their British homelands there is still a paucity of material from the likes of domestic servants and others in service jobs. There is some fine writing from the well-educated and privileged women, such as Lady Barker and Lady Martin, works which for their grace and interest have survived as popular accounts of the past into present times. On two occasions we have had to use secondary accounts of the adventures of women who by their own confession could neither read nor write, though their voices still live through the "as told to" approach of their chroniclers. Where, however, are the unsung songs of those who found no chronicler; how diminished is our heritage by their misfortune?

Most New Zealand families with their roots in the pioneer period have an oral history of their traditions. The 1990 Sesquicentennial and the consequent local celebrations have aroused a new consciousness of the pioneer past and the trend towards preserving and publishing family records must further help to fix our beginnings. When oral traditions are relied on as the only reference to the past, it is easy to reconstruct the stories to suit the fashions and judgements of each succeeding generation. In this way we have largely buried the experiences of the land wars and reinterpreted events to the point where we can comfortably live on that very land. It is only by looking back on the ferment of contemporary ideas and the political conflict which accompanied them, that it is possible to appreciate the motives and varying consciences that led both races through this uncomfortable phase.

Here are the voices of pioneer women, brave, enterprising, inspiring yet often disturbing and discomfiting. They speak directly from the past. Their words are printed largely to enjoy but there are echoes along the way which may also provoke and challenge the conscience and consciouness of many New Zealanders.

Next pages: Nikau whare in the bush, 1865, Alexander Turnbull Library.

Canterbury Pilgrims landing at Lyttelton from the ship Cressy. *From* Canterbury Old and New 1850-1900.

First Encounters

At the Mercy of the Maoris, 1824

Marianne Williams stepped ashore in the Bay of Islands in 1823, 14 years before the accession of Queen Victoria, and barely 60 years after Captain Cook 'rediscovered' New Zealand in 1769. She was then 29 years of age, married to the Reverend Henry Williams, and the mother of three small children. She has been described as intelligent, gentle and well-educated, with an unbending will . She would need all these qualities - and her reported bravery. There were few Europeans in New Zealand in the 1820's compared with the Maori population, and the new land a long way from home and not yet under the protection of the British Government.

Samuel Marsden, who had established New Zealand's first mission station at Rangihoua almost ten years earlier, set up a new mission at Paihia and installed Henry Williams at the head of it. Almost immediately Marianne began her work: the education of not only her own children and those of the other missionaries, but also the local Maori girls, to whom she taught reading, writing and household duties. The family occupied a two-roomed raupo whare, in which they were living when they found themselves at the centre of a dispute, just months after their arrival.

This excerpt from her letters, held by the Alexander Turnbull Library, reveals the risks of misunderstanding between different cultures. When a chief demands utu *or repayment for an injury to his person, Marianne Williams sees a different circumstance and places her trust in the Lord.*

Marianne eventually raised 11 children, eight of whom were born at the Paihia Mission Station, before her death in 1879 at Pakaraka, some 15 km inland from Paihia. Several of her children continued in the missionary tradition, including Samuel, Catherine (who married Octavius Hadfield, the first priest to be ordained in New Zealand) and John.

January 1824

After dinner, a most troublesome chief named Tohitapu, who lives about 2 miles from us, put us all in confusion. Mr. Fairburn who was at work at the beach saw him coming, and had the gate fastened. Instead of knocking in the usual manner for admittance, the chief sprang over the fence, made of tall thin poles. Mr. Fairburn told him he was a tangata kina, a bad man, and that it was coming in like a thief tangata tihi, and not like a gentleman, rangatira to climb over the fence. He immediately began to stamp and caper about like a madman, attracting all round him by his vociferous gabble, and flourishing his mere, a weapon of green stone, one of which they every one of them have, concealed beneath their mats, and brandishing his spear, with which he would spring like a cat and point at Mr. Fairburn apparently in real earnest. Henry upon joining them told him his conduct was very bad, and refused to shake hands with him. The savage (for so he did now in every truth appear), stripped for fighting, keeping on only a plain mat, similar to those worn by the girls. Henry and Mr. Fairburn beheld his capers with great coolness. At length upon their leaving him he sat down, to take breath, and upon their going down to the beach, he went out. Engaged with the children indoors I did not hear all that passed - Mr. Fairburn went over to the island: and Henry returned when, as he told us afterwards, he saw some mats, and wearing apparel, apparently thrown down in haste, which he imagined to be Tohitapu's, and putting them outside shut the door, and went to the newly erected blacksmith's shop, at the back of the shop. Shortly after, this furious man ran up from the beach and snatched up a long pole, with which he shoved at the door. But it not yielding to his violence he again sprang over the fence, resumed all his wild antics, and when Henry appeared, crouched and aimed his spear at him. Henry advanced, and the savage, trembling with rage, did not throw the spear. He said he had hurt his foot with jumping over the fence, and demanded a payment for it, and a great deal more, which Mr. Fairburn being absent, we did not understand. Henry told him, it was very good for him to hurt his foot with jumping over the fence, but that he should have no 'utu' payment. He walked towards the store, and having snatched up an old iron pot, in which pitch had been boiled, for the utu, was springing back towards the fence. But being retarded by his unwieldy burden, he made for the door, when Henry dashed upon him, snatched the pot out of his hands, and set his own back against the door, to stop his retreat, and called to someone, to take away the pot, which Tohitapu made several attempts to snatch away, at the same time brandishing his mere, and his spear over Henry's head with furious gestures, while Henry folded his arms, with a look of determined and cool opposition, only resisting his sudden grasp upon the contested pot, and occasionally shaking his finger, telling him to beware or exclaiming Gently sir, that is enough. As I looked through the window, with no little feeling of trepidation, I thought the scene resembled a man, who attacked by a furious wild bull, steadily eyes the monster and keeps him at bay. The blacksmith now came forward and snatched up the pot. Tohitapu still flourished about, and then began to prepare for fight, in a way which I can hardly describe. The agility of this huge man astonished me. He would run to and fro with his spear in his hand; something like a boy, playing at cricket, except that the New Zealand warrior danced sideways, slapping his sides, and stamping with a measured pace and horrid gestures, every now and then stopping or crouching down, beating his breast and panting as if trying to excite his own rage to the utmost. Mr. Fairburn came back, as he sat down, and they had much talk together. Tohi demanded his utu and said he should stay today and tomorrow and 5 days more, and he should make a great fight, and tomorrow, ten and ten and ten and ten men, holding up his fingers as he spoke would come, and set fire to the house, and burn the store. Henry and Mr. Fairburn when they could edge in a word replied in Maori 'What care I for that? A great deal of talk....' During prayers he was more quiet seated at the back of the house. His wife and some other women were looking in at the windows and one or two chiefs sat in the room. Tekoki was absent at Kaoakaoa. After prayers, Tohitapu came to the window and without any ceremony put one leg in, pointed to his foot, and demanded the utu for the little blood that was spilt. Henry told him to go away and come again tomorrow like a gentleman to knock at the gate like Tekoki and others, and he would say How do you do Tohitapu and invite him to breakfast. He answered, that his foot was so bad, he could not walk, repeated his intention of staying here many days, of burning the house etc and after talking some time again, working himself up into a terrific passion, and again stripped for fighting. It was now about eleven o'clock - and by the imperfect light he looked like some wild animal, capering about in mad frolic. Our friends looking in at the window, frequently one or the other called me 'Eh moder - Arimai - Come, tomorrow you see a great fire in the house, O yes, the children dead, all dead. A great many men. Plenty of muskets. A great fight'. Henry now came in and desired me to go to bed, closed the windows, and left Toru with strict orders to keep watch and in case of any outrage being committed to give the alarm. The friendly chiefs wrapped themselves in their shaggy mats and went to sleep upon the wood and bundle of poles - while we were preparing for rest, Tohitapu began to chant or yell a horrible little ditty, which Mr. Fairburn said was bewitching us, and this poor victim of superstition imagined he could by this means, put us to death. We were awakened early by the noise of Tohi and others, who were continually arriving until our premises were surrounded. Before breakfast Henry had been obliged to turn him out of the yard by main force, because of his having taken up in his rage, a young kid. At breakfast, I made a cup of tea for each of our friends: and having a curiosity to see how he would act upon it, we sent a tinpotful outside to Tohi, who sat on the ground in sullen majesty, surrounded by a number of his followers, who had assembled for the fight. We saw him through the paling, drink his tea, and I hope it would have proved a cooling draught. But he was soon again prancing about, inside the yard, with many other warriors, all hideous figures armed with spears, hatchets and some few muskets. They looked more formidable to me, as I caught occasional glimpses of them and listened to their overpowering jabber, feeling that Henry was in the midst of them, than if I had seen the whole. Our native girls were all out, and Mrs. Fairburn and myself were close prisoners, with our windows blocked up the whole day by ranges of native heads, looking in. I became soon so tired of them, that I ceased to be amused by their remarks. We were excluded from pure air, in an intensely hot day, and compelled to inhale a great deal of impurity. The poor children began to pine for air and liberty, and about 5 o'clock Henry came to the bedroom window, and said things were more tranquil, and many of the people dispersing. I put on the children's things, and passed Samuel and Marianne through the window. But scarcely had Marianne's feet touched the ground, when a sudden noise was heard of loud strokes apparently against the outward end of the store which appeared like chopping a breach in the wooden walls to force an entrance. Henry bundled the children in, headfirst, and ran to the spot. The noise and clamour became very great. A chief brought Edward in his arms, crying and looking pale and frightened. I asked where he was hurt. The poor child exclaimed No, mama, I am not hurt, but they are going to shoot the house and kill papa. I saw the men. I saw the guns. Marianne immediately screamed, Oh papa, poor papa, they will kill papa! As I sat in centre of the bedroom, the infant at the breast, and the three others clinging round me, I saw through a window, a man point a gun at the house, apparently making a rush to enter, and Henry step in between. My feelings were now completely excited. Yet I felt such elevation of soul, as is worth much suffering to possess even for a few moments. Oh that we did not so soon drop down to Earth again! The dear children, sobbing and crying, fell on their knees, and repeated after me a prayer prompted by the scene. The noise continued. They repeatedly shook our frail walls, but the house remained unbroken, and the children grew more calm. Edward said, he liked to say, Jesus 'thou our guardian be, Sweet it is to trust in thee'. He should like to say it for a month, and then, when the fight came again, he could pray to himself and he would pray the great God to make these poor creatures know him, and then they would leave off fighting. He would then repeat my words to Marianne and tell her a woman, and four little children could do nothing, but they would pray to God, and he would keep the people from hurting poor papa, that it was not the natives we ought to be afraid of (for they could not keep us out of Heaven, even if they killed us) but we should be afraid of sin. Marianne and Samuel soon began to be troublesome, trying to get to the windows and look out. But Edward's lesson continued. I told him, many of the natives were our friends, who would try to save Papa. Mama, exclaimed the child, what frightful creatures our friends are! Apo at length put up her good-natured face, telling me in her own language that there would be no more fighting today and that *she* had been making a great fight for us. Edward told me that he saw Aden taken a gun out of a man's hand, which was a fact. I gladly unbolted the door for Henry to enter: who told, that it was all over and that this second tumult was quite distinct from the first.

Tohitapu had remained quiet during the whole scene, rather inclined to side with us. In compliance with the united request of our friendly chiefs, Henry had given him the disputed pot, as a reward, with which he had departed. It seems that in the course of the day, the son of one of the chiefs, who came as our friend, stole a blanket, out of Mr. Fairburn's bedroom window. Some of the people charged him with it, unknown to us: and he took this mode of revenge for their exposure of his conduct. They were driven from their attempt to enter the window, forced their entrance through the door of Mr. Fairburn's room, and were mastered by our people and driven out. Poor little Betty Fairburn, had a narrow escape. These wild creatures passed and repassed over the poor little thing as she lay on the doormat which she had fallen over in her fright, while her mother had run to the baby. Several groups of natives sat on the ground outside the house. The little entrance room was full, and as many as room could be made for, inside the sitting room. Poor things! The worship in which they saw us engaged was nothing to them, but not so the rum and waters, which Henry afterwards handed round. They all talked of the great fight which was to take place on the morrow, and expressed their determination to sleep around us for our protection, as on the former night. In the morning Wednesday, all seemed quiet. Our friends began to drop off, to our great relief. But just as breakfast was begun, the boys and sawyers ran up from the beach, exclaiming that the fight was coming, that a friend of Tohitapu's was coming in his war canoes, to demand an 'utu' for the injury to his friend's foot. A general scramble ensued to preserve our property from depredations like those committed on the preceding day. The fowls (of which several had been stolen) were caught and locked up in the canoe, the pots and kettles carried into the storehouse (for we still cook out of doors). Aden...put the linen again in soak. No fight however arriving, things gradually reassumed their usual course: Henry went to Kerikeri: and in the afternoon we were again to our great joy in peace and quietness.

Next pages: Aboard an emigrant ship, 1850s, Alexander Turnbull Library.

The Longest Journey

The Longest Journey

The 25,000 km sea voyage to New Zealand was known as 'the longest emigrant journey in the world', and by its very nature - ships full of strangers sailing halfway round the world without fresh supplies - it sometimes attracted the title of 'the worst emigrant journey' as well.

Voyages varied in duration, but most took around three months. The ship Oamaru, on which one of these writers, Jane Findlayson, travelled out to New Zealand, made a fast passage of 83 days. Yet some emigrants, including a group of the first New Zealand Company settlers travelling to Wellington on the Adelaide, spent almost six months on board. The ships did not usually make a landfall between Britain and New Zealand, and often no land was sighted for months on end. Most travelled south off the coast of Africa before turning east round the Cape of Good Hope and riding the Roaring Forties to approach New Zealand from the south. This route brought a range of conditions, from equatorial heat and the delaying calms of the Doldrums to icy snowstorms in the Southern Ocean. While many passengers soon gained their sea-legs after several days on board, some suffered from mal de mer for the entire voyage.

Settlers travelling to New Zealand were divided into two classes, cabin and steerage, dubbed by the New Zealand Company 'colonists' and 'emigrants'. The cabin passengers made the voyage out in comparitive comfort and style, but conditions in steerage were fairly primitive. Living arrangements were cramped and there was little privacy. Despite the privations, steerage passengers often worked hard to stay relatively clean and tidy, and they were adequately fed - in some cases better and more regularly than they had been before leaving Britain. Although deaths at sea feature in three of our shipboard extracts, each ship had its own surgeon and those that died on the voyage were mainly young children and women during or after 'confinement'. The total mortality rate for emigrants in 1856 was said to be slightly over 1%: 0.37% for adults and 3.31% for children.

These extracts chronicle four different experiences of shipboard life: Charlotte Godley and 'Hopeful' are both cabin passengers, while Sarah Harris and Jane Findlayson had a rather more basic voyage out.

The Voyage Out

Charlotte Godley arrived at Lyttelton, then known as Port Cooper, eight months before the founding Canterbury Pilgrims in their First Four Ships. Her husband John Robert Godley was Chief Agent of the Canterbury Association, organisers of the New Zealand Company settlement on the Canterbury Plains. With a two-year-old son, Robert, they sailed from Plymouth in December 1849 aboard the Lady Nugent.

John was to oversee the construction of facilities for the planned settlement and manage the company for a term of three years. Charlotte described the building of Christchurch and the social life of the new colony in a series of letters to her mother, subsequently published for private circulation in 1936. Their value as a record of pioneer life led to their publication in 1951 as a Canterbury Centennial Edition under the title Letters from Early New Zealand by Charlotte Godley 1850-53. *The excerpts here include adventures on the voyage out and some lively comments on early Dunedin.*

January 7th, 1850
Latitude 7°9'. Thermometer 78°.

My Dear Mother,

We are now getting near the latitude for meeting the homeward bound ships, so we are getting letters ready. I do hope we shall meet one, but, of course, it is only a chance; however, I wish a good deal that we had an equal one of hearing from home. I wonder so much how you are all getting on, what you did at Christmas, etc. What we did was to sight Madeira; all the afternoon it was visible, though a long way off; but we were getting on very fast then, and in the morning there was nothing to be seen. I believe so far we have hardly made an average passage, we had such a very bad start. We left Antonie, as you know, after luncheon on Wednesday, December 12th, and got on board just before dark, and remained that night in Plymouth Sound. We sailed the next morning at about 11, and in six hours the wind came dead against us, and on the next Tuesday morning we were still not thirty miles from Plymouth, and the wretchedness of those days is not a thing to be lightly spoken of. Arthur, Powles and I were all *terrassés* at once, and I think I was the least ill of the three, for though Arthur was not so bad at the time and slept a good deal, he has not recovered the effects of it still, and looks so thin and wretched, though he is certainly better this last week. But he feels the motion as much as I do, and that is whenever it is the least rough.

My husband was very sick for two days, but his throat got perfectly well from the moment he came on board for a fortnight; now it is rather troublesome again, for we have had some hot, heavy weather, and he is not the better for it. Our stern cabin is a great comfort in this weather, as it is always airy; at first it was like sitting with the window open and no fire, and that is pretty cold at sea in December, but it will be a great thing for us now.

Please tell Aunt Jane how very acceptable the cloak was, although I cannot think of it with any coolness to-day, within eight degrees of the Line. We have had some lovely sunrises and the stars are very beautiful, but I am sorry to say we have lost the Great Bear now, which seems quite a part of home. No sharks yet, but the lines are out for them to-day. Arthur had a flying fish for his dinner on Saturday, to his great delight. It flew on to the deck, poor little thing, and the Captain made him a present of it. We have had quantities flying about for the last three days and they are beautiful little creatures, but quite small, only about eight inches long. We have seen a few of Mother Carey's chickens, too, and some shoals of porpoises. But the prettiest thing is to sit on the deck at night quite at the stern and watch the track of the vessel; last night it was like three wreaths of pale green smoke (one from each side and one from the rudder) studded with showers of bright stars. The Captain says there will be more of it, too, soon. We like him very much; he is extremely civil to us and almost too good-natured to everyone in the ship.

We are also lucky in our fellow passengers. There is only one lady, Miss Borton, quite young and rather pretty, though neither aristocratic nor very bright; but then, poor thing, she too has had a headache almost ever since she came on board. Then we have Mr. Tollemache, who sits next me in the cuddy at dinner, and who is going out to see his property in New Zealand, £15,000 worth; and he has in his suite three maids and a family whom he is helping to emigrate, whose name is Bradley, with five very naughty, dirty children, so that when Arthur cries it is the fear of being like Master B. that stops him quickly. Then we have Mr. Bulkeley, cousin to Sir Richard, going out to New Zealand to join his regiment, the 65th; Mr. Nicholson, who has just left Oxford - his father is some rich man near Leeds - and he is our chaplain; Mr. Robison, who though only about twenty-four, has been a merchant at Calcutta, and tells us Indian stories and experiences of former voyages; and a smart young Mr. Lee, one of many brothers, going out as a settler; Mr. Wakefield, only son, who is 'aide de camp' to my husband; and a Mr. Elliot, who knows all about everything but is careless about his h's and is taking out a steam engine. The Doctor is unsuccessful, as he gets very tipsy; and that is all, except the first mate, who is also *chief cabin*, a perfect likeness of Keeley and a very good seaman. There is a Durham

Canterbury Museum

cow on board going out to improve the New Zealand breed, so we get a little good milk morning and evening, but we are very glad of all our stores, beef tea, oranges etc., not forgetting the eggs, which turned out very well and have been most useful.

We have quite determined, if possible, to stop at Port Cooper instead of going on to Wellington and having to come back in three months, perhaps a fortnight's voyage in a wretched little coaster, and we hope to find things a little prepared if the October ship, by notice of which our journey was sent, has made a good passage. We are quite agreed that in spite of the phosphoric light, etc., and flying fish, any place on land will appear charming and luxurious. I can hardly conceive that you can all have a large tub of water morning and evening if you like it. Salt water is very inferior when you get it alone.

We are now in a pretty fair breeze but afraid every moment of its dropping; this is just the place for calms. Five degrees further down and the worst will be passed; in latitude 2, the breezes sometimes begin again. To-day we have opened a lottery for the time that we are to cross the line. The thermometer is today 78, in our cabin, and it is not so hot as Paris, but then of course the breeze keeps us cool so far. We are not to consider it hot till the seams on the deck begin to melt. We wake every morning before six with the pump for washing the decks and then the gentlemen all go up on deck to have buckets of water thrown over them; then the breakfast is at eight-thirty, but I have mine in the cabin; dinner is at three and tea at six, and I have that too in the cabin, and we go to bed pretty early, as between sea air and lying awake when it is rough (which Arthur does *not*) we get pretty sleepy. The worst weather we have had was on the Sunday night after we sailed, which even the Captain said was a *perfect hurricane* and seemed very frightful to me; our foretop sail was so torn that the sailors have been mending it every calm day since. I cannot bear to think how long it really must be before we get any letters and I wonder so what you are doing and how Sara is getting on and whether you all went to Stokesley; perhaps you are there now.

We had an arrival on board of a little lady passenger this morning, all very successful and the doctor very sober. Sara must manage to let us hear by the February ship. If you get this in time would you if you please send us out the Quarterly and Edinburgh Reviews for December and January and we should be very glad to have them always sent to us as they come out. Also by the first ship that is convenient will you send me eight yards of black silk, *galon* they call it in Paris, something between braid and ribbon, it is half an inch wide at least; and a piece of the narrow black silk braid such as you use for braiding with. I should be very glad too of some new books for Arthur, those he has are in such constant use here as he cannot play about when it is rough; and two new dissecting puzzles, as they call them, would be very valuable. We have got three on board, The Queen's visit to Ireland, Robinson Crusoe, and the Life of a Ship, each of which he sets up about three times a day, and he can do them quite alone, unless the ship is rolling very much.

I hope everyone will be merciful and write very much to us. We find that we cannot (as we meant to do) write a bit every day, it is only on very smooth ones that our head can stand it; I thought for a long time that I never should be able to do it at all. William, I must say, has been quite a treasure to us, *always well* and willing; he is our housemaid, and Arthur's cook, and seems very happy, especially as nearly half the emigrants are Scotch. There is one little German with a *Bath pianoforte (or Organ ?)* which he plays on festivals, and the rest of our music is composed of a mild flute and two still much milder violins.

January 9th

The breeze is over. We were woke before four on the morning after I wrote last by a thunderstorm and a squall, and then the wind went all round the compass and disappeared. The lightning was *very* vivid and *such* rain, but the rudder and its chains rattled so at our heads that we could hardly hear the thunder, and then we had a day's rolling in heavy swell and no wind, which brought us *headaches*, and a *little* shark. I have seen dog-fish quite as large, so that I was not much excited, but this morning we had a big one on our hook several times, but not caught, and two smaller ones, not four feet long, caught.

This is a beautiful, hot day, but still a *little* breeze, thermometer about 81, by the aneroid Tom gave my husband, Latitude 5° 13' at noon, and it has been really beautiful, all the day, to see the sharks playing about, with the pilot fishes all around them, down in the deep blue water under our stern windows. Arthur in delight, as you may suppose, and we each *tasted* a bit of one broiled, and very nasty we thought it. Mr. Tollemache took up one head after it had been off ten minutes and tried to frighten one of the children with it, but instead he got a good bite on his own thumb to the great amusement of the spectators, as he is the mildest and most benevolent of men, though rather eccentric. He never ventured on to the poop deck till two or three days ago as he thought he might go overboard, though it is fenced nearly all round with hen coops. He has shaved his head and *lives* quite with his three maids and the emigrants. We have five vessels in sight today, but all their heads go the same way as our own.

January 11th

We are still going on much as usual, only little puffs and squalls which are by degrees pushing us down. Yesterday the *Persia* came so near that the Captain and some more came on board. They are going to Ceylon, touching at the Cape, and so my husband sent a letter to his father enclosed, open, to Tom. She is just our size. While I am writing the *Maid of the Mill* is passing at a great rate, bound to Buenos Aires, which is very tantalizing as there is just enough wind to make it impossible to put down a boat, or it would have been a very good chance for us.

January 12th

We have now come up again with the *Maid*, and now in a calm, so my letter had better go, and I shall begin another, in case of meeting still with one homeward bound. Arthur is much better, and hopping about in only a shirt and white pinafore. It is piping hot, and now Goodbye. Yours ever, with much love to everyone. Aunt Anne would be quite amused if she knew how often Arthur has asked to go to her and Mrs. Frost. I shall direct to Sara as I am not sure where you will be. How I wish I could change places with, or get into my letter.

The Lady Nugent *was 112 days at sea from Plymouth to her first landfall at Port Chalmers, Otago Harbour. Charlotte writes of calm and storm and shipboard concerns. Their best speed is 240 miles in 24 hours. They sight the Cape of Good Hope but do not touch land, sweeping along the Roaring Forties, to approach New Zealand from the South of Stewart Island. There, in the vicinity of the Snares Islands, they are again swept up by a storm.*

Lady Nugent.
Latitude N. about 2o50'.

March 23rd

IN SIGHT OF NEW ZEALAND! but we have now had a real storm, and I should be very glad indeed to think that I should never see another. It began on Sunday the 17th, and in the afternoon we had our dead lights put in for the first time and we are still in darkness. Monday was rough, but nothing wonderful, and the two next days the same; on Thursday the wind blew very hard, and, high as we are out of the water, we were inundated even in the cuddy, great waves splashing quite over the side of the ship; and the land being due next day (Friday) the Captain got rather anxious. We had a quiet night, and some sleep, and then another sudden fall of the barometer promised another gale of wind which accordingly began after breakfast, and very beautiful the sea was when I went up about noon, to see it. The spray was blown from the top of each wave till the whole sea looked like a snow storm, white with foam. We must then have been within 100 miles of land, but it was very thick; and as we had not seen land, to prove the chronometers, for three months, it was enough to put the Captain rather in a fidget; especially as the gale increased, and the barometer was falling rapidly. There is a reef called the Snares about 40 miles south of Stewart Island, and our course ran between the two. We would have hove to, but did not dare, there was such a heavy sea on, for fear of the decks being swept, as she came round; so there was nothing for it but to go on running, which we accordingly did. All day long the wind increased, and at five in the evening the barometer had fallen one and two-tenth inches (to 29.03") in thirty-six hours. Suddenly then, the wind came round to the southward, and blew a regular hurricane; the chief mate told us afterwards he never knew it blow harder in all his experience; and the worst of it was that it blew dead on shore, and that the land according to our calculations could not be above fifteen or twenty miles to leeward. So you may imagine that we had to carry on, and take our chances of the ropes and canvas standing, instead of taking in all the sails and letting her drift, as we should have done if we had plenty of sea room. We carried a close-reefed foresail and maintopsail all night, expecting them to go every minute, but they held on, and consequently so did the ship, and we made little or no leeway. About twelve, the wind moderated again to a whole gale; the glass began to rise as soon as the hurricane came on, and though there were some tremendous squalls until four-thirty, we felt the worst of the danger was over. At day-light the Captain, calculating that he had well weathered the Cape, hauled up to the northward; there was a rumour of land at six-thirty, but it died away again, and at eight o'clock the mist cleared off a little, and there was *land* sure enough on the *larboard bow*. A most welcome sound, as you may suppose, for poor creatures on an unknown coast, in heavy weather, after being obliged for two days to take the observations by guess work, and without much faith in the accuracy of the chronometers which indeed proved wrong by about thirty-three miles, which was enough to make a very serious difference.

To complete the sadness of the whole scene the evening before we had the death of the poor steward. He was an oldish man of colour, and very trustworthy and useful in the ship, though not pleasant to the passengers, and we were none of us very fond of him. On the Thursday before dinner he fell down, and went to bed, as we all thought, tipsy; early next morning they tried very much to wake him, and at last sent for the doctor, when it turned out he was in an apoplectic fit, and his assistance came too late. All

Charlotte Godley, frontispiece from her Letters.

day long and through the storm he was lying in his berth at one end of the cuddy perfectly unconscious, and at night he died. With him lying groaning in sight of us all, and the raging of the storm, and the ship pitching and rolling, and shaking all over, I shall never forget the horrors of that evening. I did not undress, but sat up nearly all night trying to read. My husband slept but badly even in his cot, which he has found a perfect receipt for sleeping well through all other rough nights. Arthur never woke. The next morning however was very cheering; the gale sunk to a breeze, and though still a high sea, and bitterly cold wind, we had sunshine and land well in sight, and then we buried the poor steward.

I do not know whether it was the effect of New Zealand air, or the unlovable properties of poor *Ia* (the Steward) but we certainly none of us felt the sadness which I expected must follow a funeral at sea. And the afternoon was intensely exciting, with a fair wind all day; we ran up the coast at a great pace, and such a lovely mountain range as the sea view I never saw. It made me think of Wales, of course, at every yard, and there were several *Roseberry Toppins*. Nothing though quite so fine as Snowdon, except one snowcapped hill which we did not reach that day. We came up within two miles of the shore with a sunset of golden haze covering the new land and if we had had two hours more of daylight might have anchored that night. However that was not to be, and the Captain was obliged to be cautious, as we had no one in the ship who had ever been on the coast before. In the night we lay to, and then drifted too far to the northward; the breeze freshened, and kept us beating about all Sunday the 23rd, and on Monday we had another gale, almost if not quite as bad as the Friday before, only then we knew where we were. Tuesday, we were all up early and in great spirits, with a fair wind blowing straight into the harbour, and at noon in we came, at a great pace. The entrance is very narrow as there are sand banks, covered at high water, which run nearly across the Bay. But it is *so beautiful*. It is eight miles from the point up to Port Chalmers, which is a little bay in the harbour, and there *Lady Nugent* is now lying, in a perfect nest of beauty, and as snug as a ship can be.....

Charlotte first stepped on New Zealand soil in Dunedin, so the founders of the Canterbury settlement had an early chance to observe the manners of the Scottish settlement at Dunedin, founded by the Otago Association in 1848.

From Dunedin the Lady Nugent *took the Godleys on to Port Cooper (now Lyttelton). Affairs there dictated they move on to Wellington to consult with the Chief Agent of the New Zealand Company, William Fox. They spent six months there before they returned to Canterbury to await the arrival of the First Four ships.*

The harbour of Otago is eighteen miles long from the flag staff at the entrance to the town of Dunedin (as you know, the old name for Edinburgh) which is the nucleus of the settlement. Port Chalmers lies about half-way up, and there wooded islands seem to shut the entrance any higher, and at present ships do not come beyond it; but with a pilot they may come up several miles further. The Captain, with his papers, rowed off to the town as soon as we had anchored, and returned in the evening with Captain Cargill, the New Zealand Company's agent here, who came 'to pay his respects' and to press us most kindly to come up and stay with him at the town until the ship is ready to sail again; which we were very glad to do, as it is a most disagreeable time to spend on board, and almost all the people about constantly drunk, in a little place like that, where our arrival is quite an event. We find the ship that sailed about a fortnight before us has not yet been heard of, so that Captain Thomas at Port Cooper knows nothing of our coming out. But we hear there is a great deal more going on there, in road-making, etc., than we had yet heard of in England. However I believe it is settled that we now go on straight to Wellington for about two months.

I must tell you though that I am writing from Dunedin now on Easter Eve! We came up on Wednesday, in a little open boat, wind and mist dead against us, a most uncomfortable sail of nearly five hours, and are now located very comfortably in a weatherboard house, the front half of which came out as it is from England. It consists of six rooms, three bedrooms, a pantry, kitchen, and sitting room, in which I am now writing, and it is a very comfortable abode for anywhere. It is weatherboard all round, but coated with single brick at the windy end, and rough cast, and the inside is *lined*, or as we should say panelled, only roughly done, but with a pretty coloured wood, something like very dark box, which takes a very good polish, if anyone had time to rub it at all. Quite an old fashioned fireplace with dogs for burning wood (but there is coal eight miles off when they have time to fetch it); a grand pianoforte, a brass inlaid clock, red twill curtains, and at least a dozen pictures in large gilt frames! Captain and Mrs. Cargill landed here with the first settlers, just two years ago, and lived at first under canvas on the beach, under heavy rain, for three weeks, with two sons and three daughters; and very rough work it must have been, but he is an old soldier and used to such things....

It seems curious to me to come across such a different set of people from those I have been used to. Captain Cargill is a funny looking little old man with a *very* large head covered with thick upright white hair, that has been red, which also forms a white frill under his chin. He is Presbyterian, and Free Kirk, and talks broad Scotch.... I should think them a very nice family, but it seems strange to be with people who do not even know when

Easter Sunday is; though Mrs. Cargill calls herself Episcopalian, all the others are Free Kirk.

The situation of the town is of course very fine, at the head of the harbour, which opens out wider; but it looks rather bare and new, the clearings leave stumps and bare burnt branches, but it will look very different when good grass, etc., has time to grow, and the walks all about are most beautiful. There are perhaps 120 houses in the town, mostly of weatherboard; a little kirk, two butchers, three bakers, and other shops in proportion. I must say it is wonderful to see the progress made in two years, and the place looks about as grand as *Ysputty* [town in Wales], only the houses are all new and made of wood and further apart; and out of them come such smart ladies and gentlemen, what with lawyers, and doctors, and surveyors, and go-to-meeting clothes on other classes - there are heaps of them.

Indeed the black spot in Dunedin to me is the state of society there. There is a Scotch and an English party, and half of them will not visit the other half, or approve of anything that is done. I believe it is so more or less in all small communities, and here *Scotch* and *English* of course makes a capital ground of offence. The whole place is at sixes and sevens, and I am a good deal alarmed at the idea of what may be my own fate at Port Cooper, being mixed up in anything like the same state of things; but I hope it may be possible to keep out of it.

Caricature of Captain Cargill on his way to the first General Assembly from The Old Identities.

SARAH HARRIS

Confinement at Sea

Only four letters remain to tell of the early colonial experiences of Sarah Harris. Sarah and her family arrived in Taranaki in 1841, on one of the first New Zealand Company ships, possibly the William Bryant. *Although the new settlement of New Plymouth had a striking physical setting, the lack of both adequate land and a natural harbour slowed the development of the town*

The Harris's, too, had a shaky start to their life in New Zealand. They were ashore barely a month when fire destroyed their raupo whare. Sarah's husband Edwin, a surveyor, lost all his instruments, and most of the family's clothes were burnt. As most of the settlers had none to spare, Sarah was forced to use a little colonial ingenuity and make new garments out of the charred remains. These clothes, including cloth shoes for the children, made do until new ones could be sent out a year later.

Off the shores of Taranaki
April 20th 1841

Dearest Father and Sisters,

As it is doubtful whether you received my letters sent by a ship bound for New York which passed us on the 31st December I will again say something about our voyage. The weather with the exception of a few storms was as fine as it could possibly be and the Emigrants taken altogether very good sort of people, plenty of provisions, and very steady Captain (*very reserved*) a good mate and steward and kind to us, and an orderly set of sailors; the surgeon read prayers on Sundays and did it very respectably. I had my fears about the latter person who I thought very indifferent and inexperienced in his profession, but I was wrong, he certainly was forgetful. The weather was very warm before and after crossing the Line and dear Corbyn suffered much from it. He was taken ill about the 7th December of a slow fever and continued very ill for more than a month. I was fearful he would be starved as he did not eat anything for 8 or 9 days, but it was favourable to the disorder; as soon as he was better, baby was so ill as to cause everyone to think she would not survive the voyage, and I was from my own illness obliged to give her up to the woman who attended me all the time, she proved a mother to her. Before my confinement I felt very unwell for some weeks, I wanted the frequent doses of Castor Oil as was my custom in England, but from the scarcity of it on board I could not have it, and as I was induced to take two pills Emmy gave me marked strong aperient it brought on diarrhoea from which I suffered violently for 8 days and the surgeon said nothing but bringing on the labour would save my life. In less than an hour after a fine little child was born. My illness continued, the ninth day after everyone thought I was dying. Two women remained with me at night, and on that night Mr. Weeks gave me up. About the middle of the night the nurses sent for him I felt as if I was going fast. I prayed I might be restored and by the mercy of the Almighty I was so. The surgeon gave me Port Wine with a little water, I was very ill for a month and during the time we lay in Cloudy Bay I was too ill to get out of bed and remained on board for several days after all had landed. Edwin and the children went on shore. We sleep in a place that many English would not put their horses in, with the rats running over our heads. I began to recover as soon as I got on shore and poor Kate also, I could not nurse the baby but a Mrs. Croaker did for me, but for want of proper nourishment died 5 days after her birth and was buried at sea. Poor little thing, she only wanted a mother's care. Edwin I believe has told how we are situated, our clothes are a fortune to us   I like the natives, something very mild about the women. A governess is wanted. We had one wedding aboard and another takes place in a fortnight. Mrs. Cholman the cabin lady was confined a week after myself of a still-born boy. We were always very friendly on board she had a very good time; ours the only births on board. My dearest friends I cannot think of anything more to tell but give our united love to all our dear friends.... Send by the first ship direct to us New Plymouth New Zealand. I can only add I wish you were all here, Believe me your very affectionate daughter

Sarah Harris (signed)

P.S. I hope to be able to write a longer letter to all soon but the uncomfortable place we are in prevents our doing many things. Edwin sleeps in his warie [whare] with Corbyn. I remain in a place without a door with the natives looking in to me in bed and talking before I am up. They are a complete set of beggars like to have a bit of our meat and so on. We seldom take a meal without three or four about us.

JANE FINDLAYSON

Measles and Madness

Young single women like Jane Findlayson were among one of the most sought-after groups of emigrants to New Zealand last century. Single women were much in demand in the new colony, both as wives and domestic servants, and were encouraged to travel out with family members or their employers, on assisted passages. Those behind the colonisation of New Zealand saw women as being doubly useful to the growing colony: not only would the eventual birth of their children supply the new country with further population and labour force, but the women themselves would also act as a 'civilising influence' on their countrymen.

Jane and her friend Agnes left the Scottish port of Greenock, on the River Clyde near Glasgow, in September 1876, on the ship Oamaru *bound for the Otago Association settlement of Dunedin. While her diary, a transcript of which is held by the Alexander Turnbull Library, does not record her reasons for emigration, it indicates that she and Agnes were expected by friends in Invercargill. Jane mentions learning some 'nice patterns of crochet and fancy work which will be useful among the children', which suggests she may have been bound for a domestic position.*

16th [October, 1877]:- We could not get on deck this morning it being very wet, [so we were] glad when it faired as it was nearly suffocation down below. We have often heard of Equatorial heat but this is it in reality we wear nothing but our dress and shoes on our hard feet, some go without shoes but that we can't manage. There is a young Irish girl went wrong in her mind beside us, we did not get any sleep for 4 nights she talked on, so we complained to the doctor and she has tonight been taken to hospital. We are all sorry for her brother who is waiting on her till the Doctor arranges other plans for her. We met a fine vessel this afternoon, we found on speaking to her she was the *Kingdom of Fife*. I forgot to mention before I sighted land on Saturday, Cape der Verd Islands it was not visible with the naked eye. (225 miles)

....

20th:- This is another hot day we are in prospects of crossing the line in a few days. The girl who went wrong in her mind is getting worse. She is harmless as yet. She has spoken and sung continually for nearly a week. She does not know any of us now her eyes are quite vacant. The sailors had a performance tonight, they threw their 'dead horse' into the sea. It is an affair they get up at the end of the first month, we were up on the poop and saw the whole affair on the main deck below. (145 miles)

23rd:- We met a fine vessel yesterday bound for Calis, she had been 40 days at sea. We passed a restless night owing to Lizzie, she is getting fractious now and tries to belt anyone who goes near her, she is quite near us here and keeps pelting at the door with her hands and feet, she is worn to a shadow and eats nothing scarcely. We sighted a vessel this morning but was too far off to speak. (179 miles) We had [a visit] tonight from King Neptune's clerk guarded by two policemen intimating that his Royal Master would pay us a visit tomorrow afternoon in state, we got a fine laugh, he was dressed with long grey whiskers and a hat about three feet long, he laid off his discourse to the first mate who is very humoursome and answered him nicely. We got damped all of a sudden with the news of the death of a child aged one year and eight months, the funeral is to be tomorrow morning at half past 7.

24th:- We were all up and dressed by 7 o'clock and went on deck where the little child was laid out sewed in canvas and covered with the ship's flag, the service was read and at the words 'I commit this body of the deep' it was put through the porthole and with a great splash in the water it was all over, it was very solemn and we did not feel the least appetite for our breakfast. There is to be no fun today owing to the funeral. We crossed the line about 6 o'clock tonight.

25th:- This is a lovely morning we hurried on deck to see two beautiful vessels in sight, they were in full sail and looked fine at a distance. There are lots of preparations going on about the main deck preparing for the afternoon's performance. About 3 o'clock a procession came on deck consisting of King Neptune, his wife, his Doctor, clerk and barber as well as six black slaves following them. The captain received them graciously and told the King to give him a call again after he had the rest of his business done, so he went on the main deck and shaved all the new hands on board, the purser, cabin boy, (one of the cabin passengers for fun) as well as about a dozen more sailors, bakers, stewarts etc. After being shaved they were plunged into a big tank of water where the slaves were swimming about and ready to give them a proper dunking. It was two hours grand fun and that did not finish the day, the singers' names were taken down for a concert in the evening. I wished Tom had been there as comic songs were scarce and when they were sung were loudly applaused, about 8 girls and 10 men sang, the songs were enjoyed most were such as 'I'm a Scotchman born' and 'Auld Lang Syne', these put us in mind of home.... We had a birth on board about 6 o'clock tonight, a young married woman had her first baby (a daughter) both are doing well.

26th:- This is a fine day and we are going on nicely, there is another case of measles, a married man has been laid up. (111 miles)

27th:- The weather is still hot and we feel worn out in the heat of the day.

Sailing ship Oamaru *at Port Chalmers. De Maus Collection, Alexander Turnbull Library.*

We had a concert tonight amongst the cabin passengers and the single girls, the first mate danced the sailors hornpipe, we got leave out till near 10 o'clock. It was a moonlight night and we enjoyed it very much. (168 miles)

28th:- We are going on nicely but the heat is sickening, we shall be glad when the weather gets a little colder. Lizzie is no better in her mind, she tries all she can to commit suicide and many a fright she gives us. We had another concert tonight it makes the time pass pleasantly, there are some good singers among the young men and very willing they are.

29th:- This is Sunday again and the captain and doctor had an extra inspection, we were all in our places and our names called out. We had service at half past 10. Mr. Bannerman preached from the words in Rev. 3. 'Behold I stand at the door and knock.' We had our class in the evening.

30th:- This day is still hot, we sighted a beautiful vessel this morning homeward bound but was too far off to speak, believe there is a small chance of us getting any letters sent home now. We have a great job on hand for tomorrow night, Hallow'een, the single girls have permission from the doctor to entertain the cabin ladies to tea and have got extra provision for it, we expect a fine night's enjoyment. (191 miles)

31st:- We are up early this morning and have lots of cleaning on hand, we have baked our oat cakes and also seed cake. Our place is all scrubbed and by half past 5 in the afternoon were clean and ready to receive the ladies.

Of them together they were quite pleased and said we were a jolly lot of girls, they took the tea out of our tins just for a novelty. My white cup and saucer did a good service. We had a few songs and games suitable for the night and afterwards went on deck to get any amount of dancing. It brought to our minds the happy Halloweens we used to spend at home. (210 miles)

....

7th [November]:- This is a fine day tho' cold and blowing, we saw some fine birds when on deck at our class, one especially called the albatross a splendid one, it would be about 15 feet from top to tip of the wings. We also saw some smaller ones called cape pigeons, Mr. Bannerman describes them nicely to us, we enjoy his teaching more and more every day, he was saying today we will soon know as much as about New Zealand as if we had been living there for years. Lizzie has broken up the door of the hospital twice. She is more sensible than she was and when we ask her at the outside of the door how she is she knows our word fine and answers as sensible enough. She has torn up her bedclothes with her teeth and a dresser of her own she has beside her, they have taken everything out of the room, she lies on boards with a strong quilt over her, we don't know how she lives with so little sleep. (145 miles)

....

13th:- We are all in high spirits at making so good progress. We are just passing the Cape of Good Hope although we are about 200 miles off it, we don't go on deck very much, the wind is piercing cold and we feel much more comfortable below, we sit and sew and knit to pass the day profitably. We don't enter into very much intercourse with many of the girls, we feel happier by ourselves and get a laugh at what is going on around us. (215 miles)

....

25th:- Snowing hard this morning. We can't feel it much as we have not been outside since Tuesday morning. Some of the girls go on deck to have a snow balling. I never liked it at home far less here. I have learned some nice patterns of crochet and fancy work which will be useful among the children should I be spared to land safely, some of the English girls are very handy, we laugh at how they are put to a stand about their meals, they grumble sadly. We ourselves manage nicely but of course we don't eat like them. (247 miles)

26th:- Sunday morning both wet and cold the doctor gave orders not to attempt outdoors at all, it was so rough and blowy, we wearied much without a sermon and spent a good while of the day talking about home and the friends there. Mr. Bannerman came in to us in the evening and gave us a short discourse on the words 'They that are whole need not a physician, but they that are sick.' There are two more cases of measles, we are quite sure now to be kept in quarantine for a while. (262 miles)

27th:- Cold weather again but we are going on nicely, we did not sleep well last night, some way or another we felt in a mood for talking of home, we also have a good company of rats beside us, they run about in dozens, we need to take care and not leave any of our clothes in their way else they would make a gob of them. We had our salt beef today and preserved carrots, the batter we ate but we threw the beef overboard.

28th:- This day is fine, we are much the same as usual. Another birth on board. Little Mary got a young brother, she is sorry she can't get down to help her father with the rest of the children. The doctor strictly forbids single girls from going near the married quarters, he is trying what he can to prevent measles spreading amongst us here, we have disinfecting powder all over our place, it is a disagreeable smell. The doctor is very strict with us and has his eyes in every corner, he is very sharp, some do not like him but we see he is doing everything for our own good. (276 miles)

29th:- It has been snowing a lot during the day, we are going very speedily which puts everyone in fine spirits. (269 miles)

30th:- This day is snowing again we feel perishing with the cold, we were much benefited by a good cup of tea, we made for ourselves in the afternoon, our stores from Scotland are pretty well exhausted by the end of the voyage, will have nothing left in the way of eatables. (224 miles) We were sorry to hear of another child's death with measles, we went to the funeral service at 6 o'clock, the mother was pretty brave considering. We hope there will be no more deaths, it puts us all about to hear of it.

....

3rd [December]:- Unfortunately there is a fresh case of measles this morning, there is no doubt now but we will be quarantined, we are going on rapidly and as steady as can be. This is Sunday but no service on deck. Mr. Bannerman went to the married quarters and christened two of the children, their names are Elizabeth and Estherann, he will christen little Mary's brother next week, it is likely to be named after the captain, it is just now styled 'Young Oamaru'. (300 miles)

4th:- This is a very cold day, we expected warm weather 'ere now. Another case of measles into the hospital, the doctor has lots to do with them all.

5th:- There was any amount of dancing among the girls today also the skipping rope or any other game to keep the cold away. (240 miles)

6th:- Another boy seven years old went in with measles.... A married man has taken a fever of Rheumatism he can't stir himself, it will be a sad landing for his family. A great change has come during the night, we are making slow progress. (206 miles)

7th:- We are in hopes to be landed in a week or little more. I am ashamed to tell you that one of our girls was confined of a daughter last night at half past 9, the doctor sent us all off from where he was, our place is sort of two apartments with only a short stair between us so just fancy 28 girls put out of their place, some of them took their beds with them and lay on the floor, we did not do so but on a form, we spent most of the night telling stories and any little bits of fun to amuse ourselves, we got back to our beds about 6 in the morning and stayed till dinner time. This has caused a talk all over the ship, when any of us goes out the men will pass remarks such as 'Who is likely to be laid up among the single girls'. The girl is from Ireland, a farmer's daughter and had she not come away her father would have shot her, it was unfeeling of them to banish her away amongst strangers. The doctor is very kind to her, she is pretty well considering, the baby tho' small is a plump little thing. God knows what will become of her when she is well and landed. (180 miles)

8th:- We got praise from the doctor about having our place so clean, he says the inspectors who come on board are very particular. We feel a change on the weather, we are now coming into the New Zealand climate. Another case of measles and what is worse it's among us, one little girl being between 3 and 4 is away to hospital, some of the mothers beside us are in a sad state, it is almost sure to spread, there are thirteen children among us. (140 miles)

9th:- We were wakened out of our first sleep by a commotion which was on an account of the young infant being found dead beside its mother, it supposed she had overlaid it. She is a young girl not 19 without much sense, she appeared to be in a sad state about it, poor thing, its best away it puts us off our sleep for an hour or two. (180 miles)

10th:- Our names were called over this morning before the captain, we expect this is our last Sunday on board.

11th:- Last night we had a few edifying remarks and advices from Mr. Bannerman. He told us to begin a good life now that we were on the eve of standing in a new country. This is a fine day the heat is up to 62 degrees everyone is making preparations for landing, the doctor told us this morning we would be in quarantine for a week at least, we hope to get to our destination before New Year. I forgot to say there was a birth yesterday morning in the married quarters (not here) and unfortunately another child died of measles last night, the doctor was driven nearly stupid, an old man to an apoplectic fit but is partly recovered, there is a child bad with typhoid fever so that the trouble is increasing rather than diminishing. We don't eat much now and feel agitated at the thought of going ashore, we are glad that there will be time for a telegram before the New Year. (246 miles)

13th:- This is a very calm day and none of us are so happy as we were a day or two ago.... Those who are bad with measles are getting better and also the fever came, we hope with all our heart there will be no more.

....

16th:- Thank God we are safely anchored in Port Chalmers but the yellow flag has been hoisted and we are doomed to be quarantined for a week at least. We stay on the ship all night and tomorrow, [then] we go on an island for the purpose where we will have every convenience for getting our things all washed, the married folks are on one end of it and we are on another and what is most laughable is the young men are put on an island opposite us with the water between. We enjoy the sight of New Zealand very much and see it's quite true what Christie said about its being a very hilly country. Mr. Bannerman told us to get a letter ready if we wanted to send one to any of our friends and he would take them. Agnes wrote one to her brother and I to Invercargill telling them not to expect us for a week or more. I hope we will be there before Christmas. We are in expectation of getting a walk on 'terra firma' tomorrow.

17th:- This is Sunday and it is not at all like it. A great bustle and everyone is getting their beds and tins packed up for landing at quarantine Island, the married folks and single girls went off, we got landed about 2 o'clock and found a very pretty place with everything clean and comfortable, it's a large house nicely built and to all appearance like a hydropathic establishment, the rules are much the same, if you don't appear at mealtimes you get none. There is a large dining room and we sleep in small apartments for eight, we like to take a walk among the bushes.

.....

19th:- ....A sad occurence happened yesterday. A married man lost his wife, she has lost her health and fallen into a decline, she has been in hospital for more than a month and she shifted to this place from the ship. It has been too much for her, one of her young children died on board so that too was against her, she was buried today in the burial place here, it is a pretty spot and lots of nice headstones in it. Just now we are saddened very much with the news that another case of measles has broken out, the doctor says that will mean another 15 days here, we are much put about, everyone of us fancy New Year past before we get from this, it is very unfortunate but what can't be cured must be endured.

....

2nd [January, 1877]:- We landed safely in Dunedin glad to get our freedom once more, we had a very good voyage of 83 days.

Miss X Surveys the Southern Coast

'Disappointed' might perhaps have been a better nom-de-plume than 'Hopeful' for a young Englishwoman identified only as Maggie who emigrated to Christchurch in 1885. Her dislike for the growing settlement and colonial life in general is clearly shown in a collection of her letters to her brother. They were published in 1887 under the title of Taken In, *'...because there is a great deal of false information afloat respecting Colonial facts...'.*

This excerpt comes from her 'sea diary', written on the Merope, *and illustrates her dislike of New Zealand from her first sighting of its shores.*

Sunday, 26th.[July 1885]- A tremendous sea - the highest we have had yet: we went up to the companion ladder to peep, and that was all we could do; this is really the first time it has been too bad, by reason of *roughness*, to go on deck at all. *Bitterly* cold, temperature fifty-three. I read some books on New Zealand, and studied some plates of the towns and country. I can't say I was much smitten either by the views or scenery - let's hope the reality is more gratifying. This has been a *very*, *very* cold, cheerless day throughout, sea coming in everywhere, but we are making grand speed on our journey now.

Monday, 27th.- A very, very cold, stormy, blustering day; seas higher than ever; deck very slippery; several of the sailors had falls; none of us ventured on deck; great waves came even over the poop. The fierce elements seemed to stir up wild confusion in the breast of the 'Colonial' - she gave vent in the saloon to all sorts of strange socialistic and revolutionary talk. In the evening we had some long rubbers at whist, which we finished about a quarter to ten, and had just moved away from the table preparatory to our evening's trot round to get warm, when a *monstrous* wave came over the poop and poured through the canvas of the skylight right on to tables and benches and all. The poor 'Colonial' got caught in some of it, but the rest of us escaped: perhaps this was a judgement on her for all her naughty revolutionary talk; it cooled her a little for a day or two, not more! This caused great excitement, and I, as usual, was *frightened*. The ship rocked and pitched about in a mighty unpleasant manner.

Wednesday, 29th.- A bright, splendid morning, quite warm in the sun. I read some *Travelling Sketches in North Italy, the Tyrol, and the Rhine*, and was much pleased with them. In the evening we went up a minute on the poop to look at the moon and the grand sea, but it was very rough in the afternoon; the stewards were careless enough to leave the great door open near the saloon, and so an enormous wave poured in, running all along and making wet boards again. We made 240 miles today.

Thursday, 30th.- A dull, *very* cold day. We are going very well now, and are full of hope that we might reach our journey's end soon! as each day gets more monotonous than the last; *no* fresh element beyond the pranks of Old Ocean breaks in upon us.

Friday, 31st.- A *very dull, cold,* cheerless day. Nothing particular happened; we did not make such good progress; the wind was not right. The 'Colonial Spitfire' raved at breakfast over the Chinamen and their *virtues* in preference to the English; and when on deck, later, the captain gave quite another version, and certainly his word could be better credited who has been all over the world and is thrown with all nations, than such a person as the 'Colonial.' He says there is £10 a head to pay on each Chinaman who is landed in Australia; and what they call the Chinaman's quarter in Melbourne is well known, and their vices are certainly vices, and often it would be hardly safe to be in their quarters.

Saturday, August 1st.- A very dull, cheerless sort of day. After dinner we sighted a fine ship going in our direction, which created a little excitement. In the morning I saw the water blown up by a whale in the distance, but that was all. It came on to a drizzling rain by five, but not enough to prevent one's having the usual pace round. Just about tea-time a sudden gale blew up, all sails had to be taken in, and none of the officers came down to tea: there was rather a confusion, and it rained heavily. Our nearest land now is the Snares - some small uninhabited islands which we have to pass and which are rather dangerous; we had a very rough wild night.

Sunday, 2nd.- The morning opened ever so wildly, so none of us were able to go on deck.

Monday, 3rd.- Bank Holiday. A very cold, cheerless day. Land was *faintly* visible; we are going very slowly now. As we are so near to New Zealand we are beginning our little preparations for departure; we have passed the Snares today, but are making too much towards Stewart's Isle.

Tuesday, 4th.- Another cold, dull, sunless day. After breakfast I went on deck for some time to see the land, which was fairly visible on both sides, though it was rather misty. Nothing particular happened; officers all cross because we did not make a better course; we move very slowly.

Wednesday, 5th.- Ship affairs very bad. The wind is taking us much out of our course. An albatross was seen today, they always seem to prefer solitude; I have never seen but one at a time.

Thursday, 6th.- A most *exquisite* day; sun out bright and warm; we sat on deck a good deal and read and worked. Nautical affairs very bad; we are now about 300 miles from New Zealand, and might be there in a couple of days, but we make no progress and are almost *becalmed*. All hands are busy varnishing, washing and doing all sorts of jobs to make the ship look nice. Captain complained dreadfully because we make no run, I suppose it is very trying to the head of affairs, as each captain desires to make the smartest and sharpest passage, and yet the winds and waves cannot be ruled to order any more than people can 'love to order.' We saw land quite plainly.

Friday, 7th.- A *bitterly* cold day; great excitement on board on seeing land quite close. We were all on deck in the morning, with glasses, looking hard, and we saw a mountainous or rather hilly looking coast, with short stunted trees and brushwood and hills covered with snow. We passed Nugget Point and Molyneux Bay, but we are not on our right course. The officers were rather depressed that we kept tacking about, and yet did not reach our destination, though so close. After lunch I paid a visit to Miss G's cabin, and found to my surprise a little game going on there; the second mate was closeted with her, and I fancy - gathering from previous observations - *it is a case*! Grand cleanings going on on board all day. The 'Colonial' rather rude and spiteful on and off. We had our last rubber of whist in the evening and our opponents won the rubber and are now even with us, much to the joy of the 'Colonist!'

Saturday, 8th.- The coldest day we have had yet; we got on deck about eleven to see the land, which was *quite close*. We coasted along the province of Otago and passed Cape Saunders, where there is a revolving lighthouse, or rather light; this we saw most clearly and brightly at dusk. We were not so very far from Dunedin - which is the Gallic for Edinburgh, as it is supposed somewhat to resemble the place. We saw plainly little houses, huts, and cottages on the hills. It is a rugged, rough-looking shore, but still, being *shore*, after such a long absence, we tried to find beauties in it; it lacks however the noble approach to the white cliffs of Albion. Everyone felt the cold very much. There is every chance that we may not reach our destination for another week. The ship was 'turned about' several times in the day. Nothing of note happened, only extreme cold and gloom. Fourteen weeks on board to-day!

Sunday, 9th.- Fifteenth Sunday on board. *Bitterly* cold. We passed the little seaport of Oamaru; it looked to me a frightfully cold, barren, rugged, inhospitable coast, in fact the scene so depressed me that I came down and had a good cry for a few minutes - it all seemed so gloomy and melancholy and lonely; to think of having come these thousands of miles, and having left home and friends and country, and all one loves, to find nothing more cheering to meet one than black evil, hard, cruel-looking rocks and shapeless upheavals, in the place of hills; and one's mind swiftly flew back to other loved scenes; take, for instance, the charming approach to Dover, with the magnificent white cliffs standing boldly out, the stupendous Shakesperian cliff being always prominent to the eye, as also is the noble and ancient castle; and the town, so picturesquely situated at the bottom; and all along the coast the surf breaking in white, snowy foam; and the fine hotels and Admiralty pier standing clearly out. Then, again, one thought of dear old Plymouth with its grand harbour, and the soft verdant, smiling landscape all round, whichever way you looked, and beautiful Mount Edgecombe just a little way ahead. Oh! how different the present scenes; my heart sank at the sorry show!

Monday, 10th.- A very fine, bright day. The shore view today, with sunshine on it, certainly looked better than yesterday, but still very so-so. There was a range of hills all round thickly covered with snow which glistened with the sun on them; and the waves, breaking on the shore, looked also pretty; but after having seen the real Alps, the hills looked very feeble.

Tuesday, 11th.- A fine, bright, but cold, boisterous day. The ship was 'put about' - no one seemed very happy or comfortable, these evil looking rocks seemed to be surrounding us, as if we should soon be dashed on them.

Wednesday, 12th.- A rather unhappy sort of day passed. Captain and mates were restless and anxious, up and down the deck all day. The coast is dangerous here, and we seemed nearly driving into it.

Thursday, 13th.- God be praised! We reached Lyttelton Port about eight o'clock p.m. About three we began to get anxious as there was no wind, and we seemed gradually drifting on to the rocks, but soon our hearts were cheered by the sight of the pilot and his boat, and then came the steam tug soon after, and about eight we were in port - in harbour -

When the shore is won at last,
Who will count the billows past?

The evening seemed a new and cheerful one, as fresh faces kept turning up in the saloon. After so many weeks of the same faces, same voices, and same society, a change was very nice. Doctor, custom house officer, other captains, and old friends of those in command, came trooping in, and it seemed quite a pleasurable excitement.

Farewell then - thou deep and dark blue ocean -
Time writes no wrinkle on thine azure brow,
Such as creation's dawn beheld, thou rollest now.

And farewell, also, thou tight and gallant little barque, which has borne us so bravely and safely through stormy billow, and tempest - would that we all pass as safely 'through the waves of this troublesome world,' and be landed as safely in the eternal harbour!

And now let us see what the new shore will bring forth for us.

Pioneering Life

Lake Guyon, North Canterbury. Alexander Turnbull Library

A Fit Person to Emigrate

'Hopeful' did not mince her words about New Zealand. This trenchant observer summarised the qualities required to live in the colony in her book Taken In. *Her advice illustrates the need for a pioneer spirit of adventure.*

Dear Brother,

In this letter I will try and write a little on the classes who may venture out and those who should not, and this information I have gathered from most careful investigation of these matters on my own part, also from statistics and from general enquiry.

1. - THE CLASS WHO MAY VENTURE TO COME OUT.

The class who may venture to come out should be those of good and strong constitution and thoroughly prepared to *rough it*! Also men of speculative tendencies, good business habits, and sufficient money to start them in some business or mercantile speculation. For instance, labourers and country mechanics such as wheel-wrights, blacksmiths, harness-makers, rough carpenters, and a generally hard-working class, and those habituated to work for generations have, perhaps a better chance here than at home, as wages are better than in the old country, and food is cheap; but for the *town* artisan and superior mechanic there is very little demand...

2. - THE CLASS WHO SHOULD NEVER VENTURE TO COME OUT.

Well-to-do ladies and gentlemen, who have been well brought up, as also have their families for generations before them - this class is *utterly useless* in the colonies and constantly has to endure *great* hardships.

Again, ladies and gentlemen in reduced circumstances rarely succeed in the Colonies; their small income would go twice as far and give them treble the comforts at home; 30s. a week here would be no more than £1 a week at home, and as I have explained before, the price of every thing except food, is generally far higher. There is another class who would not improve their condition here, namely, that of upper servants of well-to-do families - these feel sadly disappointed at their prospects on arrival....

As I have said before, New Zealand has more than enough to do in finding employment for the numerous Colonial girls who abound in town and country. As to marriage - well that word will ever have an intense fascination to the female mind - and so one is not so surprised to find, after reading the glowing accounts given of the country, (generally by those who are interested in giving these accounts) that many females are brought out (the country is deluged with them), who discover, poor things, to their chagrin on arrival, that they have no chance of either honourable work or the much wished for husband. Many respectably, and even well educated and well brought-up girls and women, have come out in this way, to their cost, and find themselves in a sorry plight; 'they cannot dig, to beg they are ashamed,' so they go down, *down*, and the history of many, is sad indeed.

3.- THE CHARACTERS AND CONSTITUTIONS THAT SHOULD COME OUT

The constitutions well suited for Colonial life, are those that are *very strong*, and that can live and thrive on those things that are cheap. The characters, who can drive a hard bargain. Those who love money-grubbing to the depth of their souls, and care not what hardness or trouble they go through to attain this much wished for goal, and those who have little softness or refinement in their nature, will get on well.

4.- THE CHARACTERS THAT SHOULD NOT COME OUT

The characters not suited for Colonial life are those endued with sympathetic, imaginative, poetic and refined tastes, also those with affectionate and appreciative natures. The more developed these qualities are in any individual who comes out, the more he will suffer; the more painful will be the terrible roughness of Colonial life to such a soul, and the more sadly will such a one pine for home and the genial companionships of other days.

Burning Down the House

Charlotte Godley has already featured in this collection, writing of the voyage out to found the infant settlement of Christchurch. While her husband was the Company Agent for the Canterbury Settlement and they had a house servant, she was still subject to the rigours of life in the new society. Her A-frame house was as vulnerable as the next when it came to the test.

March 1, 1851

St David's day rose with a heavy mist, as I discovered by a drop which fell on my nose just as I woke; but the dust was not even laid, and it became beautiful, though not much sun, and rather windy. My husband was off early to Christchurch, as it was the day for the selection of land for the second lot of purchasers. William was sent to Lyttelton with a message, Jack for eatables to Christchurch, and I was sitting quietly in our V hut (it ought to be an A hut, oughtn't it?) thinking of former St David's days (up to the first that I can remember, when I have a distinct vision of old Mrs. Taylor at Voelas, helping you to pin an artificial leek on the shoulder of each of us, with which we were to go and wish our papa good morning), and looking on and making dots, as he calls it, for Arthur's drawing; when just about noon, I heard a great scream from Powles, and when I ran out she showed me a little bit, on fire, in the wall, as it seemed, of the kitchen chimney, but so close to the *raupo* walls that my hair was all set on ends in an instant. Powles ran off for water, about twenty yards, and I burned my hands in trying to get the spout of the kettle into the fiery hole, which was between the outer and the inner thatching, and must have caught fire from some spark lodging in a hole of the sod chimney, and gradually getting through that to the very inflammable stuff about, when it made quick work. As Powles came back, the flames burst out outside, more fortunately beginning to leeward, and then we began to carry the things out, knowing that anything else was hopeless. Most fortunately again, someone at Deans' saw our first puff of smoke, and in a minute we had Mr. William Deans himself, and six or seven men, handing out things; by which means everything was saved that was of any consequence. It was frightful to see the blaze, and hear the roar, as it spread along the roof; in five minutes it was all down, and only bare poles left standing, which burnt for some time, and then left us with nothing but a heap of black ashes.

The next thing was to get some shelter up in its stead, and we sent for some Maoris to build us another *raupo* house; in which, however, we had quite determined to have no chimney; but as they are much warmer than our huts, it is to be Arthur's sleeping-place, and the fire-place for cooking to be put to his wooden house, as being several shades less inflammable. The chimney was begun, but although it was Saturday. it could not be finished before dark, and ditto the *raupo* house. Unluckily, as it became dark, the mist that had been gathering became rain, and the rain a storm of wind, and we found ourselves without any water-tight house. We put our clothes and valuables under our tables and tubs, to keep them dry, and carefully erected an umbrella over the head of the bed. Powles' hut, having a higher pitch, kept out the rain much better than ours, and had besides an inner covering of shawls, etc., that kept at least their beds dry, and free from drops; but our umbrella was a sad failure, and the bed was positively soaked. It had not a regular mattress, only an old cover of one which we brought out here to save carrying such a big thing as ours was, and we slept on fern the first two nights, and then got this filled with the wiry grass that grows about; and though it is rather hard, and smells a little like a haystack, still that doesn't matter much for people who sleep as well as we do, after so much open air. No more did the rain, for though I woke once in the night, and found a great deal of wet, it was hopeless to do anything in the dark; so I just went to sleep again, and it was not till after six that we discovered how completely soaked we had been.

Settlers' A-frame or 'V-huts' in Christchurch early 1860s. Canterbury Museum.

JANE MARIA ATKINSON

A Personal Realisation

Jane Maria Atkinson was a formidable woman. She was described by Guy H. Scholefield, editor of the Richmond-Atkinson Papers, *as 'warm-hearted and outspoken....eminently practical [and possessing] an Amazonian spirit that shirked no dilemma and flinched at no aspect of physical danger.' Born Jane Maria Richmond, she married Arthur Samuel Atkinson in 1854, and her letters and diaries form a significant part of the Richmond-Atkinson collection, held in the Alexander Turnbull Library. The correspondence and personal records of these two prominent early New Zealand families provide one of the most complete surveys of colonial life from the 1850's to the early years of this century. Maria was an intelligent, well-educated woman who was more than equal to the challenges offered to her by conditions in New Zealand. In 1855 she became the first European woman to climb Mount Egmont - in a pair of trousers. Unfortunately her account of this adventure has never been found.*

As a preliminary to her adventures during the Taranaki wars, printed later in this book, here is a letter to a school friend, Margaret Taylor, in which she expresses her opinions - somewhat ahead of their time - on the education of women.

Nelson, 23 Mar 1870

....Whether we like it or not I feel certain the next century will see an enormous change in the position of women. It is part of Democracy. I am not sure I *like* Democracy. Power coming without, or long before, wisdom must always be bad. Whatever influence I might have in the world I should wish to use it in the cause of education. I want my girls to have a boy's education because it is a better education than what is called a girl's, since it better exercises the faculties God has given girls as well as boys. I certainly approve of any woman studying medicine or anything else she selects provided she does it earnestly. I only wish I had studied medicine myself; the mental training would have made me an infinitely more valuable member of society, to say nothing of the advantages special knowledge of the kind would have given me. I don't see how any study which strengthens the mental powers can do otherwise than make women fitter for their own special work, sick nursing included, and I believe that Nature has so provided that their own desires and affections will always lead them to discharge these duties first, except in cases where luxury, idleness and frivolity destroy Nature's promptings. My experience in the Colony shows me that the most *solidly* educated women are the most useful in every department of life, and that so called 'feminine refinement' is fatal to female usefulness. I dare say we should agree at bottom, only that you imagine (as the Confederates used to do about the Negroes) that Liberty would lead our sex into all sorts of wild vagaries and to the neglect of our own work, and I have more confidence in *us*. I believe the more we are educated, the higher we aim intellectually, the better we shall discharge our own special functions in the world. Just take my own imaginary case. Had I studied medicine till I was 28 when I left England, would it have prevented my marrying? I believe not, but it would have made me a ten times better wife and mother and a more respectable human being altogether.

Jane Maria Atkinson

SARAH AMELIA COURAGE

Encounter with a Vagrant

Few copies of the original printing of Sarah Amelia Courage's Lights and Shadows of Colonial Life *are still in existence. While 18 copies were published for private circulation late last century, nine or ten were destroyed by friends and neighbours who objected to Sarah's thin veiling of their identities using pseudonyms, and her somewhat critical portrayals of their personalities and various incidents. The book, sub-titled* Twenty-six years in Canterbury, New Zealand, *tells the story of Sarah's life on the Double Corner and Seadown sheep stations in North Canterbury in the 1860's, '70's and '80's. The stories deal mainly with domestic adventures - Sarah seemed to have more than her fair share of the colonial problem of getting and keeping servants - and social gatherings, including visiting neighbours, balls and picnics.*

Although little mention is made of family matters in her book, Sarah gave birth to four more children while in New Zealand - the eldest, Ada, was born before their emigration. Leaving Seadown in the hands of their eldest son, the Courages returned to England in 1899 and Sarah died two years later, in Tunbridge Wells. Her husband Frank married again, returning to New Zealand once more to divide the Seadown property between his children. He died in 1917. He appears in Lights and Shadows *as Fred.*

I was startled one afternoon by a loud knock on the front door. I was rather flurried, and on opening it was somewhat taken aback by the apparition of a tall black-haired, greasy looking man, who had in his hand a large brass-bound whip, which he had evidently used for hitting the door. He fixed his keen black eyes on me with a stony stare and said, 'Yer mar in, miss?'

I was so much surprised that I do not think I made any reply.

'No-o?' he said. 'I see she's not,' in a sad voice with a look of disappointment on his melancholy face. 'I wished particularly to see her with regard to several articles of utility which I am selling. I have left my van in the gully, and it is filled with every description of goods, from a beautifier of the complexion to a pair of hobnailed boots, or (glancing down at my feet) a pair of lady's French slippers, suitable for yourself.'

I interrupted him here by saying that I was not in want of anything.

'Are you the mistress?' he asked in a soft voice. 'Oh, then I am a very fortunate man, for I have a new invention with me, my dear lady, which you must see; it is a patent cushion fitted with spiral springs, which will be found invaluable in a buggy or coach where the roads are rough, and effectually prevents the spine from injury. I have them in all -'

'I do not want anything,' I interrupted in a decided tone of voice, and again I tried to close the door, but the handle of the whip was still there and I felt very angry.

'Pardon me,' he said softly. 'My two horses are dead beat and cannot go a step further tonight (it was five o'clock), and I must camp in the gully, though I am far from strong' - and he coughed in a dreadful manner - 'and the heavy dews at night are death to a consumptive man.' Here he coughed again. 'May I ask you, dear lady, to extend your hospitality to man and beast, for this night only, and I will gratefully depart at break of day.'

I felt sorry for the man, and still more sorry for the poor horses, hungry and weary. I replied that the master was not in, and I could not give the required permission myself; but he could take the horses to the stable and give them a feed, and go himself to the kitchen and have some tea, and by that time, no doubt, the master would be back. He thanked me in a most grateful tone of voice and, taking off his hat in a respectful manner, he went.

I watched him from a window bring up the horses - such wretched scarecrows, my heart ached to see them - and the huge van, too, big enough for a circus tent and for four horses instead of two to draw. Then I saw Jones, the groom, who said the 'feller looked a hawful rascal,' and he thought 'Master would never let him stay the night'. I told him not to trouble about the man but to feed the horses well.

After they had been unharnessed and fed, the fellow came round again to the door and knocked; his hands were full of Bibles and church-services, and I said again that I was well supplied with everything. Then he pressed me to accept a small book called *Crumbs of Comfort Addressed to the Sinful*, as 'a grateful offering' for my kindness to him - which was premature. However, I declined it somewhat curtly, I fear, and hurt his feelings, judging by the way he sighed as he walked off to his tea.

Half an hour afterwards Matilda appeared and asked for some money on account. (I had given her two pounds only the day before to put in a letter.) She said she wanted to buy some things she could not possibly do without, but I strongly advised her not to waste her money. On looking in my purse I found I had two £1 notes, which she saw, and begged me to let her take both.

This travelling Cheap Jack, she told me, had been all over the country, visiting the different houses on the way. By subtle flattery he ingratiated himself with the servants, feigning solicitude for their well-being, then producing his liver pills and potions, and other so-called cheap wares, and selling a quantity of rubbish. He was not particular what he took in exchange, thus offering every temptation to servants of elastic conscience to rob their employers.

That night Fred was not back till nearly seven o'clock and was naturally surprised when he reached the stables to find a huge covered van anchored there, and two strange horses without harness quietly grazing. The man had evidently made up his mind that he was going to stay by unharnessing them.

Fred came to the house to speak to me first before interviewing the stranger. I said I believed the man was ill - consumptive. 'Then in that case,' said Fred. 'I will give him a shakedown in the harness room,' and went out on kindly thoughts intent. The pedlar had undone the straps of his packs, which covered the kitchen tables, and was preparing for the display of his goods; and the barter and bargaining, which is a purely feminine weakness, was just about to begin when Fred appeared on the scene.

When he returned he said he did not like the look of the fellow at all, but he could stay, as the man had told him he was going away as soon after breakfast in the morning as possible. Later on, Fred said they were all playing cards when he again went into the kitchen. It was his opinion that the man had belonged to a circus at some period of his life. Strangely enough, I had thought the same. 'The intuition of women is the most wonderful thing on earth,' I said. '*Next* to the intuition of man,' said Fred, laughing.

Well, we both hoped that we would not be murdered in our sleep; and as we went to bed that night I carefully locked the doors. Next morning, at breakfast time, Ann came to me and said the man wouldn't eat bacon or cold mutton for his breakfast, and insisted on having chops cooked for him, and coffee. Fred was angry and said, 'Tell him to leave it then; there are no chops for him.' Ann, who was evidently afraid of him, took the message, but soon returned, saying that he had sworn and used disgraceful language but was eating his breakfast all the same.

Afterwards he lit a pipe and strolled about outside among my flower beds, where he had the audacity to pick a rose and put it in his buttonhole. Fred went up to him and said he had better be going, as his horses had finished their feed. He said he would go when it suited his convenience and not before; and using more bad language, pulled off his coat, rolled up his sleeves, and told Fred to 'come on' and he would 'let the grateful sunlight into his innerds' - an invitation, I am ashamed to say, that Fred could not resist. Quick as lightning he pulled off his coat too, and white with anger and excitement 'went for him', giving him a tremendous blow between the eyes, sending him on his back into the manuka scrub and making his nose bleed. When he got up, Fred asked if he wanted any more. 'No,' he said, 'that's enough for the present.' 'Then', said Fred, 'you clear off this place at once, and don't show your face here again.' I was an unwilling spectator of this shocking scene from the window.

The poor wretch picked up his coat and went to the kitchen for a bowl of water. As they say, 'Pity is akin to love.' Matilda pitied him (Ann told me) and, with many tears, helped to bathe his face. She was very kind and merciful to him, and mercy is one of the sweetest attributes of women.

While this little scene was being enacted in the kitchen, Jones was putting the horses in the van at the stables. Presently the man came out and went to the horses. He examined his harness with one angry and revengeful eye - the other was black - and talked and masticated wrathful words to Jones, then went back to the kitchen again, and returned, accompanied by Matilda carrying her carpet bag and hatbox. For pride, which supplies its caustic though severe remedy for the wounds of affection, came rapidly to her aid; and she told Ann she was going too.

'Great occasions call for great exertions.' I sent Ann running to tell Matilda to come and speak to me, and she came a few yards. Just then the man whipped up the horses and started, and Matilda turned and fled to the van, shouting, 'Don't run away from me, you naughty unfeeling man.' He pulled up and she scrambled in, and they went off together. She had overdrawn her wages by a sovereign, but I did not think of it till too late. For a moment I was so bewildered and amazed that I could hardly realise what had taken place.

Then Fred came over to me and said with real concern, 'You look as scared as if you had seen a ghost. Come in and sit down.'

I did as I was bidden, and tried to think what was best to be done. I felt quite stunned, for a knock-down blow stuns for a time and the victim cannot do much when prostrated. I told Fred that I was disgusted with the events of the morning; that he had forfeited his character for niceness; and that it was an easy matter when he had forfeited his reputation to descend into unfathomable depths of degradation, and I hoped it would be the last time such a disgraceful contretemps should take place wherever I was mistress....

Matilda was never seen or heard of again. I often wondered what had become of her, and I decided, once and for all, never again to take a written character.

Three days after Matilda left I was putting away the linen which Ann had ironed and found that a large pair of sheets were missing. Of course I could not tell which of the 'twain' took them, but they had gone.

SARAH AMELIA COURAGE

A Fashionable Ball on the Frontier

With homesteads scattered so far apart across the Canterbury Plains, and domestic and family duties taking much of the time of settlers like Sarah Amelia Courage, formal social events were few and far between. Thus Sarah describes the prospect of a garden party and dance at a neighbouring station as 'a vision delightful to contemplate'. The names in this account are thinly veiled pseudonymns which upset her neighbours of the time. The station Sarah refers to as Sunnylands was in fact Seadown, which Frank Courage bought in 1873. The party was held at Mount Grey Station (Greyrocks), run by a widow Sarah O'Connell (Mrs. Fitzpatrick) and her brother John Russell (Mr. Fussell). The gathering is a welcome slice of England on the other side of world: croquet is followed by 'high tea', civilised conversation and dancing.

It was late Autumn - April - but our Indian summer still remained and the weather was perfectly lovely. Mrs. Fitzpatrick of Greyrocks sent her neighbours all an invitation for the following week, to a garden party and dance afterwards. The coming dissipation was to me a vision delightful to contemplate; and this would be quite a new experience.

As the day approached, I unearthed from a big packing case used as a dressing table a festive garment of pale green French cambric, trimmed with fine black lace, which I had never had any occasion to wear out here, and found to my satisfaction that it still fitted me and was quite the latest fashion in the colonies, though I had had it three years.

Having collected shoes, gloves, fan and other minor appendages, I ironed out the creases in my dress due to its having lain so long folded together. Fred came in and said it looked very pretty and made him feel quite festive to look at it.

Tuesday came, and we started at three o'clock, for it was a long drive. The neighbours were all assembled; the female portion of them wore the airiest and prettiest of dresses - the most voluminous of petticoats, and crinolines in moderation. Our hostess looked very nice in maize muslin. So did Mrs. Iscariot in white muslin, dressed just like her daughters; but she was not a woman to trouble about public opinion. After all, why should she? Her figure was slight and wiry still.

There were four strangers from Christchurch, Mrs. and Mr. Jolliboy of course (he, as usual, beaming with smiles), the Coltons, and Miss Sinikel from Sunnylands, who was going to be married to Dr. Siedlitz before Mrs. Iscariot left there.

The garden looked very pretty. Some played croquet, others sat and talked under the trees, and others again rambled off in pairs. The fruit was all over, except an occasional plum or apple.

Mr. Fussell introduced me to a Dr. -, a tall, shy young man of about twenty-three, I should think, who gazed about in an absent-minded sort of way and remarked with an effort that it was 'a very warm day'. One always feels sorry for shy men; it must have been a terrible ordeal for him, I thought, to be launched among strangers in a strange land. After a time we talked together and he was less shy. He said he had only just arrived in the colony, and thought of settling in Christchurch and practising his profession.

We had several games of croquet. Then the shadows of evening had gathered, and the sun fell and all around was dark. The bell was rung and we all trooped into the dining room. The windows were wide open to the veranda, with its graceful creepers festooned from side to side, the warm air flowing in revivingly and sweetly from the great bed of mignonette before the windows. How vividly all these minutiae return to one! I think I can see it all at the present moment.

The table was spread with materials for the heterogeneous meal called by some people 'high tea', a class of refection welcomed by all who live in the country, and very prettily decorated with fruit and flowers, great dishes piled high with plums and late peaches, whipped cream and trifle etc. The bowls of roses, too, must not be forgotten, for Greyrocks was ever noted for its roses, and is so still. Then for those who were unable to subsist on 'a glass of water and the scent of a lily' there were plenty of substantial viands as well.

Everyone laughed and talked together; but my new acquaintance, the doctor, who sat opposite me, was out of it all and seemed dimly to imagine that he had fallen among thieves.

Mr. Jolliboy on that evening surpassed himself. He was carving at a side table and knocked over a handbell, whereupon a maid appeared to see what was wanted. When she had gone he said, ' "Sometimes you ring to say that you did not ring", as Newman Noggs said to his employer, Ralph Nickleby,' at which everyone seemed as if they felt in duty bound to laugh. The young doctor seemed surprised at so much laughter being the result of so tame a remark, as well he might be.

I suppose everyone that evening felt in good spirits, and when one is happy laughter is very near one's lips - even those who felt that the laugh was not entirely with them. The whole thing had a certain resemblance to the jokes which Goldsmith's schoolmaster cracked to the trembling scholars, who could trace coming events in his morning face.

When tea was over the moon had risen, and we all sauntered outside while the room was cleared for dancing. Mrs. Iscariot and I sat on a seat under the veranda, and I wondered if she would speak about leaving Sunnylands; but she did not, nor did I, for I hate prying into people's affairs. Mrs. Jolliboy, who had known her longer than I had, came up and sat beside Mrs. Iscariot, and said, 'I hope there is no truth in the report we have heard that you are leaving the neighbourhood.' Mrs. Iscariot turned sharply round and said, 'I am not going to be questioned by anybody, or to be called upon to go into particulars to people I don't care a pin about just to gratify their curiosity. All that need be known will appear in the newspaper in a few weeks.'

Poor Mrs. Jolliboy reddened and looked snubbed. At that moment a few chords were struck on the piano. The room was ready and we went in. The ladies were to play in turns.

The shy doctor asks me to dance with him and we begin. It is a quadrille; as it proceeds great beads of perspiration stand out on his forehead. When we stop and I look about me, I see Mr. Jolliboy's short, stout figure blandly backing between Mrs. Iscariot and Mrs. Fitzpatrick, whom he is dancing with, for he is a great admirer of fine women.

When we reach the fifth figure in the quadrille, everybody prepares to gallop round in a frantic manner. Occasionally I get glimpses of my better half - all arms and legs, like a windmill - at the bottom of the room, which seems to be one struggling mass of muslin. My poor partner gasps and

Photograph: Alexander Turnbull Library.

puffs apopletically, saying the heat is stifling and he feels giddy, but he gives no sign by which I can infer that he has had enough of it - and when the time comes, he goes through it all over again with Miss Fitzpatrick.

Between every dance we all walk about outside on the lawn. The moon being at the full, it is as light as noonday. A waltz was the next item, and the music began vigorously. I did not dance it but sat under a tree and chatted with Mrs. Iscariot, who, for once, was in a most amiable mood.

She told me she was leaving Sunnylands; that it was a great sorrow, but she, like many others, had failed in her efforts to make farming pay, and she would try her energies in a fresh direction. She said with a bitter smile that she did not think she was leaving many friends behind - 'The world loves man when riches on him flow,' she said sadly. I felt sorry for her, though I did not say so. She was such a peculiar woman; in my own mind I had always likened her to a turkey with a querulous kind of note, never seeming to become sociable, or to make one of the human family in any sense save the numerical. There is no character so perplexing as the character which always thinks itself in the right and everyone else in the wrong. Further conversation became impossible, for the music was ending in a series of shrieks.

Then Mr. Jolliboy comes up with an unwelcome alacrity to claim me for the next - the lancers. He was an untiring mover and an active dancer for his age; and he bows, sets and shuffles most valiantly, while the poor doctor gets hopelessly muddled in the figures; but we get through at last in a satisfactory manner.

On the celerity with which the evening glided by, and on the happiness I enjoyed, I will not dilate, nor say how sorry I was to hear from Fred that the clocks had struck eleven, the hour we had beforehand decided to leave, having a long drive before us. I could have willingly stayed all night, and begged him to let me have one more dance before bringing the horses round, and he did so. I danced with the doctor, who had quite lost his shyness and was very amusing. He commenced to discuss the various persons who were floating past. We both admired Mrs. Fitzpatrick, who was, he said, a countrywoman of his.

'Look at Fussell!' he exclaimed. 'He dances like a broken umbrella; and Jolliboy - upon my word, in a small room Jolliboy is positively dangerous,' and so on. I could scarcely answer for laughing. He said, 'The society here seems to be of a homely sort of country-neighbour style, and very jolly all the same.' The music stopped; the dance was over; and I felt tired out - and cold and creepy, as I wondered when I should have another.

I was roused out of my reverie by hearing Fred's voice speaking sharply to the horses, who were fidgety; and putting on my wraps, farewells were said. The buggy came round and we were soon leaving the merry dancers -

'light and life' it seemed to *me*, endowed by nature with more than my share of animal spirits.

As we drove away the 'Adieu' waltz was being played - strangely appropriate to the moment; and I could hear its trilling strains floating out to us through the open windows in the still, warm night long after we had driven away.

Our horses were very fidgety. The music seemed to have got into their feet as they pranced and curvetted along, requiring a whole vocabulary of strong language to keep them in the middle of the road. For a few miles we trotted in a straight road over tussocks, not a house or tree visible. The sea was shining in the bright moonlight, calm and beautiful; and the air was as sweet as hay and the evening primrose, which grew luxuriously by the roadside, could make it.

When one is young, happiness seems to be our right. This evening was to me a thing of light and joy to look back upon, but with feelings of regret that another slide had passed into life's magic lantern. There is a chill of change as we go back to 'enjoy', forsooth, solitude and communion with nature - the daydream is over and one feels that

Joy so seldom weaves a chain
Like this tonight, that oh! 'tis pain
To break its links so soon.

- Moore.

CATHERINE VALPY

Chased by a Lunatic

The Valpy family, who travelled in Dunedin on the Ajax *in January 1849, arrived just a year after the first Otago Association immigrants landed at the Dunedin settlement. Catherine's father, schoolmaster William Henry Valpy, was of the British upper class and had money to spend, fitting perfectly Edward Gibbon Wakefield's concept of 'gentry' for the new colony. The social set in which the Valpy sisters mixed included the daughters of Captain William Cargill, the leader of the Otago settlers. After two years of living in the growing town, the Valpys moved to a 48 ha farm, Forbury, south of Dunedin, where according to the 1940* Dictionary of New Zealand Biography, *William farmed 'in the English style.' Catherine later married James Fulton and moved to a sheep station near East Taieri, 10 km inland of Dunedin.*

The area in which Catherine and her sisters had their scare is today less than a kilometre from the centre of the Octagon. But in the 1850's the girls had scarcely walked 500 metres from their home, in what is now Stafford Street, before being 'quite in the country'.

Mary Jeffreys with my sisters and myself had an exciting adventure one afternoon. We wished to call on an emigrant named Mrs. McFie who lived in rather an out of the way place, surrounded by bush, flax and fern.

The day was fine and sunny so we walked merrily along Mud Terrace (which is now transformed into Princes Street South), and we then turned up a pretty winding track towards the hill.

One of our party suddenly called out 'Oh, there is a man in a red blanket with a great stick following us', so we quickened our steps, and he did also. Then we ran, having to go single file because of the track. We reached the gate first and burst in at the door causing great astonishment to Mrs. McFie.

We helped her to put her table with chairs and boxes against the door and then waited, trembling all over. Soon a ponderous banging on the door frightened us still more, and the man called out 'I am waiting for the young ladies!'. My youngest sister and my cousin Mary Jeffreys became hysterical, half laughing and half crying.

Time went on, tramp, tramp, around the house continued with occasional thunderous bangs on the door. We asked Mrs. McFie 'When will your husband be home?' 'Not until after dark', was her reply.

Presently we screwed up our courage and cautiously sallied forth accompanied by Mrs. McFie with her broom. We went at quick march with the man close at our heels. Up Mud Terrace we almost ran, and joyful sight! at our garden gate (in what is now Stafford Street) stood our father and Mr. Strode, who looked astonished at our agitated condition.

They quickly relieved us of our tormentor and we rushed through the glass door into our sitting room, where breathing more quietly we recounted our unpleasant experience to our anxious mother.

The man was eventually sent back to the Home country as a dangerous lunatic, he had frightened other women also in isolated dwellings.

Manor Place had been the scene of our adventure - imprisoned in the cottage it seemed to us quite in the country.

A 'Bush' section on Green Island, Dunedin (Fox Lodge) from S. Hursthouse, New Zealand the Britain of the South, 1857.

A Meeting with Queen Victoria

Born in New Zealand, Elizabeth Colenso was already a mature woman when the first of the immigrant ships arrived. Her parents worked for the Church Missionary Society and the family were living at Otahuhu when Bishop Selwyn insisted she marry the mission's printer, William Colenso. Elizabeth taught Maori children while her husband combined his work as a deacon with some of the pioneer explorations of New Zealand. They served at Waimate North, then Ahuriri, in the vicinity of Napier. The arranged marriage was not successful and after William fathered a child by a Maori woman in their household, Elizabeth took their children back to her family in Auckland. She then went to London, spending her early forties translating Maori texts for the Church Missionary Society. Several prominent Maori visited London during this time and Elizabeth helped them find their way in that community. Her adventure here concerns the presentation of Hare and Hariata Pomare and their new-born son to Queen Victoria. The child, born in London, attracted the notice of the Queen, who asked to become one of the godparents. An official's wife stood in for Her Majesty at the Christening but the Queen asked that the boy, named Albert Victor in honour of the Royal couple, be brought to her at Windsor by Elizabeth Colenso.

Friday, 4th Dec., 1863

A most lovely day - we Hare Pomare, Hariata and child and I started at 8.30 this morning in a fly for Paddington Station, took train and changing at Slough, reached Windsor about 11 a.m. Took a cab to the Castle where we were ushered into a warm cosy sitting room where refreshments were brought us - tea, coffee, and bread and butter, cake and wine. Sir Thomas came in to see baby and many ladies. After a time the Queen sent the Hon. Mrs. Bruce to say she wished to see the baby but first enquired what time we had arranged to go back - I told her Mr. Dealtry had named 4.30 p.m. Mrs. B. went back to her Majesty and then came and said that the Duke of Newcastle had requested that they might not be detained late for fear of cold etc. I said they were often out at parties late in the evening and as we had a fly I did not think they could hurt, but that of course we would do whatever her Majesty wished. Mrs. Bruce went and returned, saying that the Queen did not wish on any account to alter the arrangement which had been made etc etc so we stayed till 4.30. Soon after Mrs. B. came and took us to see the Queen. We went along a magnificently ornamented winding corridor, full of paintings, statues, etc etc with soft seats at intervals and splendid carpet. We waited some minutes in the corridor as the Queen was

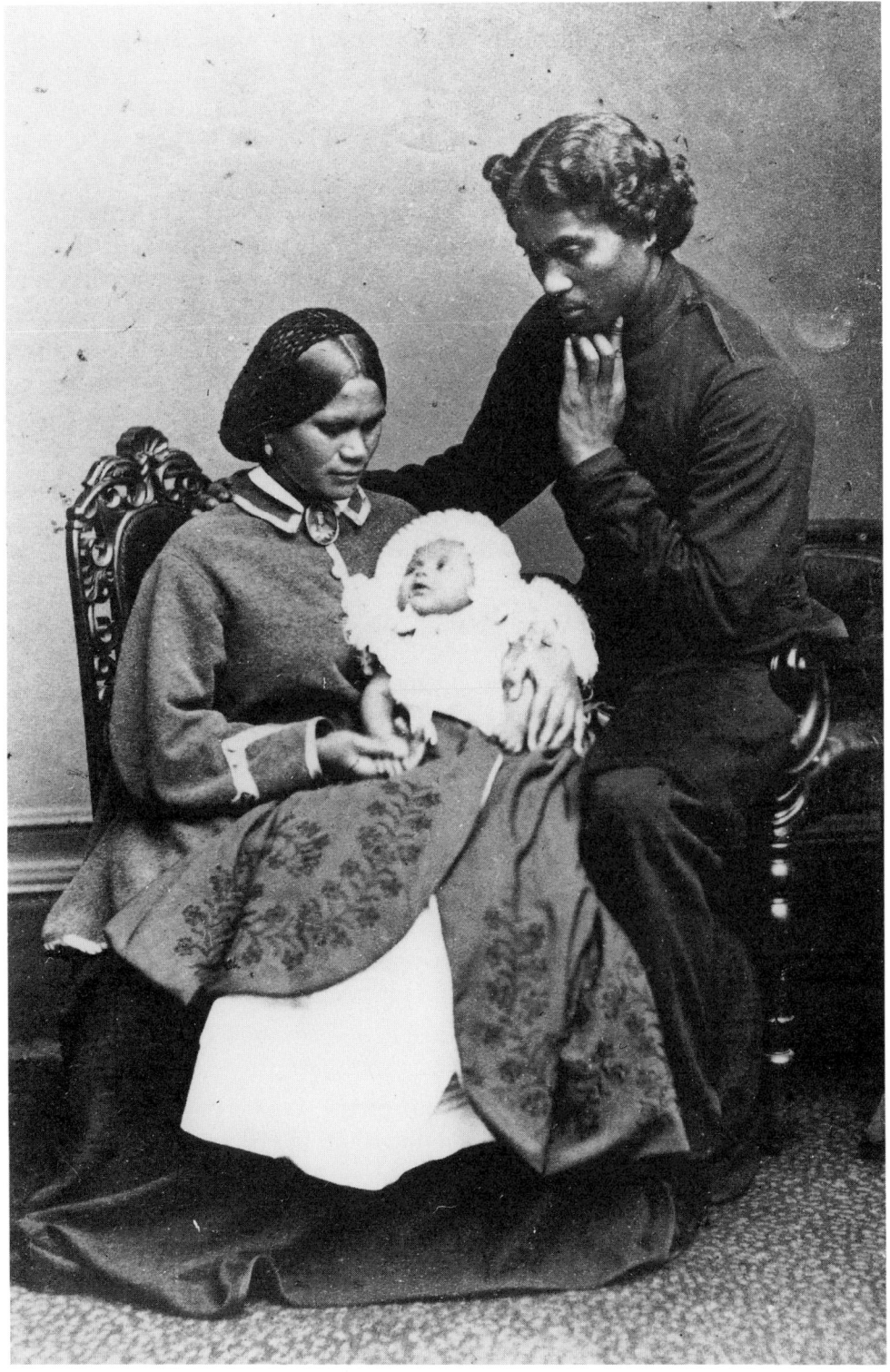

Hare Pomare, his wife Hariata and their child Victor Albert, photographed by Royal Command, in London, 1864. Alexander Turnbull Library.

not quite ready. The Housekeeper then proposed taking us to see the drawing rooms and dining rooms full of rich and beautiful and costly furniture - in the Second drawing room was the table where her Majesty takes her coffee and the Etiquette is for the gentlemen to stand, and on going into the Second drawing room they may sit down. We walked all round the Royal family's dining table which was laid for dinner and was resplendent with gold and silver plates. The Queen's seat was pointed out to us in the middle at one side opposite a magnificent gold, or gilt? flower vase filled with flowers. We admired the view from the windows - and now we were hastily re-called as her M. was ready to see us. We were led into an audience chamber adjoining the drawing-room and stood awaiting our Monarch's approach. She came preceded by attendants opening the doors and was followed by 4 of her daughters, the princesses, and the interesting little Princess Beatrice, about 5 or 6 years old. The Queen came forward with a sweetly! sweetly! smiling face bowing to each of us in turn. We bent the knee and bowed to our gracious sovereign - the Queen came and kissed the baby and admired his healthy fine appearance and said how pleased she was to see him. She spoke of the war in N.Z. and said how much it troubled her and she earnestly hoped it would soon be over. She said she should always feel a great interest in the child and hoped he would be a good man etc etc interpreted to Hare Pomare. He made a suitable reply and then returned grateful thanks to the Queen for all her *great* kindness to them and also for the splendid present to the baby and £25 to Hariata. Her Majesty smiled most graciously. Baby then happened to cry out lustily and the Queen and Princesses retired. They turned round two or three times and smiled and bowed a goodbye till out of sight.

We were then shewn by the Housekeeper all through the State apartments - arrived at the Banqueting Hall an attendant came up with Prince Leopold, an interesting and pleasing looking boy, but who seemed rather bashful. He wished to see baby who was shown to him and kissed by him.

We then proceeded on our tour of inspection through the rooms which were most magnificent.

We saw Mr. Frith painting the picture of the Prince of Wales and the Princess Alexandra's wedding and also the room the princess occupied the night before her wedding, the Waterloo room, the rooms containing the celebrated Bayeux ? Tapestry - *most beautiful* - the whole history of Queen Esther in the Bible portrayed in beautiful *needle*work. We saw a splendid doll's house which had been presented to the Princess Royal when a child by her Nurse, cost about £400 (four hundred pounds).

At length we got back to the large banqueting hall where Prince Leopold saw the baby - I forgot to say that we saw the room where her Majesty bestows the Order of the Garter in which hangs a full length picture of the

Queen in the dress worn by her Majesty on such occasions. A raised arm chair (ascending by steps) made of most beautifully and elaborately carved ivory which came out of the Exhibition of '51. We each sat for a minute or so in it and Hare laid the Baby in it.

As soon as we had returned to the corridor from whence we had set out, an intimation came from the Queen that she wished to see the Baby again. We waited till the Honourable Mrs. Bruce came who said we were to wait a little her Majesty was not quite ready. In the meanwhile crowds of her Majesty's female etc attendants came to see and nurse the baby, the attendants and children of the Crown Princess of Prussia (Princess Royal) and the Princess Beatrice, with her brother Prince Leopold holding the hand of his little nephew Prince William were all there. The four children came round the Baby, the Princess Charlotte a little pretty thing in white took hold of his hand and said 'What a pretty little hand he has' 'What pretty fingers' and I ventured to ask if I might kiss the little one year old prince's hand (Henry) and was permitted to do so. Mr. Bainbridge formerly of Waimate Bay of Islands now appeared having received the Queen's command to take Hare Pomare's likeness which he did taking him away with him for the purpose.

The Queen now sent for me with the Baby to her private audience room and received me most graciously so that I felt at ease immediately. Her Maj. made many enquiries as to Hariata's health both before and since her confinement. She then enquired how long I had been in New Z. I told her I was born there and well remembered the times of cannibalism. The Queen lifted up her hands saying 'Good gracious' and looked at Mrs. Bruce. She then asked how long had I been in England and when I returned - I answered nearly three years and I thought of going back in October next; she then said she supposed I could speak the N.Z. language well I said yes better than English. The Queen smiled sweetly and said she should always feel a great interest in the child and that I must write from time to time and let her know how it got on. Mrs. Bruce asked the Queen to take it in her arms and try its weight which she did and said it was the finest child of its age (six weeks) she had ever seen. She gave me back the child, smiled most sweetly, wished me goodbye and retired. I returned to the room where Hariata was and Mrs. Bruce appeared and conducted us back to the room we were first received in.

The housekeeper then came and refreshments were ordered for us. A messenger came to ask if two ladies and my lady Canning could see the baby. They came and pronounced the universal opinion, 'the finest child of his age they had seen.'

Hare returned and a cab being ordered the housekeeper saw us safely into it, giving me the address and name, she having promised to show Fanny and Latimer and myself the private rooms in the spring or summer if I write and let her know a day or two beforehand.

Footnote: Albert Victor was born in 1863 and is said by some writers to have been lost at sea as a young man. By coincidence the same edition of the Auckland Sun newspaper which carries the tale of Caroline Ngoungou in this book, also reports on Maori claims for the baptismal gifts from the Queen which were then held at Bishopscourt, Auckland. It appears from this that Hariata Pomare died in New Zealand and that Albert Victor was taken in by an Anglican orphanage in Auckland, aged four. Queen Victoria had wished him join the navy. Albert Victor is variously reported by the Sun to have died of an illness after sailing to San Francisco, or alternatively settling in Canada but his whereabouts were unknown when his relatives claimed the Royal Christening presents in 1929.

Missionary Elizabeth Colenso in later life, photographed in Auckland. Alexander Turnbull Library.

Opposite: On the way to Mount Cook. Ross Collection, Alexander Turnbull Library.

Explorations

SARAH MATHEW

Climbing the Volcano of Rangitoto

Sarah married her cousin Felton in Sydney in 1835 and was present at the founding of Auckland in 1840. Her husband was to serve temporarily as Surveyor-General to the infant colony. Both keen diarists, their records, now in the Alexander Turnbull Library, tell of early settlement about the time of the Treaty of Waitangi and feelings among the officials who established the new capital at Auckland. It was from there Sarah Mathew made this trip to the young volcano of Rangitoto, situated at the mouth of the Waitemata Harbour, virtually in the ocean entry to Auckland.

I think it was in the second year of the Settlement, that the city being now all laid out, the streets marked out and named, the sale of the Allotments took place, and my husband bought two of them, in order to include the pretty spot on which our tents had first stood, and then our house was begun. A ship came in from Van Diemen's land or Tasmania as it is now called with a cargo of superior timber for building purposes, & of this our house was built; its durability has been well tested, for now, after the lapse of more than 30 years, I understand the dear old house is as good as ever, it cost upwards of £2000, though of very moderate dimensions & simple construction, much after the fashion of an Indian Bungalow, all on the ground floor, with windows to the ground opening on a wide Verandah, and a terrace, beyond which a sloping lawn with flower beds and then a belt of shrubbery partly native trees, but sown with acorns, chestnuts, walnuts, & planted with vines & fig trees, which we brought from Sydney. The Acorns were from the Oaks at Hobartville, the estate of our old friends the Coes - great changes have taken place, but I hear the Oaks are flourishing still. 12 years ago, when I last saw the place, they were goodly trees. But we continued to inhabit our little Warre [whare] for some time after our return from the cruise to the South, making several expeditions by land exploring the country round Auckland, sometimes on foot, but generally on horseback, or in our boat, on the Manukao [Manakau] or Waitemata. One of our most fatiguing expeditions was to the top of the highest of the Volcanic Peaks on the Island of Rangitoto: we were accompanied on this occasion by our young friend, John du Moulin, who was indeed at that time one of our family, Captain Rough, the Harbour Master, and Captain England, a retired officer who had come out to settle in the new Colony, poor fellow he was killed by the Natives a few years afterwards. But at that time, all was bright & hopeful, and no one had the least apprehension of hostilities. We started early in our boat, taking provisions with us, it was a

Maori fishing party with Rangitoto in view by Charles Heaphy VC.

beautiful day I remember in early spring time, when all the trees and shrubs were in flower, the bright yellow balls or tufts of the Acacias, with numbers of those beautiful birds the Tui, which specially affect these trees as if aware that their shining black plumage appeared to great advantage in contrast with the golden blossoms and graceful foliage of the Acacia, then the Rata with its small red flowers, & the Fuchsias with varied flowers, red or white or purple, & largest of all the Pohutukawa which grows quite down to the coast covered with large crimson tufted blossoms shaped like a bottle-brush; but besides all these, & climbing over all, are the largest flowered white clematis I ever saw; and many other shrubs we noticed, as we clambered over the broken masses of Scoria of which the whole island seems to be composed, track or path there was none, after we left the Beach; and the extraordinary richness of the vegetation covering all this bed of Scoria was remarkable. We were more than 3 hours in the ascent, every step over huge masses of brittle substance, sometimes so thin as to break under our feet, every interstice filled with fern or shrubs and parasitic plants, which were in some places a help, their tough streamers giving us something to hold on by, when the Scoria & broken rocks rolled from our feet. The height is by measurement only 900 or a thousand feet above sea level, but the nature of the ground to be trodden, & the steepness of the ascent, makes it more fatiguing than many higher mountains; and there were deep hollows, extinct craters, which we had to go round, or descend into & ascend on the other side, here the ground was bare of all vegetation, & was only a mass of fine cinders, into which the feet would sink, as on a shingly beach, so we tried to keep to the steeper parts of the hill. The heat was excessive & not a drop of water was to be found all through that toilsome day. At last we reached the summit, all quite exhausted, & sat down to rest and breathe. We found the top of the mountain was a deep hollow and surrounded by irregular Peaks, apparently formed by the action of the Volcano, throwing up heaps of ashes or scoria in several directions, probably at different periods; it must have been long extinct by the quantity and size of the vegetation; but what a wonderfully extensive view we gained from this point, all the Firth of Thames studded with its islands, the great and little Barrier islands with their rich Copper mines, the dense forest of the island Waiheke, the Mercury isles [sic], Coromandel with its gold diggings, then suspected but all as yet unknown, & then Kareho sleeping in the sunshine & the little busy hive we had left this morning scarcely to be distinguished from the unknown forest. The wind blew so strongly on the summit, we could scarcely stand, & after resting awhile, and making a fire of the dead wood, which burned for some days, we began our descent, trying what appeared an easier way, than that by which we ascended; it seemed from the top of the mountain as if a stream of Scoria and stones had poured over the lip of the crater, quite down to the shore: but this was broken by deep fissures, and in places so covered with vegetation that our progress was often impeded, the sharp rocks & scoria had worn my boots to pieces, & my dress of grey merino was torn in shreds, struggling through the thorny brush wood, & by the sharp edges of the rocks - thankful was I to see the shore & boat at last, where we had some wine, but no water had been found, tho' the men left with the boat had searched half round the island for some spring or stream: this absence of water would account for there being no living creature on it; we saw nothing, not even a bird. We were all quite exhausted, & after a short rest returned to Auckland. It was quite dark when we landed, and we had scarcely reached our house, when my husband was taken with faintness & shivering which alarmed me very much. I sent for Dr. Johnson who administered brandy, & sat with him some time after he got to bed; he told me it was exhaustion from over-exertion, & that he would be well in the morning, which was indeed the case after a night's rest. This alarm quite cured my fatigue, I watched the greater part of the night, and felt no want of sleep, tho' previously in the boat I had scarcely been able to keep my eyes open.

Thames to Tauranga by Litter

Lady Mary Ann Martin was regarded as an invalid yet she made several long journeys from Auckland, sometimes being carried in a Maori litter. As wife of the Chief Justice of New Zealand she lived in Judge's Bay, Auckland, receiving visits from the official community, including Governor and Mrs. Grey, and Bishop and Mrs. Sarah Selwyn. Lady Martin arrived in New Zealand during 1842 and lived in Auckland until 1874 when she returned to Britain with her husband. There she wrote Our Maoris, *a book far more interesting than its now unfashionable title suggests. It includes accounts of her work in establishing a hospital for Maori in Auckland and her interest in providing for their education. There is much, too, of the settlers' reactions to war and public affairs. This extract, however, recounts adventures in the hinterland.*

We started for Tauranga and the Lake District in the spring of 1846, accompanied by a faithful party of Waiheke natives. The Bishop took us all in his little cutter, *Flying Fish*, across the Gulf of Hauraki to the valley of the Thames. We went on board on a lovely evening, our patients and their friends all coming out to wish us good-bye and to watch our departure. We ran by moonlight between the mainland and islands. The Bishop stood at the helm steering. I lay, wrapped in cloaks, on the deck, enjoying at once the beauty of the moonlit waters and of the cliffs fringed with trees, and the deep talk of the two friends. The captain was an Englishman, a tall, handsome man, and the only sailor was an equally tall, noble-looking Maori, from the Southern Island. At a late hour we turned in to the tiny cabin, furnished with two bunks of canvas. The Bishop, wrapped in his shepherd's plaid, lay on the deck outside, and our men found some place forward. There was hardly a breath of wind stirring the next day. Long sweeps were used to propel us along, our Maoris willingly offering their services. At sunset we put to shore, opposite to a native village called Tararu, which nestled under the long range of wooded hills. The people came swarming down to the beach to welcome us and to crowd round the Bishop. The still evening, the water like a lake, the little ship, the boat upon the shore, the eager, upturned faces, all reminded one of scenes on another lake long ago.

Our men soon pitched our little tent on the sand, and piled up freshly-cut fern for a bed. The natives do this in an artistic way. The stems are bent underneath the branchy heads of the strong ferns, so that they are as elastic as a spring bed. The smell of the fronds is as agreeable as heather; over the fern was laid a piece of waterproof and our blankets. I had heard so much from travellers of the sweetness of the notes of the birds in the bush, that I was grievously disappointed when only cocks crowed shrilly, at intervals, all night! Half the village had gathered round the tent when we emerged, and after a friendly chatter, a canoe was lent to us for six weeks on very easy terms, and we were soon paddling along the coast till we entered the wide mouth of the Waihou River, called by the English the Thames. To our right another river ran into the gulf, fringed at the mouth by an extensive wood of white pine trees. All day, as we paddled up against the stream, we passed by villages with fleets of canoes drawn up on the beach, or by great jungles of flax and reed-bushes. We stopped at sunset, and in a few minutes our canoe was made fast to a bush on the bank; the tent, bedding, and food box were brought on shore, and in ten minutes more the tent was pitched, our bed made, and a bright fire lit, over which our camp kettle was hung. Tea, biscuits, and a slice or two of bacon, frizzled over the hot embers, made a capital supper. The men over their fire cooked a mess of rice and potatoes, and long after we had settled for the night, we heard their merry laugh and chatter as they hunted for eels in the mud of the river's bank. We did hear the birds next morning, at sunrise, in all their sweetness, as Captain Cook had described; first, the bell bird gave its one clear, full note, and then came such a 'jargoning' as made one's heart glad; and looking out at the tent door we saw the rising sun lighting up the woods and flax-bushes in ruddy glory. By seven o'clock we were in the canoe again, and paddled all day long, save when we rested at mid-day for dinner. The men did not row with the steadiness of Englishmen. They had spurts when they dashed along at a tremendous pace, encouraging one another with cries and snatches of old boat songs. Their paddles flashed in the sunlight. Then would come a season of dreamy dawdling and silence. We passed our Sunday at a little village perched on a cliff above the river. After service in Maori, the people came to the tent door; some for teaching and friendly chat, some sick folk for medicine. I had brought a box of pills on the chance, and they received them with much gratitude and entire faith. One poor old woman prayed us to give her spectacles.

The banks of the river, up to this time, had been low, without any special beauty; but on Monday morning a sharp bend brought us into sight of loveliness, such as one can never forget. The river became deep and narrow, and wound for many miles through a forest. It was spring-time, and the great white clematis and the yellow kowhai blossoms hung over the brim of the river in masses of gold and silver, which were reflected in the clear blue water. We thought of the twelve princesses in Grimm's fairy stories, who saw trees with gold and silver branches. The great forest came down to the water's edge. Once we came to a little opening where a pathway had been made, just wide enough to drag a newly-made canoe down to the river. Far away up this vista, some thin blue smoke went up from a bush fire. Now and then the forest receded, and a range of hills with grassy slopes appeared instead. Some day, doubtless, stately mansions will be built there, and the park-like ground stocked with deer. As we slowly paddled past one of these ranges, one of our men pointed out a hill and said: 'That is part of my property. I have got a store of potatoes up there. If we had but time to stop, I would run and get you some.' Yet it is sometimes asserted that the greater part of the country is untilled and ownerless. As far as we could learn, every man had his share in the tribal property, and knew as well as any old English squire what tracts belonged to him.

We had to stop one whole day in our encampment; there was such a steady rain. We did not find time pass heavily. We had Guizot's *Histoire de la Civilisation* to read, as a contrast to our rude surroundings; and our men sat by the fire and smoked, and were very merry. Towards evening the weather cleared, and an old man, attracted by our camp fire, came from a distance to visit us. He had learned to read, and was well disposed to impart his knowledge of Scripture and to gain more. He told us, in the most naive, graphic way, the story of the cleansing of Naaman, and made seven distinct stages in the process, till at last the leper came out with a man's skin. He might have stayed longer, had not his quick eye caught sight of a wild pig, and he went off stealthily to catch it. The next day we reached the highest point of the river that we needed to ascend. The canoe was dragged on shore and half-hid among some bushes to keep it from the heat of the sun, and the paddles stuck upright beside it. On one of these a word or two was scratched, to say to whom they belonged, and that no one must take them away. We pitched for the night at the foot of a high hill, over the face of which a grand waterfall dashed headlong into the valley below. We encamped beside a mountain stream, which hurried down over great boulders to the river. The distant roar of the waterfall, the brawling of the stream and the hoarse cry of the night-owl made us wakeful, and by five in the morning every one was astir, as we had a long day's march before us.

We had engaged, the night before, eight bearers from a neighbouring village to carry me. Breakfast was over, prayers read with the people, and the tent taken down, when the men struck for higher pay. One of them, a tall, powerful, wild-looking fellow, began to run up and down, brandishing his spear as he delivered his speech. He spoke for himself and for his kinsmen; the way was long, the burden great, they must have higher wages. Our own people dared not interfere. I am afraid, as I sat and shivered in the valley, I should soon have given in, but my husband remained quite quiet, and after half-an-hour's vigorous declamation on the part of the insurgents, he calmly turned to our boy Josiah, directing him to go over to Tauranga,

A Maori litter for carrying sick or wounded. Detail of construction also shown. From The Story of New Zealand *by Arthur S. Thomson.*

where we were bound to spend Sunday, and to bring back with him a party of men on the the Monday. A stage aside from him that our meat was nearly gone and the bread running short, met with no reply; so he packed up his knapsack and blanket, and, waving his hand, began his solitary march. Before he had gone a hundred yards, the leader of the strike burst out laughing and said: 'Oh, friend, it was only fun of mine, we'll go on your terms,' and in a few minutes, with good-humour beaming on all our faces, we began the steep ascent. The native litter was very light. It consisted of two thin, elastic poles tied at each end, with a light network of flax in the middle and bits of wood across for head and foot rest; a pillow and cloak completed the arrangement; the bearers changed every three minutes, and wore pads on their shoulders. They had proposed to tie me in, but I indignantly declined, till I found myself apparently standing nearly upright in the air, with a fall of 100 feet below me, and my hands too cold to be able to hold on to the poles; when I was obliged meekly to request them to make me safe; they strapped a long rope of flax across my waist and feet, and I felt as safe as an Indian papoose in its bark cradle. We had a glorious view from the top of the hill; the river lay like a silver thread below, and far away in the distance rose the snow-capped peak of

Tongariro; we could not but picture to ourselves what the stir and hum of life will be in years to come, in this well-watered plain, now laying solitary and waste.

Our way down the mountain lay for many miles through a tangled forest; no word-painting can describe the beauty of the trees, their trunks green with parasitical plants and ferns, while tangled masses of supplejack hung down from the branches; the daylight was almost shut out by the luxuriant foliage. We got on but slowly, as our track often lay down a steep, sharp bank to a clear mountain stream, the men clustering round the litter to lift me over the boulders, or over some huge tree that lay prone across the path; sometimes they had to clear away the tangled brushwood with hatchets; and so we went on again, struggling upward till we came to some sunny little opening - 'places of light,' as the natives call them - where the sun greeted us, and the birds sang, and the weary men laid me down among flowering, sweet-smelling shrubs; we could hear parrots screaming in the distance. My wild bearers, ten in number, were very kind; they could not make out why I wanted to look at some of the delicate little ferns which grew on the trees, but when I expressed a wish for one, they threw so many, all dripping with moisture, into my lap, that I had to cry 'Enough.' By one p.m. we had passed through the forest, and came out on a wide plain, from which we saw the sea and the coast, stretching far away, and a mountain at the entrance of the harbour standing out against the blue sky; but our fatigues were not over: we knocked about till dark in a whale-boat on a rough sea, and when we landed the first sight that greeted us was a raging fire in the pah on an opposite hill. My bearers put me down on the beach, and rushed off to help extinguish the flames. A kind Maori woman, whose English husband was away, received us into her house, and gave us bread and coffee, and when, after stumbling along in the dark to the crossing-place and shouting in vain for a boat, we returned to her, she brought out a pile of new blankets and made a bed for us on the floor. About midnight, however, our host, Archdeacon Brown, arrived, and soon after we reached his comfortable Mission-house. After ten nights in the bush, an English bedroom seemed a great luxury.

I stayed for three weeks at Tauranga, while my husband went on to the hot springs. The house was all of native workmanship; the outer walls were of raupo, and the inner walls and ceilings receded after the best Maori pattern. The windows of the bedroom were overhung with roses. One hardy shoot had worked its way in through the roof, and hung down in the room. I was ill for the first week, and was tenderly nursed by a Maori woman, who, but for skin and speech, might be taken for a well-trained English maid. Her name was Margaret, and she had lived from childhood with Mrs. Brown, and had nursed her through many illnesses. She was delighted to find that I could talk Maori with her; every morning she used to come in, duster in hand, and steal gently about the room, dusting, and folding, and arranging; and then helping me to dress with so much care and tenderness that I used to long to show her to English people as a sample of a so-called savage. Her history is a pretty one; she was sent to be the little slave-girl of a damsel of her own age entrusted to Mrs. Brown's care. The latter, a chief's daughter, was to be taught English ways, and might sew or help 'Mother' in any genteel way; but her father gave many strict injunctions as to her never preparing food or doing anything menial. So little Margaret came to do the rough work; and after a while a slave-boy was sent to Mrs. Brown's school, who had nursed the little heiress in her babyhood, carrying her on his back, and waiting on her all day long. They all grew up together, and the heiress loved the boy, now grown into a man. Wonderful to say, the old father, in consideration of the lad's early care of her, consented to the match. But the course of true love never did run smooth; by a strange perversity the young man loved the maid instead of the mistress, and the maid loved him. The young mistress was very wroth when she found how matters stood, and for a long time refused her consent. At last Mr. Brown won her over by the dignity of giving a written consent to the match. She issued a sort of marriage licence, and she went to the wedding. Poor girl! she died some months after (not of a broken heart).

Everything went on after such a quiet fashion, just as in an English rectory and village, that it was strangely interesting to hear stories from the Browns of their experiences ten or fifteen years before. 'Do you see those patches in these dimity curtains?' said my hostess to me one evening as she sat by my bedside. 'I mended them when we recovered our property after the great Rotorua War. They had been torn up to make garments by the spoilers. The war, which lasted for several years, and in which hundreds of lives were sacrificed and acts of heathen ferocity committed which must not be recorded, was begun through the revenge of one Rotorua man. A powerful member of his own tribe had offended him, and others stood by the offender. The wretched man went off to Tauranga to a tribe long hostile to his own, and slew one of its members in cold blood. Of course, the Tauranga people came down with a war-party to take 'utu'. They not only attacked the Rotorua natives, but they sacked the Mission station and burnt down the house. Not that they had any grudge against the good old missionary, Mr. Chapman, and his wife, but because they were their enemies' Pakehas. And then the Rotoruas sacked the Tauranga Mission station.' Mrs. Chapman was staying with the Browns for rest and change, for her heart was sad through the terrible sights and scenes of war around her, when she heard the wild shouts of a war-party, headed by the renowned Maori chief Waharoa (Long Mouth), as they returned in triumph home. She saw the men rushing by, loaded with spoils. One huge fellow had her neat, black silk bonnet (his only article of clothing) stuck on his head. Another had her much-prized wedding-gown thrown as a shawl across his shoulders, and she soon found that she was houseless. Dear little woman! she had a great dread of savages when she left England; but she followed her husband without a murmur, and as long as she remained in the north at the Waimate, where all was comparatively quiet, she was timid and unsettled; but, as soon as she was called to accompany Mr. Chapman into the heart of the country among fierce heathens, her fears vanished. She became a mother to all around her, and the eyes of the roughest would glisten as they spoke of 'Mother,' and of her kindness to them.

A NATIVE SCHOOL.

Night camp in the Rangiora Bush as painted by Frederick Weld. Alexander Turnbull Library.

CHARLOTTE GODLEY

A Long Ride on the Canterbury Plains

Before the arrival of the Canterbury Pilgrims on their First Four Ships, Charlotte Godley made a journey across the barely populated plains. Her Letters *tell of accompanying her husband, while caring for a three-year-old boy, on a journey to the present locality of Oxford and back to Lyttelton.*

December 13, 1850

On Wednesday we were to start for an expedition across the plains, to make sure of seeing something of the country before any of our first ships could arrive, and while we had Mr. Weld with us.

It turned out most fortunately that we did go then, but I was rather alarmed at the idea of introducing Arthur suddenly to bush life, and bush fare; sleeping in a tent and so on, in possible rain. However, we were already leading such a rough uncomfortable life that the change was no so much for the worse, in those respects, and it was important that my husband should go without delay, while he could; and I could not well have stayed *quite* alone here, and in short, off we went on Wednesday, December 4th. Captain Stokes had *most* good-naturedly insisted on John's bringing his two horses with us, which was I need not say a great stretch of kindness, and he offered us every kind of store, from ship biscuits, to wine and green tea. When he heard of our expedition, in spite of all I could say, he sent me a chicken-pie, and some tins of preserved meat, etc. He sent Arthur a present of a little puppy, the grandchild of his own favourite pointer, for which Arthur, to his great amusement, wrote him a letter of thanks....

Our first day's journey was only as far as Mr. Deans' station on the plain, about ten miles, but we had to climb over the hill. I conclude you know that the great road is still very unfinished; several shoulders of rock that come in the way, and have to be blasted, stop it up completely, and in some places along the line even the path is quite a climb, with a rope to pull yourself up by. Since the money was lent to the Governor for carrying on the works (five weeks ago) about £300 has been devoted to making a bridle path, over the hill, immediately above the port which is about two miles shorter than the line of the road, but will only be meant for horses. When we went up there was still a bit at the top where no one can ride; man and horses must climb over rough stones and rocks, and on the other side the descent is steep enough to make most people prefer walking, too, until the path is completed. From the top of the hill, we had a lovely view, the day was so very clear. We had rocky hills all round us, and, below, the plain; a dead flat for forty or fifty miles each way, sea beach on one side, and hills, or rather mountains, on all the others. To the North, as far as we could see, were the Kaikouras; magnificent hills nearly 10,000 feet high, covered with snow, and clear to the eye as Snowdon on our finest days, though it was 106 miles from us, as the crow flies.

We got into Mr. Deans' between five and six, in time for a heavy tea; and a walk afterwards, to see his station, which is a very good picture of colonial life, before the ornamental has begun to be considered. There are on the plain five patches of bush, or rather, as we should say, of woods, some of them very large. Near the smallest, and nearest to Lyttelton, of them, perhaps fifty yards from the last tree, Mr. Deans has built his house, on the bank of a beautiful stream, as clear as those about Llanberis, and ornamented with green bushes growing at the side, and stretching over like long branches; making a perfect paradise for the geese, two ducks, and one wild one with a young one which was diving about there and is not molested. Arthur thought it perfection to stand on the edge and watch them, and pronounced them exactly like himself and his Father, because they too went into cold water every morning. He is beginning to think a great deal of his Father and try to be like him, in which, by the by, he succeeds pretty well naturally; at breakfast, for instance, he eats oatmeal porridge, which he used not to like, for the sole purpose of eating the same, and so on. Mr. Deans' house is of weatherboard and lined (panelled) throughout; there is a good sized kitchen, and out of it two little bedrooms, meant for himself and his brother, Mr. William Deans, who was not at home when we were there, but he has now so many visitors that one may be almost called a spare room. There is, just behind, a house, much larger, and more roughly built, (no ceiling) where his workmen live, and the cooking is done. The principal one is married, and Mrs. Todd, who is cook, housekeeper, and housemaid, has already four children; the three youngest born there, and doing credit to the place, quite prize children anywhere, and she is the only woman about the place. Then there are buildings round for cattle, and for sheep; some of them across the stream, over which there is a very picturesque bridge on piles. The fare at Mr. Deans' was very plentiful; fresh-killed mutton, salt beef which all the people here keep in barrels for their men's rations, bread which is generally rather sour, and capital scones; flour and water baked on a girdle, and made good *á plaisir* by the addition of milk and soda, or butter, or sugar; and there too we had damper, the regular bush fare, - it is flour and water, kneaded, and baked on a stone under the wood ashes. Then we had plenty of butter and milk, and tea three times a day.

We did not start very early from Deans' as the morning was rather threatening, and we had a few drops of rain. He tells us that they have not had so wet a spring as this in the seven years that he has been here, and that in ordinary seasons there would not have been a green leaf in *our* garden. His own, which stands between the bush and the river, is *most* flourishing, and in it we had planted half of all our English seeds, most fortunately, as the other half, sown here, have all failed. It is *unusual* for them to grow at all here, but ours have a good many of them come up at Deans'. Almost all ordinary garden seeds are to be bought at Wellington, and the roses, etc. are beautiful there. I heard, before I came, of geranium hedges, but truth compels me to own that they are not visible; very few people have any at all. Those settlers who came out in ships touching at the Cape, generally brought supplies of flowers and shrubs from there, and they all do uncommonly well, and even bear the wind pretty well, which the roses do not. It was quite curious to see the burst of bloom on all the trees in our Wellington garden, when a few calm days came, just before we left....

After we left the fence of Deans' paddock, we saw nothing but unvaried *plain*, with surveyors' poles for landmarks, all covered with grass of different kinds, looking something like hay, and very tiring to walk through, for about twelve miles, when we came to the banks of the Courtenay [Waimakariri] on which we *camped* for the night. The little tent, just big enough for a bed for us three, was soon pitched, while some more cut toi-toi grass and fern, to spread at the bottom. Then the horses, nine altogether, were let loose to feed themselves, one or two tethered, in hopes that the rest would stay to keep them company, but it could not be done to all, as some horses always cut themselves with the rope. For instance, the one I ride did, the first night, and had to be let loose afterwards.

I assure you *camping* is the best fun possible, excepting at dressing-time. I packed all our things in a bit of india-rubber, in a tub, which was a great luxury, and just went on one side of a horse; as though the gentlemen could go down the river, Arthur and I could not quite manage so, but had to confine our evolutions to the top of our bed and kneel, as we could not stand upright in the tent, and of course no looking glass, so it was rather a scramble; but the evening, after the fire was lighted, was very pleasant. The flax bushes and grass grew all about, higher than our tent, so that we seemed almost in a shrubbery; about ten yards behind our tent, along the little native path by the river, the fire was lighted, with drift wood from the river, and round it we all established ourselves most comfortably, waiting for tea, which was soon ready; three flax stalks were tied together, gypsy fashion, and on them we hung just such a tin can and cover as one of your Welsh women, with a family of six, would bring for broth; they are the lightest to carry. When the water boiled, a quantity of tea was put in, and after a few minutes it was served round; to us, by way of distinction in pint mugs, and the rest of the party produced each man his tin pannikin, generally worn on the belt, to be ready for occasional refreshment at the streams, and for the first night we all had milk, a most unusual luxury. It was great fun sitting round the blaze, which the evening was just cold enough to make us appreciate; Arthur and I quite wrapped in Mr. Weld's opossum-skin cloak, which he used to lend me, such as they have in Australia, and which is as good as a house to live in.

As it got a little dark, a party of natives, who had been assembling at some huts just across the river, came over in a canoe to pay us a visit, and sit down by our fire. The chief was funnily dressed out for the evening, in white cotton stockings without shoes, white trowsers, a black waistcoat and jacket, and most wonderful beaver hat. The gentlemen had a sort of shed, built of long sticks, and sail cloth laid over it, with one side open to the fire; but till we were all asleep in the tent we heard them singing and laughing.

Next morning we were up early, and found the fire lighted, and tea but no milk; broiled eels, which the natives had caught for us in the river, during the night etc.; and as soon as breakfast was over, we had to pack up all our goods and tents, and then cross the river in a canoe, the horses having to be swum over. After a very short walk, we went the rest of our morning's journey in a canoe up the river, the banks of which were very pretty, as we got to the bush. My husband shot some wild ducks, and we lay in the boat, very pleasantly, and were paddled to the spot where we were to get on our horses again.

There we found assembled a party of natives, who were expecting us to come and feast with them. So we had to stay and dine there and a very pretty place it was; but, as a feast *with* natives, it was rather a failure. For they just gave us some *infantine* potatoes, much too young to eat, and some capital little fish, just like whitebait, from the river; and then sat round and looked at us, and smoked, and sucked fern root, while our men cooked, and then spread out the dinner, in a shed, built there by the surveyors, and here we ate alone. It was pleasant sitting in shade, though, for the sun was really very hot that day, and gave me a great sickness and headache, during the afternoon ride. But it all got well with the cool sunset, and the sight of our beautiful camp for that evening, at the edge of Rangiora bush, the next to the one where we had dined. You never saw anything prettier than it was, but I am a bad hand at describing, and you must imagine us there, just on the edge of thick, almost impenetrable wood, with very fine trees; and our little tent, with a fire at the door, quite shaded over by the tall waving toi-toi grass, and the large one for the gentlemen a little beyond, with such a magnificent fire.

Mr. Weld, often as he had camped, in every kind of country, quite

Frederick Weld's painting of the crossing of the Waimakariri includes the Maori camp across the water. Canterbury Museum.

exclaimed in admiration at it. He is quite a practised bushman, and did all kinds of things for us, better than anyone else. He even went and got me a bouquet, that I wish I could send home for some of you to take to a ball! It was the flower of the cabbage tree, in size like an aloe, with a bunch of small whitish flowers, perhaps eighteen inches high, and sweet like hyacinths, growing straight up out of the green leaves. We all sat round till the stars shone out, oh, so bright, and the owls began to hoot in the wood. It was a most lovely evening. Our only contretemps was, the loss of Arthur's little blue trowsers, which, in spite of the heat, he wore as a protection from mosquitos, and which were, in the dark, put bodily onto the fire by his Father, with the branch on which they were hung. A melancholy reminder of scraps of serge, and black buttons, was all we found in the morning. You would have laughed so to see how completely he took to the bush life, always talking of making 'little *warris*' [whares] (as they call the little huts for a night), as we used to build 'houses' with little sticks. Even his Father was obliged to own that he was no trouble, and very funny.

The next morning we had with much sorrow to say goodbye to Mr. Weld, whose course no longer lay with ours, as he was going to walk up the coast to his station, Flaxbourne, nearly opposite to Wellington. It was a great undertaking, about 150 miles, that had scarcely *been walked* before, several rivers to cross, and 19 miles running by the beach, along the rocks where you must hang on by your hands to the rocks above, and so on; but he wanted to see the country, and to get back to his station, so as to make preparations for going home, which he hopes to do by the *Lord William Bentinck*, to sail on the 20th January next. Mr. Fox and some troops go home by it too, and I should not a little like to know that a cabin was engaged for us....

Our next day's ride, about twenty long miles, took us to Harewood Forest [Oxford] where there is a surveyor's station (shed) just under the hills, across the plain, and this was to be the end of our journey. We spent all Sunday, the next day, there, and *I* was quite glad of the rest. It is a pretty place, from the beauty of the woods, which are extensive, and run over the hills, leaving patches of grass, so as to look just like fine park scenery. We settled that those Colonists who aspire to a fine place, will locate themselves somewhere, there, where there are such magnificent situations. A good sized river comes through a deep wooded rent in the rocks, two or three miles from the place we were at, and another small one only quarter of a mile from us, across the plain. We were on the very edge of the wood and consequently a prey to mosquitos, and sand-flies, which are *much* the worst here: they light on you silently without the smallest notice of their approach, and bite instantly, and then the bite is so venomous, and lasts such an immense time! Arthur of course was *the* victim, and really could hardly sleep for one night, he was in such a state of irritation all over. It was lucky we *had* arranged to stay where we were, for the next morning six of the horses, including both of ours, were not be found, and our horsebreaker rode fifty miles after them, and then walked in another direction, and at last they were discovered, a very few miles off, brought home, and measures taken to prevent a similar escapade in the night.

We had a very long day on the Monday, about thirty-five miles, and got into Deans' at tea-time, and pretty much tired. The principal features of the day were a *pig hunt* and the crossing of the river Courtenay. I did not join in the hunt, but saw the black boar's head with its fine tusks brought back. My husband was rather disappointed with it, as sport; either the dogs were *too good*, or else the pig not fast enough; it was caught directly, by a dog at each ear and then 'a hunter' sticks it with a long knife, behind the shoulder, and the whole thing is over. However, everyone says that with a good boar, and a fair start, you do often get a capital run of a mile or two. Much the best sport is with the wild dogs, of which there are a great number on the hills, sad nuisances to the sheep runs; they have become very much like foxes and run straight off just in the same way. The pigs get along very fast, but cannot help stopping and turning round occasionally, to see what is going on!

The crossing of the river was most disagreeable, and I am sure is a most dangerous thing for strangers to attempt. The bed is of shingle and about three-quarters of a mile broad, over which run eight or nine streams, most of them about the size of the Conway at Voelas (just above the bridge), and very rapid; but the bad part of it is, that the streams are always shifting their bed, besides that an extra warm day sends down more or less flood from the snow mountains; and so, though quite safe one day, you may find the same place impassable the next, and the water runs so clear that it is difficult to guess at the depth. None of our party had crossed where we did before, and though I was quite safe, myself, with Holland leading my horse, who understands these rivers well, it was not quite so with my husband, who *of course* would go first, though he had taken Arthur before him for the crossing, and in one stream, just at the edge, I had the pleasure of seeing his horse, and Mr. Boys', sink in over their tails as they tried to rise at the bank; the place was too deep, and the bottom not firm. Arthur was tossed off on to the ground, and they all scrambled out, very little wet, but it was very unpleasant to *see* from the other side, where I was. One very disagreeable part is that, when the water runs so fast, it makes everyone who is not used to it as giddy as possible. I fancied the horse was standing still, pawing the ground, and the stream getting more and more rapid, and so I hear others say.

We took half an hour's rest, after the river, and then left my husband to bathe, and made the best of our way towards Deans'; passing a number of paradise ducks, and putting up quail constantly, from under the horses' feet, but this is not the season for shooting them. There was a hot wind, and threatening sky, that made us press on to a good shelter, but the evening turned out lovely, and the bad weather came only in the shape of a *tremendous* blow next day, as we were crossing the hills back to Lyttelton.

Journey in the Old Waikato

The interest of Mary Ann Martin and her husband in Maori life is reflected throughout her autobiographical account of New Zealand, called Our Maoris. *Despite delicate health, Lady Martin made several adventurous trips with her husband. Here she describes a journey from Auckland into the Waikato and Waipa valleys, at a time before the region was devastated by the wars of the 1860s.*

In 1852 the Judge was asked to go as one of the Government Inspectors of native schools, and I gladly accompanied him. A cart was engaged to take me and our belongings for the first fourteen miles, as far as any road went. It had become very bad, and our driver, a cautious Scotchman, at every deep rut or boggy bit, would turn to me and say, 'I doubt if Jimmy will do it'; and when he bravely floundered through, he would mutter, 'I doubt if Jimmy'll do it going back.' It was pleasant to change to the light litter; the men trotted across the plain with me in a far easier way. When we got to a wide, well-known creek, called the Slippery Creek, from the uncertain footing, they were full of jokes, and called out to those who had already crossed to stand at ease and see our downfall into the water. The next day was very rainy, and the road was up and down steep wooded hills. The droppings from the branches came like a shower-bath on us as we pushed our way through the trees. We stopped to dine in the mid-day, and the men lit a roaring fire in an open space, and we warmed ourselves and dried our clothes. Our way led afterwards along a narrow muddy pig track. The poor fellows slipped and stumbled with me, and I felt like a daughter of the Pharaohs to oppress them so heavily. But they were good-tempered, and never grumbled, except at the cook, whose mess of flour had been made too thin, and they chaffed him unmercifully as the cause of every slip. We halted just before sunset in a dismal valley beside a stream. A great tree lay across the path, and our men soon detected a smouldering fire within the hollow trunk, and blew it up to a ruddy glow. We walked up and down, enjoying the luxury of a foot-warmer. The rain was over by the next morning, and we ascended up a steep bank into the forest again. For about a mile we travelled under an avenue of tree-ferns. The morning sun lit up the warm stems, and delicate drooping fronds; and the gossamer webs on the branches of the trees, still wet with rain-drops, glittered like diamonds. One man had to go in front of us, and with an axe chop a way through masses of supplejack and brushwood, so rich was the vegetation. At last we emerged from the forest, and far below us lay the broad Waikato river.

We had sent on a trusty native man ten days before to engage a canoe, and there he was quietly awaiting our arrival. We slept beside an old dry swamp, and had rushes for our beds instead of fern. The place was populous with large black birds, called by the Maoris pukeko. They have a harsh cry like a corn-crake. By early dawn we were afloat, and our men paddled steadily against the rapid current till evening. We passed many villages, and the people came to the bank to hear news, and to invite us to stay and eat. But there was no time for that, and not till after dark did we arrive at the first Mission station. Native teachers and their wives, and the whole school, boys and girls, came running to the bank to greet us, and to escort us up to the Rev. B. Y. Ashwells'. The other Government Inspectors arrived an hour or two later, and the next day the examinations began in geography, arithmetic, English and Scripture history. The girls sang part-songs in the evening with great spirit. We stayed over Sunday, and attended native service in the large reeded church built by the Maoris. The church was full of well-dressed, plump-looking boys and girls, with a good sprinkling of older people from the villages around. We heard of elementary schools being kept in all of these, and of monthly gatherings of the teachers to this central station for instruction. We lingered on the verandah in the evening to admire the quiet beauty of the scene. It was spring-time, and between us and the brimming river lay a paddock full of peach-trees in blossom, with a hedge of flowering white acacias, and on the opposite bank rose the wooded peak of Taupiri.

We had to start again up the river in pouring rain, which lasted all day. We went on shore for dinner, and scrambled up a bank to a very miserable village. We sheltered under a ti-manga, *i.e.*, a large square potato store set up on the top of high poles to prevent the rats attacking the food; the villagers gave us fire-wood, and we enjoyed our meal *al fresco*. It was hard work to get me up the slippery cliff at night, but the men were most patient and friendly. The ground was soaking and the ferns wet, but the good lads dashed the rain-drops off and lit a roaring fire. 'Noah,' our cook, acted as lady's maid, and dried all my wraps, and brought them back warmed, and with a strong smell of smoke (both of wood and tobacco). The total-abstainers in this country would rejoice to know that none of our party suffered from colds, though we had been sitting in the wet for twelve hours, with the exception of one, who took some brandy and water to keep off a chill; all the rest drank tea, and got up the next morning warm and unharmed. The weather had become lovely and intensely hot. Our men pulled lazily along up the Waipa river, a tributary of the Waikato, running between high wooded banks. It was a luxury to live on such a day, and to glide along past one bend after another, and watch the wild ducks rise.

While at Otawhao, the Mission station, we rode across to look at a mill which had been put up by the aid of the Government. The day was very hot, but a keen wind from the snow mountains cooled the air. Our path lay across a wide plain, and our eyes were gladdened on all sides by sights of peaceful industry. For miles we saw one great wheat field. The blade was just showing, of a vivid green, and all along the way, on either side, were wild peach-trees in full blossom. Carts were driven to and from the mill by their native owners; the women sat under the trees sewing flour bags; fat, healthy children and babies swarmed around, presenting a floury appearance. In the two villages we passed, there were wooden churches, built by the people themselves. We little dreamed that in ten years the peaceful industry of the whole district would cease and the land become a desert through our unhappy war. We went down to the river to the mouth of the Waikato, where Archdeacon Maunsell's Mission schools were to be inspected. It was easy work to go down the stream. We slept one night on a little island in the loveliest part of the Waikato. There was a wood on one side. As we came back from exploring its deep shade the scene was most picturesque - our white tent by the river's brink, the canoe made fast beside it, a large fire burning brightly, round which our men were busy cooking their evening meal. It was a moonlit night, and we stood looking at the wooded mainland, and the many islands, and the rushing river, rejoicing in the beauty all around. We heard the bittern sound his drum, booming in 'the sedgy shallow' in the early dawn. The men were up betimes, and made themselves very smart, as we expected to arrive early at Kohanga. They washed their hair and stuck bunches of wild scarlet geranium in it. We found hearty work going on at Kohanga. A wooden church with a spire had just been built, and beside it were the school buildings, filled with boys from eight to eighteen, who passed a good examination. We heard Archdeacon Maunsell preach on Sunday to a large native congregation. He spoke Maori with great fluency and precision. We could not help thinking of St. Augustine's mode of teaching his Africans as we listened to the good man's illustrations and saw him pause and look keenly at one and another as he walked up and down, to elicit an answer or to keep up attention.

We passed a volcanic hill on our way back, and I told the men how the scoria which lay scattered in masses about the terraced slopes had once been liquid fire. Our head bearer listened, and then said gravely, 'Mother, that's a fib of yours.' He was too gentlemanly to use the stronger word, falsehood, so he took the reduplicated form of the noun, which softens the force of it. Thus was a scientific discourse quenched on the spot.

By Canoe Up the Wanganui River

Married to a British Army officer, Rhoda Carleton Coote experienced many different aspects of life in early New Zealand. The Cootes first came out in 1852 and were based at Wellington for seven years before returning to England, where Henry Coote retired in 1859. He then decided to settle in the colony. The couple first ran a sheep station in Canterbury for several years before moving to Matahiwi, 10 km northwest of Masterton, where they farmed until Henry's health failed in 1867. They spent his last weeks travelling the country before he died in March. Rhoda returned to England with Bishop and Sarah Selwyn in July 1867.

In this excerpt from Rhoda's reminiscences, held in the Alexander Turnbull Library, the couple travel up the Wanganui River to a pa at Pipiriki, 20 km west of Raetihi, in 1857. They travelled with missionary Richard Taylor and his daughter Mary, later Mrs. Medley. While the men of the party venture further up the river to settle a tribal dispute, Rhoda and Mary are free to explore the surrounding area, including persuading one of the Maori to show them 'where the natives threw the remains of their Chiefs' and 'the caves where the natives used to cook and hold their Cannibal Feasts'.

October 2nd. [1857] Left home on our trip up the west coast in the afternoon, on horseback with our kits. I on 'Puck' and Henry on 'Gipsy' and went about 20 miles to Porirua. Here we found the Foxes, with whom we were to travel, at a wretched little Inn where we stopped for the night and for our breakfast next morning. Henry got a pail of water and started at 9 a.m. on October 3rd. and reached Otaki that evening after a magnificent drive through the beautiful valley of Walariki [?], such a view at the summit of the coast for hundreds of miles, and a splendid gallop on the sands till we reached the river at Otaki which we crossed without difficulty though it is sometimes very dangerous from snags and quicksands - the latter is a danger all the way up the coast where there are a number of river mouths to cross, for there was no road in those days. Otaki was the first Missionary Station in these parts and most highly interesting as well as beautiful.

Sunday 4th. Having stayed at the comfortable hotels we found here, we went to the Service at the Maori Church, a beautiful specimen of native architecture, which was quite full of natives all seated on the floor, and taking hearty part in the service, and all with books. The singing was very good, and altogether it was a bright service and a gratifying sight. Archdeacon Hadfield and his family have lived here for many years. He was very ill at this time so we did not see him, but went to enquire for him and afterwards to see a famous Chief Rauperapa [Te Rauparaha], who had a very fine and well furnished house in the English style. His wife gave us tea consisting of tea, bread and butter with roast pork and wild duck. After this we had a lovely walk whilst Henry sketched. In the evening Rauperapa [Te Rauparaha] dined with us at the Inn. He had been to England and behaved and spoke like an Englishman, and was a fine specimen of this noble race. Here we saw the sun set for the first time since we came to New Zealand without being interrupted by hills.

Monday 5th. The ride to-day took us to the Horowhenua Lake where we found some natives and they gave us some eels and potatoes for lunch all cooked together, except for the want of salt not too bad, but we had shells from the shore for plates and reeds for forks. We gave them sandwiches for their elaborate meal. The scenery is lovely with snow on the top of near mountains, and Henry made a beautiful sketch. After leaving the Horowhenua Lake we passed some well cultivated Maori lands, and then a dreary ride through sand-hills to the Manawata [Manawatu] River, a very large one, and being flooded, we had to wait a long time in bitterly cold wind for a canoe, which came at last. The horses were sent round and we all got safely to the very good Inn at Manawata [Manawatu].

Tuesday 6th. Off by 8 a.m., and had another windy ride to the Rangitiki [Rangitikei] River, and a very disagreeable crossing again in consequence of the floods, and it was hours before we got the horses over, and one of ours having kicked Mrs. Fox's mare, she was very vexed, and it spoiled our day's ride, besides which the long delay made it necessary to make as much haste as possible and neither Puck or Miss Poole's horse were inclined to go fast, so we had some difficulty in keeping up with the Foxes and to keep them in sight as it was getting very dark, but Henry kept them and us in view, and we arrived at last at Mrs. Fox's beautiful property at Rangitiki [Rangitikei], some 20 miles from the coast. It was too dark to see anything, and we were all very tired, so after a welcome supper we retired early to bed.

Wednesday 7th. Henry and I left Rangitiki [Rangitikei] and the Foxes and made our way to Wanganui, about thirty miles; Puck so tired she would not get up to be saddled, but we had no time to spare as Mr. Taylor and the natives had already waited for us to join them for several days. Happily we found someone going to Wanganui, who showed us the way. We had to cross one or two rivers but had no difficulty, and reached Putiki, a native village, where Mr. Taylor lived, on this side of the Wanganui River. It was a sweet home with a wilderness of choice shrubs and flowers surrounding, and we met with the warmest of welcomes from its dear inmates, Mr. and Mrs. Taylor and their daughters. The natives being impatient to start, the

Scene on the Old Wanganui from an album by Frank J. Denton, Wellington.

canoe was ordered for 6 o'clock the next morning, but, alas, we had no change of clothes, having nothing but what we brought with us on horseback, our boxes not having arrived from Wellington by steamer. However, we borrowed of our friends, and after a good night's rest and early breakfast, started in a splendid canoe, with about twenty natives to paddle it, taking all our provisions with us for the journey.

October 8th. Nothing could exceed the enjoyment or interest of this mode of travelling. Weather exquisite, scenery perfectly beautiful and varied, and sitting at perfect ease in the canoe with Mr. Taylor joking with the natives and telling us legends or true stories of every turn of the river. We stopped in the middle of the day, and again towards evening for the night, in one of the numerous Pahs on this river, most of them having classical names such as Athens, Zion, London, only much changed by the native spelling and pronouncing. In all the larger Pahs there are churches, and we found that whatever the natives were doing they would cease and go to the church for service whenever the [bells] rang, and they had both morning and evening services when there was any missionary or Catechist to conduct it. At night we pitched our tents inside one of the Maori huts or Wharis [whares] and gladly turned in after our evening meal which we had to get entirely ourselves, for the natives did not wait on us at all. Mary Medley and I shared our bed of fern covered with rugs and blankets in one tent, and Mr. Taylor and Henry in the other - but sleep was quite impossible, for a rat kept us company, and the Maoris outside kept up a conversation in their usual loud voice; they always talk over business matters at night, till 4 o'clock when the cocks took it up, and we gave up sleep as a bad job and were quite ready at 6 o'clock to prepare for breakfast and an early start. We now came across several rapids in the river and the excitement at passing them was very great. At every village we passed we were joined by other canoes all going to the Hui or meeting for which we were bound, and the shouting and talking on the rapids was very amusing, each canoe trying to pass the other. We stopped the night at a large and important Pah called London (Raheria) where there was a hut built for Mr. Taylor by the natives - so that we had a nice quiet night's sleep. There were some beautiful tombs here of which Henry got a sketch, as the natives pay great regard to the graves of their Chiefs and principal people, always choosing picturesque spots to put them in. Each day the river becomes more beautiful - the banks, all precipitous rocks covered with the exquisite trees of the New Zealand forest.

Saturday 10th. As we approached Pipiriki where the meeting was to be held, the scene became most exciting, and great numbers of canoes, some thirty or forty, all full of people, had joined us, and regaled us with guns firing and shouts and blowing of horns, and all kinds of friendly demonstrations, and at our landing it was intensified and the uproar was considerable. Bugles sounded and when we set foot on shore the assembled natives in hundreds cheered us vociferously with good English hurrahs. After shaking hands with some of the principal Chiefs, we went to the Catechist Mr. Booth's house, and were most hospitably received by his wife. The Chief of this important Pah had invited Mr. Taylor to come and settle a dispute between him and other Chiefs further up the river together with other natives of other villages to be present at the Korero, and also to partake of the Sacrament which Mr. Taylor was to administer. The first thing done at the meeting soon after we arrived was the calling together of all the tribes to feed, for which purpose the Chief had provided vast heaps of potatoes and pork, each tribe having a heap allotted to them. To us also was given a certain portion. As there were between 800 and 1,000 people present, it must have been a considerable expense. After the feast came the speaking, and a wonderful sight it was to see and hear the natives, though we could not follow their eloquent words and appropriate similes. Their gestures were most expressive and impressive, they took a few steps and then slapping their sides, spoke for some little time, and would then go back and return again till they had finished their say. Mr. Taylor spoke to them and then they called for Major Coote, who they chose to call Te Kawana, the Governor, because he was a Government Officer. What he said was interpreted by Mr. Taylor, and they were much pleased with his words - he made a capital speech. Whilst the speeches were going on, Henry had made a capital sketch of the scene. The heaps of food and natives in every variety of costume, some in native mats, others in blankets, and several in semi-English garments. We had King George, Hori Kingi, and Queen Victoria and other distinguished representatives in the crew of our canoe, and they, of course, were in full European dress. One very old man remembered pigs and potatoes being introduced to New Zealand, no doubt by Captain Cook.

Sunday 11th. We had service in the church here and afterwards received the Sacrament with about three hundred natives all certificated as fit to take it. It was a wonderful scene, the church crowded with these almost savages, seated or rather half kneeling on the floor, receiving the Sacrament from their beloved and respected pastor. The service lasted three hours, but all were quiet and reverent the whole time. In the afternoon we strolled through the Pah to some tombs on the hill at one end and found some orchids and unknown flowers during the walk. The natives and our gentlemen had great talks till late at night as to what was to be done. Mr. Taylor wishing to go on to settle the dispute between the Tribes, and our Maoris not liking him to run the risk - however, it was agreed that they should start the next day taking Mr. Booth, and, of course, Henry would not let Mr. Taylor go without him, so early on

Monday 12th. they left Mary Medley and myself, both eager to

accompany them, but that the natives would not allow, saying there would be shooting if not fighting, so we remained with Mrs. Booth thinking they would return the next day, in which we were greatly mistaken in that they did not come back till Friday. They had a large canoe, and all the best natives of our party, the Chief of Pikiriki [Pipiriki] and other Chiefs, and a good strong set of men, but the length of time they were away made us very anxious as we knew the natives were not friendly, and they were met in two or three Pahs with war dances and shots of blank cartridges and other signs of hostility. But dear old Mr. Taylor was not be frightened, and went on shore everywhere without taking any notice of their threats, and at last after three or four days further journey up this wonderful river of which Henry made several sketches, they reached the principal Chief Taupera, with whom the quarrel originated (over some stones for crushing corn, I believe). By this time their food supply had run quite short, having come all the way from Wanganui, not being good, so they told Taupera they could not stop without food, upon which he killed a pig for them and that in such hot weather was not very wholesome, but they returned to their anxious belongings in fair health and safety at the end of the week. In the meantime, Mary Medley and I made the most of our time in getting walks up the mountains, one a very high one to see Tongariro, the active volcano of New Zealand, which amply repaid us though the pull was tremendous. Tongariro and Ruapehu, two grand mountains, stood out some miles off, and from the top of the first we saw a cloud of something which proved to be smoke, and we saw it roll off majestically to our great satisfaction. It was a cone shape. Ruapehu was much larger and covered with snow from summit to base. That has since become active, I believe, when or since the Terraces were destroyed in 1886. Between us and the mountains was one grand forest, forming a magnificent view, which I sketched in a fashion, with a large river at the foot of the hill we were on, but looking like a little stream from our great height. Another walk we had to the top of a very steep hill covered in ferns as high as ourselves, to see where the natives threw the remains of their Chiefs. We got a Maori to take us to the spot, but he was either very reluctant to let us see the spot or very lazy, but Mary made him show us the way. There being no path he had at times to pull us up by main force, but we did at last get to the chasm in the rock and I hope it was the right place. We had to descend the mountain by a water course and slid a great part of the way, the native being in a great hurry to get down and telling us the canoe had come back with Te Tera and Te Kawana, Mr. Taylor and Major Coote - but that was not the case and we had to wait a day or two longer, which we spent in sketching different parts of the Pah and we were shown caves where the natives used to cook and hold their Cannibal Feasts, but they were highly offended if we alluded to such things now, though three years later they had many of them forsaken Christianity and taken to a new religion Hau-hau-ism, when they drank the blood of their enemies in this very place, it was said.

THE BURIAL PLACE AT PUKE TAPU ATENE ON THE WANGANUI.

Friday 16th. Our dear gentlemen returned safe and sound and *Saturday 17th.* we left the good Mr. Booth and his wife and returned in one day to Putiki - Mr. Taylor's village. It was a most exciting voyage down the river, the natives in great delight at the dispute being settled they sounded their horns and made great demonstrations at every Pah we passed, jokingly calling Mr. Taylor the 'Bone of Contention' from some old connection in their minds with his having settled the quarrel about the stone - but after a time he got tired of his name being handed about in that fashion, and as we neared Wanganui he no longer allowed it. We remained at Mr. Taylor's charming home at Putiki about ten days, and then had to leave them most reluctantly after the delightful time we had spent together and return to Wellington. The first day Mr. Taylor accompanied us to show us the way, but unfortunately he got lost in the sandhills amongst which we had to travel, and we wandered about until we reached the Turakina River where we bade him adieu and getting on to the beach made our way as fast as we could to save the day-light, which we were just able to do, having to turn inland and nothing to guide us but a small cross which we could only just discern, and it was in the light of the moon which we found our way to the Inn, where at last we dismounted, having been on horse-back eleven hours, except for twice dismounting to cross rivers and swim the horses. The last part of the journey was considered a four hour ride, and we did it in a little over two, and of course were rather tired at the end, but the next day found us in the saddle again, and we reached Wellington by the expiration of Henry's leave of absence without any further adventure.

A Visit to the Volcanic Region

Eliza Rachel Jean Jones was one of several single women who accompanied a missionary party on a trip overland from the Bay of Plenty to Rotorua and the thermal region in 1858. She had emigrated to New Zealand with her brother Humphrey the year before, but he had remarried within months of their arrival, leaving Eliza free to explore her adopted home. The party travelled by canoe and foot around the lakes of the district, with the young women of the party collecting examples of the native ferns. On her way home to Auckland through the Waikato, Eliza stayed at the Te Kohanga Mission station, where her future husband James Stack was serving. The couple married in 1861 and spent much of their married life in church service in Canterbury. Eliza died aged 91 in Worthing, England.

This extract, from Eliza's Jottings from my New Zealand Journal, 1858, *describes the party's visit to the famous Pink and White Terraces, destroyed in the Tarawera eruption in 1886.*

The first thing which attracted my notice was seeing our guide walking, as it seemed to me, on a field of ice; and yet it could not be ice, for great volumes of steam were rising all round the edge of it, and that certainly did not suggest cold. It looked slippery, but proved not to be at all. I could not understand what formed the crust which enabled us to walk over the boiling water, and felt thoroughly mystified.

No sooner had I joined the party who were proceeding over the icy-looking surface, than I saw what filled me with the greatest amusement and delight.

Above this wide spread field of apparent ice on which I stood, rose terrace upon terrace of dazzling white incrustation, in countless numbers, to a height of several hundred feet.

As we mounted higher and higher, the water which flowed over everything in a shallow stream two or three inches deep, became warmer and warmer to our feet.

When we got half way up, we turned round to look upon the marvellous scene below us. It was indeed a strange and lovely sight which met our wondering eyes; shallow basins and pools of every variety of size and shape covered the top of each terrace, in which the pale blue water contrasted beautifully with the dazzling whiteness of the basins containing it.

We found an immense basin at the very top of the Terraces, from which the boiling water was welling over all round; a conical mound completely covered with herbaceous vegetation crowned the topmost terrace, adjoining the great pool. This we ascended at no small risk of scalding our feet, as boiling water flowed all round it.

It is only occasionally that guides venture to take people on to this mound, as it is sometimes drenched with boiling water thrown up by the spring, and shakes so violently that it is impossible for anyone to stand upon it.

We were very proud of having achieved the rarely accomplished feat, and seized the opportunity to gather specimens of mosses and ferns which have never been dry and never felt cold. Some of the mosses were a foot high, and we got three varieties of ferns which grow on the brink of the boiling pool, and procured healthy leaves which were dipping in the hot water. Manuka shrubs were thriving in the moist heat, as well as ferns and mosses.

The fascinating charms of this wonderful place were brought into greater prominence by the contrast which the colour of the terraces presented to that of the surrounding landscape.

Warned by our guide not to prolong our stay in what was really a dangerous position, we slowly descended, feeling loth to leave what seemed to us a new world of rare beauty and wonder.

Before doing so, as it was time for our mid-day meal, we looked about for a suitable spot to have it in. I saw what I thought a good place, and pointed it out to our guide, who said, 'Oh no, you must not go there, the Atua [god] would be very angry if you defiled his sacred place with food, and he would kill you.' So we begged him to show us where we could take our lunch in safety. And well we did, for before we had finished it, a vast column of boiling water shot up, without any warning, to a great height, from the very place I had chosen, and had we been seated there we should all have been swept into the boiling cauldron by the returning waters as they fell back into the basin of the huge geyser.

Leaving the Tarata behind us, we followed our guide along the shore of the lake to Ohapu, where every beauty we had been admiring from the top of the Terraces was reversed - where everything we saw was ugly, foul, and hateful.

We had to follow closely in the guide's footsteps, as the slightest deviation to the right or left of his track might result in the unwary follower being precipitated into boiling water or boiling black mud. We were walking on a thin crust, which was all that separated us from the boiling stuff beneath it.

While we stood in the middle of this veritable Inferno, surrounded by

The White Terraces. Auckland Institute and Museum.

deep holes full of boiling black mud, our guide rushed forward and called aloud to the Spirit who presides over it, to pile on more fire, because the White People had come to see all the marvellous things he could do.

The bronze coloured figure of our scantily dressed guide, as he stamped his bare feet and shouted and waved his bare arms, in the midst of clouds of smoke and steam, and surrounded by bubbling pools of foul-smelling slime, made him look the very personification of the Demon Stoker of this sulphurous region.

I felt rather sorry that I had been brought to such a place so soon after enjoying the vision of beauty presented by the Tarata. It was too sudden a transition from Heavenly scenes of loveliness to Infernal scenes of Ugliness.

But it was done with a purpose. It was done to enhance my admiration of a still more lovely vision of Nature's marvellous handiwork, to which I was soon to be introduced.

I was glad to escape from the sulphurous fumes of Ohapu, and to obtain relief from the choky sensations caused by them, and heard with pleasure that we were going by canoe to another part of the Lake.

We had not gone far, and I had not yet recovered from the startling effect of what I had just seen, when I was told to stand up and look round.

Wonder of Wonders! What a fairy vision burst upon my sight. I felt quite overwhelmed by it; my only wish as I looked at it was that I could be alone, and give vent to my overwrought feelings in a flood of tears.

The golden rays of the setting sun, just disappearing behind the distant hills, shone with an unearthly brilliance upon a magnificent celestial staircase, over which the blue waters of the Hot Spring gently flowed. Each drop, as it fell from the points of the coral-like surface of the Terraces, glittered in the sunshine, producing a dazzling effect of surpassing brilliance and splendour. The whole surface of the Terrace from top to bottom seemed studded with diamonds and rubies and sapphires, and every brilliant gem in existence. No Eastern monarch's crown ever shone with such magnificent lustre as O Tu Kapua-rangi [Otukapuarangi] in the setting rays of the sun the first time my eyes rested in its unearthly loveliness.

It was but for a few minutes that this celestial vision, which was probably due to the peculiar atmospheric conditions under which it was seen, lasted. It disappeared with the disappearing sun, and then the scene we looked upon resumed its usual every-day appearance. But even then, it was still a thing of exceeding beauty and a joy to look upon.

And as I gazed at it, I could not help saying to myself - Can it be possible that this spot on earth's surface has escaped the primaeval curse and continues to be the same beautiful thing as it was when it came fresh from the Creator's hand in the day when 'God saw everything that He had made, and behold, it was very good.'

Few visitors reach this place, as the old Chief who owns the surrounding country, makes it 'Tapu' for eight months in the year, that the ducks which come to this part of the Lake to moult may not be disturbed. It is during the moulting season that great quantities of these birds are caught in nets by the natives; and that is why they keep this end of the Lake a close preserve for them. Travellers in the Summer months have to be content with a view of the Terraces from the opposite side of the Lake.

We lost no time in making a closer inspection of the magic Pink Terraces. They extended about fifty or sixty yards at the base, and gradually get shorter as they ascend. The pools available for bathing were more numerous than at the Tarata, and the water within them was found to be of a variety of colours, and every variety of heat.

We walked entirely round the huge steaming basin at the top, from which the clear blue boiling water flows down over everything.

The crust round the edge of it, upon which we stood, seemed frightfully thin, and the heat of our feet was hardly bearable. So dangerous was it thought to go near it, that only one man of our party would venture to guide us. We could see far under the crust of the rim, on which we stood - and down into the depths of the clear boiling water beneath us. And strange

Tourists at Otukapuarangi, (Pink Terraces) Rotomahana, from Round About New Zealand *by E.W. Payton.*

and beautiful were some of the fantastic forms taken by the dazzling white incrustations. One, deep down under water, looked like an old woman, with outstretched hands, and head covered with a cap - bent forward looking into the depths below.

The name of this wonderful place is 'O tu Kapua-rangi.'

In getting back to the canoe, I was delighted to find that our tents were going to be pitched close enough to enable me to listen to the drip, drip, dripping of the lovely waters down the Fairy Staircase. And that I should have plenty of time to study its beauties at my leisure.

The part of Rotomahana into which O tu Kapua discharges itself is quite hot, and boiling springs were bubbling everywhere around our tents. In one of them, not a yard away, we boiled the potatoes for our evening meal; but we could not use this water for making tea, as the taste is peculiar, owing to its mineral properties.

Mr. Spencer, who was with us on this occasion, told me that the last time he came here one of his Maoris got fearfully scalded on reaching the landing place. He jumped out of the canoe on to a spot where the crust, being too thin to bear his weight, broke, and his legs sank into the boiling water past his knees. I was warned to be very careful if I wished to escape his fate.

Before going to bed, I had a bathe, such a bathe as I have never had before, and suppose I never shall again.

The moon was at its full, and as I walked up the Fairy Terraces by its silvery light, I felt more than ever like one transported into a new world.

Celia and I were alone, and I was glad of it, for I longed to hold converse with myself, and think about what these earthly wonders suggested, those Heavenly wonders which eye hath not seen, no ear heard, neither hath it entered into the heart of man to conceive, but which our Heavenly Father will one day reveal to us.

While walking up the terraces, Celia urged me to select one of the numerous pink or straw coloured basins, and get into it. But I must confess that in spite of the enchanting beauty of my surroundings, and the romance of a hot bath by moonlight under such novel conditions, I felt a little nervous and awestruck. And it needed a good deal of persuasion, and the sight of my companion's evident enjoyment before I ventured into the blue water. But once immersed in it, I experienced the most delicious sensations - too ecstatic to be real. I seemed to be dreaming that I was translated by Genii into a Palace of Enchantment.

We tried five different basins, each higher than the other, till the water became too hot to be endurable. Then we descended, and although we had some distance to walk in our wet things before reaching our tent, I felt all in a glow when I entered it, and got into my sack.

The ceaseless throbbing of the ground on which we were lying, and the steam issuing from every crack, which wetted everything in our tent, did not let us forget where we were; but in spite of it all, we slept well, and enjoyed pleasant dreams.

An Eventful Crossing of Cook Strait

The Victorian novelist, Mrs. J. E. 'Isabella' Aylmer, never visited the strange new land she described in Distant Homes or The Graham Family in New Zealand. *Published in 1862, the book was based on the letters of Isabella's relatives in New Zealand and embroidered with information from various emigrants' handbooks - plus a fair dash of imagination. Her book gives a perception of how people in Britain viewed the adventures of their emigrant relatives. Here Isabella Aylmer presents her heroines with a startling array of perceived colonial hazards, including a volcanic eruption of Mount Egmont, while crossing Cook Strait.*

Although Mrs. Graham had avoided saying anything she thought might depress her husband, or add to the anxiety he already felt at leaving her and the children, when she was left alone, she could not altogether cast aside a sad apprehension as if some evil was about to happen; but this feeling was natural enough, when you remember that she was alone in a new country, surrounded by perfect strangers, who, although very hospitable and kind, were all so much occupied in their own affairs, that they had not time to devote to strangers. Another and perfectly unexpected cause for anxiety arose the very day of her husband's departure. A merchant vessel, heavily laden, and under an engagement to deliver her cargo at Lyttleton upon a certain day, was seen off the mouth of the bay, labouring against the wind, which was blowing a perfect gale. A pilot boat was sent out, and came back for a tug, with the intelligence that the ship had run upon a sand-bank, broken both paddles, and sustained such damage, that if she was not in harbour in a few hours, she would be lost.

The little town was in a great state of excitement, and a couple of steamers were speedily sent out to the assistance of the unfortunate ship, and, in about two hours, they were in sight again with her in tow; the aid had come just in time. Although the whole strength of the crew had been working at the pumps, the water was gaining upon them.

The captain was in despair; he had staked a large sum of money as security that he would fulfil his engagement as to time; and now it seemed perfectly impossible, and the hard-earned savings of many years must all go as forfeit. One hope only remained, and that was to re-ship the cargo in another vessel, and proceed immediately. This would have been easy enough, if another ship had been there, but the only one that could be got ready was that in which the Grahams had just arrived. After a good deal of persuasion the captain consented to load his ship with the cargo, which consisted of various inflammable articles, such as candles, cottons, silks, &c., and a number of barrels containing whiskey.

By dint of hiring all the labour they could command, and working all through the night, they succeeded in clearing the sinking ship, and transferring the goods to the other; and about two o'clock the following day, Mrs. Graham, who had been anxiously watching the busy scene, received information that she must be on board in an hour, to be ready to catch the tide and afternoon breeze.

When she had settled the children in their cabin, she proceeded on deck to take a last glimpse of Nelson. The day had changed very much, the atmosphere being hot and oppressive; and although the sky looked as clear and bright as before, the horizon had a pale pinkish haze hanging round it, such as she had never remarked before. But there was little time for such thoughts; the tide was turning, and in a few minutes, with a parting cheer, the anchor was shipped, and the sails spread to catch the expected breeze.

Blind Bay is one of the most picturesque in New Zealand, and almost shut in by a long sand-bank, which, covering its mouth, obtained for it its name. The shores rise to a great height, and on three sides join the mountain range; so that it is completely secure from high winds, and however violent a storm may be in the straits, inside the bay all is peace and safety.

The ebb tide was running very strong, and as the breeze gradually and quickly freshened, no time was lost in making their way down the bay, so that just as the sky grew red with the sunset, they ran through the narrow spit of water between the mainland and the sand-bank, and entered Cook's Straits.

Here a brisk breeze was blowing; and, crowding on all the sail he could, the captain took advantage of it. Nothing could be more beautiful than the picture on which the last light of day was lingering; the snowy mountains upon the North Island were all tinged with pink, the woods near the shore looking almost black, while, just on the horizon, a faint white pillar of smoke rose from the volcano of Mount Egmont. Twilight does not last so long in New Zealand as in England, and the last streak of light soon faded out, leaving a dark cloudy night, the moon, which was almost full, being completely hidden. The breeze suddenly fell, and the sails flapped lazily against the rigging. Lucy and her Mamma were on the deck at the moment, and were equally startled at the sudden clap of the canvas, more resembling the shutting of a door than anything else. When the wind fell, the heaving of the ship became very unpleasant, and Lucy, although not actually sea-sick, felt very uncomfortable, and would have liked to have gone to bed, only she saw her Mamma looked pale and anxious, and as poor Beatrice had a bad headache, she would not leave her mother alone, so sat still, resting her head against the side of the ship.

Presently, an exclamation from one of the crew, who stood near, made them look round, and a sight that one who has once seen never forgets, burst upon them - the volcano in action.

The pillar of smoke had become a crown of fire, above which, hung a thick and dreadfully dark cloud. The sides of the mountain, though at such a great distance, were distinctly visible, and looked as sharp as if cut with a knife.

Both Lucy and her mother had sprung to their feet, and stood silent and awe struck. They were still gazing, and neither had spoken, when a low, rumbling sound crept along the water; it only lasted a minute, and might have been the echo of distant thunder, or the firing of cannon; Lucy thought so, and whispered an enquiry to her mother.

'No, Lucy,' replied Mrs. Graham; 'it is an earthquake. Let us pray to God to protect your father and all of us.'

The blood rushed to Lucy's heart; a cold shiver shook her limbs.

'Oh, Mamma!' was all she could say, and trembling, crept up to her side, trying not to look at the volcano, but still gazing with fascinated eyes. Just then Beatrice stole up, and put her arms round her mother.

'I heard it, dear, and could not stay below; my head is better now.'

'Is it dear,' said Mrs. Graham, absently.

'I am afraid we are going to have rough work, madam,' said the captain, passing with the pilot.

Embossed cover detail from Distant Homes or The Graham Family in New Zealand *by Isabella E. Aylmer, published in London, 1862*

'Yes, sir, that we shall,' said the pilot; 'the old mountain never gives us warning in vain.'

Mrs. Graham drew her children closer to her, for an instant, and then told them to stand still, while she went to look at Aps.

He was lying sound asleep in his berth, his curls all tossed, and his pretty, white, fat legs thrown over the coverlet.

Mrs. Graham knelt down by his side, and prayed God to guard them through the perils and dangers of the night; then kissing her child, she went on deck again.

A couple of hours passed very slowly away, the ship lying like a log upon the heaving ocean; the pillar of fire growing sometimes brighter, sometimes almost disappearing; not a sound broke the stillness, except the straining and groaning of the labouring vessel; and Lucy, who would have borne up very well if a storm had come, got terribly frightened and nervous in the strange calm, and kept tormenting her Mamma by a thousand foolish questions, until at last she began to cry, and would have cried herself to sleep, if a tremendous clap of thunder had not made her start to her feet with a loud shriek, which she was heartily ashamed of giving way to the next minute, when she met her mother's eye.

'Go down below, Lucy, if you cannot behave more sensibly, here,' she said.

'Oh, Mamma, it is so dreadful; it came so suddenly. Did you see the lightning? If I had, I don't think I should have got in such a fright.' But Lucy was wrong, for while she was uttering the last word, a vivid flash darted across the sky, and putting her hands up to her eyes, she gave a louder shriek than before, and then, throwing herself into her mother's arms, began crying and sobbing.

'You are very silly, Lucy,' said her Mamma, 'and very ungrateful to God. He has taken care of you all your life, and will never desert any one who trusts in His care.' But Lucy only sobbed the more, thinking her Mamma was unkind not to pity her.

'Oh, if Papa was here,' she sighed, 'I should not be so frightened.'

'Papa could not help you, dear; but your heavenly Father can. Why would you trust and be happy if Papa was here, who could do nothing more than those with you now?'

'Because I love him, and I know he would do anything for me, and save me.'

'And would God not do so?'

Lucy could not answer, and held down her head, with a burning blush.

'Now,' said her Mamma, 'go below, and lie down beside Aps; I will call you, if I want you; but first, Lucy, ask God to give you faith in Him.'

Lucy would have liked to have stayed; but when Mrs. Graham said a thing she always meant it, and saw that it was done; so the little girl kissed her Mamma, and did as she was told.

All through the night the thunder rattled, coming with deafening peals, such as are never heard in England. Still there was no wind, and the ship made no progress. Morning broke at last, the thunder-clouds dispersed, and the pilot began to talk of the danger having passed; it was, however, only beginning. Far away, to the east, a white cloud seemed to lie on the bosom of the sea, running along the top of the waves.

Mrs. Graham saw the captain's expression change, as he watched it, and heard him exclaim, 'Thank God!' as it passed by.

'What is it, captain?' she asked, in a breathless whisper.

'A squall, madam; if it had struck us, there would have been no cause to ask that question.'

'Do they occur often in these parts, captain?'

'No, madam; but when Nature is in the mood she is in to-day, anything may occur: "They that go down to the sea in ships, that do business in deep waters, these see the works of the Lord, and His wonders in the deep; for He commandeth and raiseth the stormy wind, which lifteth up the waves thereof; they mount up to the heaven, they go down again to the depths; their soul is melted because of trouble; they reel to and fro, and stagger like a drunken man, and are at their wits' end. Then they cry unto the Lord in their trouble, and He bringeth them out of their distresses."'

As the captain repeated these beautiful words, he uncovered his head.

'Thank you,' said Mrs. Graham, holding out her hand. 'You have comforted me more than I can tell you.'

The captain grasped her hand warmly and passed on.

As the morning advanced, the heat became almost unbearable, and once or twice the same low, grumbling sound broke the stillness.

Presently the great pillar of smoke rushing up from the volcano disappeared, the air grew heavy and tremulous, and the waves as quiet as a millpond. Every one rushed on deck, and stood waiting, pale and awe-stricken.

The silence lasted for nearly three minutes; then a faint roll, like thunder, was heard; it grew louder, and the vessel seemed to tremble, just as you have heard a window do when cannon are firing near; then one or two sharp cracks, and the water became agitated; a wave rose up here and there, as if trying to escape from something, and immediately to the leeward, a jet of water, like that from a fountain, rose about thirty feet in the air; three or four more broke out in different directions, and, almost at the same moment, the volcano began to smoke again. The ship now commenced rocking with a short, sharp motion, which gradually increased, until it was difficult to remain on deck, even when holding on by different things. This continued about ten minutes, though it seemed much longer to the frightened passengers; then a gentle breeze came singing through the rigging, and, with a cheerful voice, the captain gave orders to hoist sail. The danger was past, and the earthquake over.

What they had felt so mildly at this distance, had caused great alarm and destruction at Wellington, where a number of houses had been thrown down, and a great many people injured, while many more were drowned by the sudden ebb and flow of the tide, which rushed up from above high-water mark, and carried away several men, women and children in its recoil.

Footnote: *Geologists believe Mount Egmont may have erupted as recently as 200 years ago, perhaps when it was shrouded in cloud, for there is no historic record of this.*

Mabel Smith milking a cow, Taranaki. W.A. Collis Collection, Alexander Turnbull Library.

CAROLINE CHEVALIER

Across the Southern Alps on Horseback

*Caroline Chevalier claimed to be 'the first lady who ever rode across the [South] Island,'
crossing the Southern Alps in 1866. Married to the artist Nicholas Chevalier, she
accompanied his journeyings through Australia and New Zealand, expeditions which
inspired a series of romantic paintings which show a wild New Zealand with more affinity
to his native Switzerland than this raw, young country. Their crossing of the Hurunui
Saddle, now known as Harper Pass, led them down the Taramakau River into Westland.
From field sketches of this journey, Nicholas later painted his 'Crossing the Taramakau',
the picture shown in part on page 115 of this book. Caroline is shown fording the river
on horseback. The Chevaliers spent some months in Otago before their expedition
through Canterbury to the West Coast goldfields in 1866. That journey is recalled in
reminiscences now in the care of the Alexander Turnbull Library.*

 The spelling of Caroline's husband's name as 'Nicolas' in this extract is her own.

Having heard there was a building used as a wool shed, and that we should
find it open, & would be a cover for the night, onward we pushed. Now the
way was a narrow or from time to time a rider path only, & we began to
follow in file. On & on we went, but no wool shed, until it was growing
dark & I was getting tired for we had been in the saddle from very early
morning. SO the path becoming steep & narrow, N. decided to stop. There
was good grass along the slopes & here & there flat places for the horses &
they were hobbled for the first night. No doubt the little mare chaffed
much, but I was too busy in helping with the unpacking & pitching our first
tent to think of horses. There was no place for the tent level enough & free
from wind gusts save on the path & so across it our camp was placed. As it
was quite dry, we lay on the earth, afterwards we made luxurious beds of
cut fern, sweet & soft, but then we had more experience. Nicolas thought
nothing of the hard ground, I thought it hard. Our pillows were our saddles
& I remember always how terribly mine smelt & how very light it seemed,
with only the canvas of a tent. Strange how kindly nature is, & I slept
soundly, the senses of smelling & seeing both forgotten. As to tasting well
we had our supper, my first camp one. The tin pannikin with the hot tea
burnt my lips, & with no milk, was not very nice, but we had bread brought
with us & really delicacies, some butter or cheese, & no doubt some they
cooked for I remember the frying pan was used & there was a great

splutter. I sat & watched the moon rise over the hill on the other side of the river, which rushed & roared beneath our path, & one had to mind how far one went to the edge as it was a steep decline. That crescent moon looked down so calmly on us, then hid behind the hill & all seemed so dark, & I crept into the tent, & put my head into the not sweet scented saddle. Scott rose from his sleeping place several times during the night to see if the horses had not wandered far; they were all four hobbled still it was a nasty stooping ground & not much herbage. Sleeping in a tent is an extraordinary sensation. You seem to be in the open air, & the thin kind of calico, appears lighter somehow than when out in the open. You wake up & all seems white & dazzling, but certainly one sleeps well in that pure air & I never once suffered from insomnia. Not as one often does in a luxurious bed & beautiful room. And then one is not tempted to lay in bed, once awake one is only too glad to rise, and then one has to find a little creek or bend in the river or lake, & make one's ablution, & a still pool for a looking glass, if you should desire to look tidy even. All these matters were soon settled & Scott made the tea, & if we had not a tempting breakfast, we had better - excellent appetites. We were soon on the move, & in about half an hour came upon the wool shed which was intended to have been our hotel for the night.

Very shortly we had to cross the river (Hurunui) for our path was too abrupt on the left side, & as soon as a narrow rocky bed showed, Nicolas went over. My horse did not like facing the rushing water & swerved to the left with the result, that we got into a deep pool & water up to my knees. It was sharp work to get out & alarmed me but it was a caution for Scott & the pack horse. A good lesson to me, but I had several yet to learn.

We travelled on this narrow path through a gorge all day, never meeting a person & in the afternoon emerged into a plateau surrounded by hills. Lake Coleridge [actually Lake Sumner - Ed.] is beautifully embossed in hills, with grassy slopes & sheep runs traversing all about & you see hundreds of sheep winding up the sides of the hills in long lines following one another. It was very tranquil only the bleating of the sheep, & the sighing of the wind. On the banks of the lake, we camped & a pretty camp we had, & the horses there were on the level & had good food. We had had a very long day & I was glad indeed to get out of the saddle & lie me down. Nicolas sketched until too dark, & Scott was extra busy no doubt boiling rice & I attempting some dainty out of the materials we had, which were not numerous. Tinned meat & such delicacies were unknown.

It will be impossible to remember each day's camp or to attempt to describe the beautiful scenery lakes & woods we traversed & then the entry at the foot of the range of grand forest scenery. Immense trees clothed with lichens of many colours all hanging around their stems like grey beards &

'Wet or Fine? 1866,' a sketch by Nicholas Chevalier shows Caroline emerging from a tent on their journey across the Southern Alps. Alexander Turnbull Library.

all looking very weird & as though they were hundreds of years old as they may have been. From the lovely placid lake to the wild solemn forest with its ghostlyness, was indeed a great change & on the one day one seemed to pass from the freshness of lovely spring, all nature clear & bright & fresh & green the lake most beautiful blue, then the heat & fatigue of mid day sun, and closing in of the evening & night amidst the stern realities of life & old age tried worn & decrepit. A shiver seems to come over me as I think of that camp. It was so dark, so damp, & so sad. I was deputed to cut bracken to make our beds on, for the grass was dank, & cold. Scott made a big fire, & the artist sketched & cooked. Our bread had by this time been eaten, so a damper or large round cake must be made. This is only made of flour & water & a little salt, well stirred up & the consistency of dough as the baker makes bread. But the oven had to be made, nay built, and that took a long time. Plenty of wood had to be gathered & a large fire made & continually fed, until there was a large heap of red hot ashes, broad & high enough for the oven. Then the centre is scooped out & laid flat & even & done quickly, so that the embers remain red hot. Into this the damper is laid, & covered very quickly entirely with the red hot embers, & a good thickness of them it requires. The fire is continually fed, but kept smouldering, & the baking lasts a long time. This said loaf was very large quite eight inches across & took a long time, but when finished was really very nice indeed. In those days one did not suffer from indigestion. It was all right that night for supper, but the next day - I could not bite it, it was hard as possible but the others thought it perfection, & I had to make up my mind to eat it some how, or go without.

This camp was not at all inviting & long before day light I was longing to be out of the tent. The moaning of the trees the ghostly swaying of the long hanging mosses & lichens, the creepy sounds, as of gnomes, & queer beasts, made me long for daylight, & though my husband was very tired & slept well, yet we were astir very early, for we had a steep journey & a trying day before us. We were now about to follow the Hurunui to its source. Crossing from Lake Coleridge [Sumner] we had left it making a big detour, we now took it up again. It was much narrower & rushing past over boulders, which grew larger & larger as we mounted higher & higher. The poor horses, for it was not only steep but there was little foot hold, all rolling stones. As we had to get to the head of the pass & must get over the other side before night we had to press on, & no stop was made save now & then when we saw a bit of good grass, for the horses. Little by little we rose, & curved in & out, often unseen to one another, & when nearly at the top, with the straining of my horse & the position of the girths, my saddle got looser & looser & I felt myself slipping round. The rapid torrent was on my left side, deep down, on my right rose the wall of boulders. I called loudly to Nicolas who was on before & out of sight, but the noise of the roaring torrent drowned every sound. I looked for Scott, & only saw the poor pack horse struggling under his heavy load. Suddenly round went my saddle under the horse & how I managed to disentangle myself I scarcely know. There was no place for me at the horse's side, so I just left the reins, & let him go on & I followed calling as loud as I could possibly, but the roar of waters drowned every sound. The consternation of the artist when he turned & saw the horse can be imagined, for anyone could have fallen & been carried down that torrent & no one could have heard a sound. In that condition we reached the head of the Hurunui a wild mountain torrent, with scarcely the slightest plateau at its head & an immediate descent on the other side, where the fine river Taramakau rises. The soil seemed to change & after an hour of boulders; we came into patches of trees wild scrubby little bushes, with soil at the roots which was simply liquified mud. It was impossible for any of us to ride here for the tangle of the roots under the mud made it terrible for the horses & my husband was sorely afraid they would hurt or break their fetlocks & was particularly anxious about the pack horse. Several times both he & Scott had to lighten the load & carry portions long distances. We were all far above our ankles in mud, & once or twice nearly up to the knee. I had luckily two pieces of American cloth to keep off the wet from my sketch book & these I bound round my legs like putties, & so really did not get very wet, but my boots well I thought they would never reach Hokitika: but they did.

I thought the boulders were dreadful, & rejoiced when we could turn from them, but the mud was worse & seemed endless. The track was the only

Crossing the Taramakau 1866, a detail from a romantic watercolour by Nicholas Chevalier showing Caroline, the artist and their companion Scott, painted some 20 years after their journey across the Southern Alps. National Art Gallery, Wellington.

one, & over it passed any cattle or sheep that were going to the West Coast, & although but very few went, still they completely worked up the ground & the running water, kept it in a constant slush. We emerged at last as evening was fast coming on, then had to make the first crossing of the Teramakau. It looked nothing at all to do & most picturesque, but it was far from agreeable huge moving boulders & all more or less slimy, so that one had to be on the look out, & make a dash at a given moment.

My husband crossed & I was intently watching & just starting, when the wretched lawyer a hanging plant with long reversed hook or thorns all down its long spray caught my hat & my hair & nearly made me a second Absolom.

Now we made up for lost time for we were on a nice open bit of ground at any rate wide enough for the horses, & we hurried on & on, anxiously looking for a resting place. This was at last found, a flat sandy kind of Island where the river had opened into open ground. We crossed the shallow water & were indeed thankful that day was over.

An Inhospitable Inn

Caroline Chevalier's expedition with her artist husband and a companion called Scott involved a journey from Canterbury to Westland across the Harper Pass in 1866. After struggling down the wild river flats of the Taramakau River, into Westland, the party approached a junction with the new coach road over Arthur Pass. The prospect of civilisation, however, was quickly dispelled as they found themselves in an inn which catered for gold-miners on the journey through the Southern Alps.

We journeyed till sunset & arrived at a small accommodation house, where the road forks to the Otira Gorge. We had struck the coach road which had been made by Arthur Dobson, & whose name was given to the pass over the Otira Gorge. Having been directed that this house existed, we were all looking forward for a most delightful supper & bed. Coming up to it, it really looked most inviting, a pretty little place with a square foot & a skillion back. Of course of wood but a big chimney. The proprietor, a young fellow, came out immediately to welcome us, but what was my disappointment to find the only bed room he had, was just taken by a man & his wife & three children, a rather large party for a little place of a few feet square, & a kind of wooden stretcher or two, no other furniture. Still it was a covering from rain. They were common people journeying on the road to Hokitika, there hoping to find work or make a fortune digging.

We were all too tired to travel farther & the horses done up, so Nicolas decided to take what we could get, & really it was much worse than camping. The house consisted of a front room for eating & a bar, over it *the* one sleeping room, behind, a skillion kitchen with a big fire, & one end of this skillion had a kind of shed, or one would call it a stable. It was divided from the kitchen by boards or slabs about an inch from each other, & against this was put two flat slabs to form shelves for people to sleep on. The proprietor showed us these with great satisfaction & considered they were most desirable sleeping accommodation & I have no doubt asked a good price. I know he asked a very big price for some oats for our horses, & gave them very little. We had to accept this or go on & find a camping ground & it was late & we were done up. So we unpacked & stored the things in the shed & the horses were hobbled, but from that moment N. had no rest, for horses & saddles were most valuable in these quarters, & there were a set of horrible fellows, squatting about drinking & smoking, & they would think nothing of taking horses or any thing they could lay their hands on. Indeed during the next few months occurrences showed that desperate characters were on those very roads, for poor Arthur Dobson mentioned above was murdered by a set of ruffians who mistook him for a store keeper returning with gold dust. And one of the dreadful rascals turned Queen's evidence & acknowledged they had killed 20 or 30 (I think) poor unfortunate people. You can imagine that the faces of these kind of men gave you fear, but I had no idea that they might go off with the horses. Had they done so, we were undone. We got a kind of supper, & some tea, & Scott had his pipe with the party of diggers & rascals in the kitchen. Our supper was taken with the family party, & I really was greatly interested with the poor woman & her nice little children. What a life the poor creature [had] & what became of her I have often wondered. The terrible things I heard of after, frightened me for any women's lives thrown into such places.

Naturally we hoped to be down - I can't say go to bed - early & we took our blanket, & the man gave us each a dirty thing which we could not use. We entered our apartment - earth floor, old rubbish about, wood & some tools. I managed to scramble with assistance to the upper berth or rather shelf, & lay me down & N. took the under one. But sleep - how could one, there between the inch chinks I looked at these men, many half drunk, all noisy, some miserable, some wild there were about a dozen. They were drinking beer I suppose and smoking. The big fire blazed & made the darkness cheerful, for there was but one candle. Their conversation was not agreeable, some were most quarrelsome, & we unfortunate people seemed the theme of a deal of unpleasantness. We were talked of indirectly as confounded aristocrats, and upstarts & every name they could think of because I had not gone in and sat down with them, & I began to wonder how the night would end, when suddenly about 10 o'clock the proprietor opened the door, & shouted 'now then all out.' Then began a scrimmage some would go & some would not, but he absolutely drove them, little fellow as he was, & then he went out himself & turned the key & we heard him mount a horse & ride away. Now we thought we should have a quiet night, Scott was to sleep in some out house & after N. had gone out & seen all four horses he was more content & we composed ourselves for a sleep. Alas, alas - in less than ten minutes the place was alive, not with people but with rats - rats that rushed up & down on the table over the chairs along the rafters all around the fire & packed along close to the chinks, squeaking and rushing. This was too dreadful. I could see them of course plainly, I knocked, I called out, but they cared for nothing, and nothing could be done but get a candle & sit up till morning, and this we did until the proprietor returned & his presence seemed to drive the beasts away. It was one of the most dreadful nights I have passed. Camping out was peaceful & healthful compared to it. I never shall forget those horrid creatures sitting on the table on their hind legs & eating every scrap & crumb they could find & fighting with each other. New Zealand is a terrible place for rats, they say they go about in shoals under the ground & have their exits here and there. It is so extraordinary, because New Zealand is like Ireland & has no reptiles, & yet the rat swarms.

We were thankful when day light returned, & as soon as we had had some hot coffee, and some nasty bread and butter for which we paid exorbitantly we bade adieu to the accommodation house to which we had so looked forward as a quiet resting place.

'The Shoot after passing the Hurunui Saddle' showing Caroline and the artist Nicholas Chevalier with Scott on the West Coast side of the Harper Pass. Alexander Turnbull Library.

'My First and Last Experience of "Camping Out"'

Lady Mary Anne Barker (later Lady Broome) is perhaps the best-known and best-loved of the chroniclers of New Zealand life last century. Her books, including the classic Station Life in New Zealand *(1870), deal mainly with sheep station life in the 1860's. A series of letters 'home' cover a range of topics from domestic details to major events such as the great snowstorm of 1867.*

Lady Barker came to New Zealand after marrying Frederick Napier Broome in 1865, following the death of her first husband, Sir George Barker. The couple took up the Steventon station in the Malvern hills, inland from Christchurch, and renamed it Broomielaw. Although they lived on the station for only three years, the wealth of information and experience Lady Barker obtained during her time there filled several books, including Station Amusements in New Zealand *(1873) and the children's novel* A Christmas Cake in Four Quarters *(1871).*

Although officially Mrs., and later Lady Broome when her second husband was knighted in 1883, she called herself Lady Barker for the purposes of her writing. The F. of this story is of course Frederick Broome.

Broomielaw, April 1867

I have nothing to tell you this mail, except of a rather ridiculous expedition which we made last week, and which involved our spending the whole night on the top of the highest hill on our run. You will probably wonder what put such an idea into our heads, so I must preface my account by a little explanation. Whenever I meet any people who came here in the very early days of the colony - only sixteen years ago, after all! - I delight in persuading them to tell me about their adventures and hardships during those primitive times, and these narratives have the greatest fascination for me, as they always end happily. No one ever seems to have died of his miseries, or even to have suffered seriously in any way from them, so I find the greatest delight in listening to the stories of the Pilgrims. I envy them dreadfully for having gone through so much with spirit and cheerfulness, and ever since I came here I have regretted that the rapid advance of civilization in New Zealand precludes the possibility of being really uncomfortable; this makes me feel like an imposter, for I am convinced that my English friends think of me with the deepest pity, as of one cut off from the refinements and comforts of life, wheras I really am surrounded by every necessary, and many of its luxuries, and there is no reason but that of expense why one should not have all of these.

One class of narratives is peculiarly attractive to me. I like to hear of benighted or belated travellers when they have had to 'camp out,' as it is technically called; and have lived in constant hope of meeting with an adventure which would give me a similar experience. But I am gradually becoming convinced that this is almost impossible by fair means, so I have been trying for some time past to excite in the breasts of our home party and of our nearest neighbours an ardent desire to see the sun rise from the top of 'Flagpole', a hill 3,000 feet above the level of the sea, and only a couple of miles from the house. As soon as they were sufficiently enthusiastic on the subject, I broached my favourite project of our all going up there over-night, and camping out on the highest peak. Strange to say, the plan did not meet with any opposition, even from F., who has had to camp out many a winter's night, and with whom, therefore, the novelty may be said to have worn off. Two gentlemen of the proposed party were 'new chums' like myself, and were strongly in favour of a little roughing; new chums always are, I observe. F. hesitated a little about giving a final consent on the score of it being rather too late in the year, and talked of a postponement till next summer, but we would not listen to such an idea; so he ended by entering so heartily into it, that when at last the happy day and hour came, an untoward shower had not the least effect in discouraging him.

There was a great bustle about the little homestead on that eventful Tuesday afternoon. Two very steady old horses were saddled, one for me and the other for one of the 'new chums,' who was not supposed to be in good form for a long walk, owing to a weak knee. Everything which we thought we could possibly want was heaped on and around us after we had mounted; the rest of the gentlemen, four in number, walked, and we reached the first stage of our expedition in about an hour. Here we dismounted, as the horses could go no further in safety. The first thing done was to see to their comfort and security; the saddles were carefully deposited under a large flax-bush in case of rain, and the long tether ropes were arranged so as to ensure plenty of good feed and water for both horses, without the possibility of the ropes becoming entangled in each other or in anything else. Then came a time of great excitement and laughing and talking, for all the 'swags' had to be packed and apportioned for the very long and steep ascent before us.

And I now must tell you exactly what we took up. A pair of large double blankets to make the tent of, - that was one swag, and a very unwieldy one it was, strapped knapsack fashion, with the straps of flax leaves, on the

Lady Barker and her husband Frederick Broome from the frontispiece of her popular book, Station Life in New Zealand, *first published in 1870.*

back, and the bearer's coat and waistcoat fastened on the top of the whole. The next load consisted of one small single blanket for my sole use, inside of which was packed a cold leg of lamb. I carried the luncheon basket, also strapped on my shoulders, filled with two large bottles of cream, some tea and sugar, and I think, teaspoons. It looked a very insignificant load by the side of the others, but I assure you I found it frightfully heavy long before I had gone half-way up the hill. The rest distributed among them a couple of large heavy axes, a small coil of rope, some bread, a cake, tin plates and pannikins, knives and forks, and a fine pigeon-pie. Concerning this pie there were two abominable propositions; one was to leave it behind, and the other was to eat it then and there: both of these suggestions were, however, indignantly rejected. I must not forget to say we included in the commissariat department two bottles of whisky, and a tiny bottle of essence of lemon, for the manufacture of toddy. We never see a real lemon, except two or three times a year when a ship arrives from the Fiji islands, and then they are sixpence or a shilling apiece. All these things were divided into two large heavy 'swags,' and to poor F. was assigned the heaviest and most difficult load of all - the water. He must have suffered great anxiety all the way, for if any accident had happened to his load, he would have had to go back again to refill his big kettle; this he carried in his hand, whilst a large tin vessel with a screw lid over its mouth was strapped on his back also full of water, but he was particularly charged not to let a drop escape from the spout of the kettle; and I may mention here, that though he took a long time about it, for he could not go as straight up the hill as we did, he reached the top with the kettle full to the brim - the other vessel was of course quite safe. All these packings and repackings, and the comfortable adjustment of the 'swags,' occupied a long time, so it was past five when we began our climb, and half-past six when we reached the top of the hill, and getting so rapidly dark that we had to hurry our preparations for the night, though we were all so breathless that a 'spell' (do you know that means *rest* ?) would have been most acceptable. The ascent was very steep, and there were no sheep tracks to guide us; our way lay through thick high flax-bushes, and we never could have got on without their help. I started with a stick, but soon threw it aside and pulled myself up by the flax, hand over hand. Of course I had to stop every now and then to rest, and once I chose the same flax-bush where three young wild pigs had retired for the night, having first made themselves the most beautiful bed of tussock grass bitten into short lengths; the tussocks are very much scattered here, so it must have been an afternoon's work for them; but the shepherds say these wild pigs make themselves a fresh bed every night.

The first thing to be done was to pitch the tent on the little flat at the very top of the hill: it was a very primitive affair; two of the thinnest and longest pieces of totara, with which Flagpole is strewed, we used for poles, fastening another piece lengthwise to these upright sticks as a roof-tree: this frame was then covered with the large double blanket, whose ends were kept down on the ground by a row of the heaviest stones to be found. The rope we had brought up served to tie the poles together at the top, and to fasten the blanket on them; but as soon as the tent had reached this stage, it was discovered that the wind blew through it from end to end, and that it afforded very little protection. We also found it much colder at the top of this hill than in our valley; so under these circumstances it became necessary to appropriate my solitary blanket to block up one end of the tent and make it more comfortable for the whole party. It was very little shelter before this was done. The next step was to collect wood for a fire, which was not difficult, for at some distant time the whole of the hill must have been covered by a forest of totara trees; it has apparently been destroyed by fire, for the huge trunks and branches which still strew the steep sides are charred and half burnt. It is a beautiful wood, with a strong aromatic odour, and blazed and crackled splendidly in the clear, cool evening air, as we piled up a huge bonfire, and put the kettle on to boil. It was quite dusk by this time, so the gentlemen worked hard at collecting a great supply of wood, as the night promised to be a very cold one, whilst I remained to watch the kettle, full of that precious liquid poor F. had carried up with such care, and to prevent the wekas from carrying off our supper, which I had arranged just inside the tent. In this latter task I was nobly assisted by my little black terrier Dick of whose sad fate I must tell you later.

By eight o'clock a noble pile of firewood had been collected, and we were very tired and hungry; so we all crept inside the tent, which did not afford very spacious accommodation, and began our supper. At this point of the entertainment everybody voted it a great success; although the wind was slowly rising and blowing from a cold point, and our blanket-tent did not afford the perfect warmth and shelter we had fondly credited it with. The gentlemen began to button up their coats. I had only a light serge jacket on, so I coaxed Dick to sit at my back and keep it warm; for whilst our faces were roasted by the huge beacon-fire, there was a keen and icy draught behind us. The hot tea was a great comfort, and we enjoyed it thoroughly, and after it was over the gentlemen lit their pipes, and I told them a story: presently we had glees, but by ten o'clock there was no concealing the fact that we were all sleepy indeed; however, we still loudly declared that camping out was the most delightful experiment. F. and another gentleman (that kind and most good-natured Mr. U., who lives with us) went outside the tent, armed with knives, and cut all the tussocks they could feel in the darkness, to make me a bed after the fashion of the pigs; they brought in several armfuls, and the warmest corner of the tent was heaped with them; I had my luncheon-basket for a pillow, and announced that I had turned in and was very comfortable, and that camping out was charming; the gentlemen were still cheery, though sleepy; and the last thing I remember was seeing preparations for what a Frenchman of my acquaintance always will call a 'grogs'. When I awoke, I thought I must have slept several hours. Though the fire was blazing grandly, the cold was intense: I was so stiff I could hardly move; all my limbs ached dreadfully, and my sensations altogether were new and very disagreeable. I sat up with great difficulty and many groans, and looked around: two figures were coiled up, like huge dogs, near me; two more, moody and sulky, were smoking by the fire, with their knees drawn up to their noses and their hands in their pockets, collars well up round their throats - statues of cold and disgust. To my inquiries about the hour, the answer, given in tones of the deepest despondency, was 'Only eleven o'clock, and the sun doesn't rise till six, and it's going to be the coldest night we've had this year.' The speaker added, 'If it wasn't so dark that we'd break our necks on the way, we might go home.'

Here was a pretty end to our amusement. I slowly let myself down again, and tried to go to sleep, but *that* relief was at an end for the night; the ground seemed to grow harder every moment, or, at all events, I ached more, and the wind certainly blew higher and keener. Dick proved himself a most selfish doggie; he would creep around to leeward of *me*, whilst I wanted him to let me get leeward of him, but he would not consent to this arrangement. Whenever I heard a deeper moan or sigh than usual, I whispered an inquiry as to the hour, but the usual reply, in the most cynical voice, was, 'Oh, you need not whisper, nobody is asleep.' I heard one plaintive murmur: 'Think of all our warm beds, and of our coming up here from choice.' I must say I felt dreadfully ashamed of myself for my plan; it was impossible to express my contrition and remorse, for, always excepting Mr. U., they were all too cross to be spoken to. It certainly was a weary, long night. About one o'clock I pretended to want some hot tea, and the preparation for that got us through half an hour, and it warmed us a little; but everybody still was deeply dejected, not to say morose. After an interval of only two hours more of thorough and intense wretchedness we had a 'grogs,' but there was no attempt at conviviality - subdued savageness was the prevailing state of mind. I tried to infuse a little hope into the party, by suggestions of a speedy termination to our misery, but my own private opinion was that we should all be laid up for weeks to come with illness. I allotted to myself in this imaginary distribution of ills a severe rheumatic fever; oh! how I ached, and I felt as if I never could be warm again. The fire was no use, except to afford occupation in putting on wood; it roasted a little bit of you at a time, and that bit suffered doubly from the cold when it was obliged to take its share of exposure to the wind. I cannot say whether the proverb is true of other nights, but this particular night, certainly, was both darkest and coldest just before dawn.

At last, to our deep joy, and after many false alarms, we really all agreed that there was a faint streak of grey in the east. My first impulse was to set off home, and I believe I tried to get up expressing some such intention, but F. recalled me to myself by saying, in great surprise, 'Are you not going to stop and see the sun rise?' I had quite forgotten that this was the avowed object of the expedition, but I was far too stiff to walk a yard, so I was obliged to wait and see what effect the sunrise would have on my frozen limbs, for I could not think of any higher motive. Presently someone called out 'There's the sea' and so it was, as distinct as though it were not fifty miles off; none of us had seen it since we landed; to all of us it is associated with the idea of going home some day: whilst we were feasting our eyes on it a golden line seemed drawn on the horizon; it spread and spread, and as all the water became flooded with a light and glory which hardly seemed to belong to this world, the blessed sun came up to restore us all to life and warmth again. In a moment, in less than a moment, all our little privations and sufferings vanished as if they had never existed, or existed only to be laughed at. Who could think of their 'Ego' in such a glorious presence, and with such a panorama before them? I did not know which side to turn to first. Behind me rose a giant forest in the far hills to the west - a deep shadow for miles, till the dark outline of the pines stood out against the dazzling snow of the mountains behind it; here the sky was still sheltering the flying night, and the white outlines looked ghostly against the dull neutral tints, though every peak was sharply and clearly defined; then I turned around to see before me such a glow of light and beauty! For an immense distance I could see the vast Canterbury plains; to the left the Waimakariri river, flowing in many streams, 'like a tangled bunch of silver ribbons' (as Mr. Butler calls it in his charming book on New Zealand), down to the sea; beyond its banks the sun shone on the windows of the houses at Oxford, thirty miles off as the crow would fly, and threw its dense bush into strong relief against the yellow plains. The Port Hills took the most lovely lights and shadows as we gazed on them; beyond them lay the hills of Akaroa, beyond the power of words to describe. Christchurch looked quite a large place from the great extent of ground it appeared to cover. We looked on to the south: there was a slight haze over the great Ellesmere Lake, the water of which is quite fresh, though only separated from the sea by a slight bar of sand; the high banks of the Rakaia made a deep dark line extending back into the mountains, and beyond it we could see the Rangitata faintly gleaming in the distance; between us and the coast were green patches and tiny homesteads, but still few and far between; close under our feet, and looking like a thread beneath the shadow of the mountain, ran the Selwyn in a narrow gorge, and on its bank stood the shepherd's hut that I have told you once afforded us such a good luncheon; it looked a mere toy, as if it came out of a child's box of playthings, and yet so snug for all its lonely position. On the other hand lay our own little home, with the faint wreath of smoke stealing up through the calm air (for the wind had dropped at sunrise). Here and there we saw strings of sheep going down from their high camping-grounds to feed on the sunny slopes and in the warm valleys. Every moment added to our delight and enjoyment; but unfortunately it was a sort of happiness which one can neither speak of at the time, nor write about afterwards: silence is its most expressive language. Whilst I was drinking in all the glory and beauty before me, some of the others had been busy striking the tent, repacking the loads, - very much lighter without the provisions; and we had one more excellent cup of tea before abandoning the encampment to the wekas, who must have breakfasted splendidly that morning. Our last act was to collect all the stones we could move into a huge cairn, which was built around a tall pole of totara; on the summit of this we tied securely, with flax, the largest and strongest pocket-handkerchief, and then, after one look round to the west - now as glowing and bright as the radiant east - we set off homewards about seven o'clock; but it was long before we reached the place where we left the horses, for the gentlemen began rolling huge rocks down the sides of the hills and watching them crashing and thundering into the valleys, sometimes striking another rock and then bounding high into the air. They were all as eager and excited as schoolboys, and I could not go on and leave them, lest I should get below them and be crushed under a small stone of twenty tons or so. I was therefore forced to keep well *above* them all the time. At last we reached the spur where the horses were tethered, re-saddled and loaded them, and arrived quite safely at home in time for baths and breakfast. I was amused to see that no one seemed to remember or allude to the miseries and aches of that long cold night; all were full of professions of enjoyment. But I noticed that the day was unusually quiet; the gentlemen preferred a bask in the verandah to any other amusement, and I have reason to believe they indulged in a good many naps.

NIGHT ENCAMPMENT.

Child Explorer on the Milford Track

Eleanor Adams was just 11 years old when she walked what is now the world-famous Milford Track in Fiordland, in 1888. Eleanor joined a survey party including her father, Charles Adams, then chief surveyor of the Otago province, and Quinton Mackinnon, who gave his name to the main pass of the track. Their journey from Milford Sound to Lake Te Anau, which now takes guided walkers travelling east to west just four days, took around four weeks.

It was only a short while after my Father had returned from the Sounds where he had surveyed the Sutherland Falls - finding them to be only 1904 ft. high instead of about 4000 much to the disappointment of the discoverers - that he and I left the Bluff in one of the Union Co's boats to return to Milford early in 1889.

We had a very rough trip, and my Father being a very bad sailor was very glad to get into the perfectly calm waters of the Sound in the late afternoon. There were a number of English tourists on board and they were delighted that the ship had to call at Milford to land my Father and myself there giving them a chance to see Milford Sound, but the Captain was not at all pleased as it delayed his arrival in Melbourne. We had expected to find two survey parties awaiting us at Milford but there was no sign of them. However the Captain put us ashore in one of the ship's boats as soon as we reached the head of the Sound, and as soon as possible put to sea again. The tourists were distressed at leaving us there by ourselves - my father looked frail after the rough sea trip and I was only eleven - and they persuaded the Captain to let us have some food to take ashore with us. Sutherland was away and I never met him at all - but he had left his hut open for us to use.

My father and I watched the steamer until out of sight. It was terribly lonely with not another soul there and surrounded by such huge mountains and thick bush to the water's edge. Luckily I did not know how anxious my Father was at the non-arrival of the survey parties. They had planned to be at Milford days before we arrived - but bad weather and numerous avalanches near the Pass had delayed them.

We went to bed early - at least I did - and in the early hours of the morning my Father heard a coo-ee from across the water and knew that at least some of the party had arrived safely. Soon after daylight a tiny little canvas boat came over, and I think we started off the same day.

That little canvas boat was the only boat we had and it held only 2 or 3 at a time and it took some time getting the party over the river or lakes. Some one had to squat down in the bow and watch for any snags - Lake Ada was full of them - that might hole the canvas. We had a very rough walk from the Sound to the Ball (now called Quentin) huts and it took a long time getting us up Lake Ada in the canvas boat - I think some of the party scrambled round the lake. It was lucky there were the two huts near the Sutherland Falls for we had to stay many days there on account of bad weather. The huts were very primitive affairs but they, as well as Sutherland's hut, all had some very pretty curtains and I wondered where the material came from. One of the surveyors told me that it had been torn from a French Countess's dress, when she had tried to walk up from Milford to see the Falls, she had returned to the Tourist ship with only the lining of her dress left and no shoes.

One day while we were at the Ball huts we had a frightening thunder storm - in the flashes of lightning the mountains seemed to tower over us.

At the Ball huts the bush rats were dreadful but luckily I was not afraid of mice and rats, but all the same did not like their running all over me as soon as the lights were out. I begged a yard of the white calico - used for the survey pegs - from my father and cut a good many holes in it so that I could breathe, and put it right over my head. I felt quite happy that way. During this bad weather my Father was quite anxious and wondered when we could get over the Pass.

One day we saw the Sutherland Falls - we were about quarter of a mile away I think, but we were covered with spray. I lost all sense of distance among those huge mountains and thought I could throw a stone into the pool at the foot of the Falls.

At last a good day came and the party for Te Anau and ourselves started off over the Pass. It was hard work pulling ourselves up through the heavy bush but above the bush line the way looked very dangerous, especially skirting Mt. Balloon where the rocky ground was all slimy with moss and water. Quintin Mackinnon roped me to himself and my Father and we all got safely to the top of the Pass. The little tarn on top was called after me - Lake Ella. Looking down the thousands of feet into the valley we had left was awe-inspiring. The only way I could look was to lie down flat and pull myself to the edge of the cliff and get my Father to hold my ankles!

We camped somewhere near the foot of the Pass and all night long were kept awake with avalanches falling. Just over the Pass above the heavy bush we went through acres of the large flowered houhere or ribbonwood - it was like a cherry orchard in Spring.

Going down the Clinton Valley was the easiest part of the journey and very lovely. When we came to the Clinton River it was a raging torrent with huge boulders, and the younger of the Quill brothers carried me across. We could see the river coming out from a huge ice cave at the head of the valley, and also saw an avalanche falling near.

The track to Te Anau was fairly level and we caught lovely glimpses of the Clinton River with its clear greenish waters. The native birds were so tame, and the little robins would come a perch on our toes and hats while we had our meals, ready for any crumbs. And nearly always while my Father was surveying a robin would perch on his hat or theodolite. Wood hens were plentiful in the Clinton Valley and would run off with anything bright they could find in your tent. If you imitated their call they would come right up to you.

Above the bush line at the Pass there were many native flowers - unfortunately I did not know the names of many of them. I saw one big white mountain daisy and mountain lily and at the Sound the rata was ablaze.

The bush was magnificent - huge trees with their trunks covered with lovely mosses and ferns and long trails of moss hanging from their boughs. Wherever you put a foot down you had to tread on lovely kidney and other ferns and mosses and masses of tiny native plants. And waterfalls and lovely mountain streams were everywhere. I think it took us three weeks to reach Lake Te Anau, then we had three days in Mackinnon's boat on a perfectly calm lake rowing all the way and camping two nights on lovely little beaches - once on the West side and once on the East.

Mackinnon shot some duck and cooked our dinners over a fire in a kerosene tin in the boat. One day we stopped under a huge bluff for our dinner and when we dropped our duck bones over the side of the boat we could see them sinking down and down for ages - the water was so wonderfully clear.

We stayed at a sheep station on the East side of the Lake for the night and next day we rode on horse back to Lumsden station where we got a train to Dunedin.

Hauhau attack on a farmstead, painted by Ferdinand von Tempsky (at right). Hocken Library, Dunedin.

Conflict with the Maori

From the beginning there was conflict between settler and Maori over land. The Treaty of Waitangi in 1840 was about sovereignty over resources and much of the political history of pioneer New Zealand was fuelled by the hunger for land and the resistance of Maori to these pressures. Armed conflict began early, with war in the north and skirmishes elsewhere, in 1845. War between the Government and various tribes broke out again, in several parts of the North Island, during the 1860s and the history of many settlements was shaped by the presence of military. The episodes recounted here come from different times and places.

Elizabeth Holman writes of the mood in Whangarei and Auckland during the war of 1845 in the nearby Bay of Islands. Jane Maria Atkinson reveals settler concern about the handling of affairs and of raids in the opening phases of the Taranaki War in the 1860s. Elizabeth Caldwell experiences the side effects of tribal loyalties with Taranaki, from the comparative security of Golden Bay. Maria Morris is captured by the messianic Te Kooti on his trail of revenge in Poverty Bay. These tales in no way reflect the full progress of the New Zealand wars but they reveal some of the disparate settler views and experiences of those unhappy times.

ELIZABETH HOLMAN

The Evacuation of Whangarei

During her 93 eventful years, Elizabeth Holman experienced a wide and varied slice of colonial life in New Zealand and Australia. Raised in Sydney where her father was Official Assignee, Elizabeth first crossed the Tasman on an expedition to extract kauri spars from the Hokianga in 1840. She returned to New Zealand the next year and married Henry Holman in Kororareka (now Russell, Bay of Islands). During their 53 years of marriage the couple lived in Auckland (where Henry was Superintendent of Public Works), Sydney, Mimiwhangata, Whangarei, Riverhead on the Waitemata, the Thames goldfields and Kamo. Among the major events in her reminiscences, held in the Alexander Turnbull Library, is the sacking of Kororareka by Hone Heke and his followers, and the subsequent evacuation of Whangarei when settlers there feared attack by the Maori. Written by Elizabeth in a 'stream of consciousness' style, this extract has been punctuated to make the story easier to follow.

Elizabeth's reminiscences were adapted into a very readable first-person narrative biography by Florence Keene and published in 1972 under the title With Flags Flying.

When my husband arrived in Whangarei with our things from Mimiwhangata, Mr. Mair let us have a three room cottage to put our things in close to their dwelling house. We lived in this cottage but still had our meals with the Mairs as my husband was often away from home on business for Mr. Mair, sometimes in Auckland. At this time Governor Fitzroy was in Command; he took the rule in 1843.... Early in the next year he went South to visit the principal towns in the Colony and to inquire into the quarrels between the Natives and Europeans. He appears to have given great offence to both races during this visit as he pardoned the Wairau murders and this displeased the English as the Natives laughed at him and said he was afraid of them. Then Fitzroy made a law that the natives might make their own bargains with the people but for every acre bought from the Maoris the people should pay 10 [?] to the Government but it was found after a time that this plan would not answer and many other plans were brought forward too numerous to mention. At that time there were a lot of mischievous people about who took delight in making the Natives discontented putting foolish ideas into their heads. (Those American Whaler Sailors) did a deal of mischief that way particularly in Auckland. The Maoris began to think they were far better off in the old Bay of Islands Whaling time and it was these together with the French Whaler sailors, a bad lot, [who] would tell the Maoris that it was through that flag flying up there that they could not now do as they formerly used to do. These worthless men so influenced a lot of the Natives that it became a serious matter and at last they did cut down the flag & early one morning the Natives made an attack on the farther end of the town close to the Church. Captn. Robertson of the *Hazard* landed with his sailors to support the soldiers & 13 of the poor sailors were slain and Captn Robertson had a bullet in his arm. While this was going on Hone Heke and his men cut the flag staff down. The Europeans collected in a fortified house on the beach and defended themselves for some time. After three hours fighting the Natives asked for time to be allowed to carry off their wounded. Taking advantage of this truce the Europeans thought it best to escape while they could and there were three ships in the bay into which all the people of Kororareka crowded and gave the place up to Maoris. As soon as all were on board the Maoris came from the hills and burnt & plundered the town.

I could tell a lot about this. Mrs. Ford & the Dr. with their 4 children and servant were hurrying through the town when it was being sacked by the Natives and things lying about in the streets. One of the little girls picked up a jug. Of course it was taken from her. The child cried and Hone Heke came to the child putting the jug in her hand saying she shall have it (and they took that jug to Auckland and it was always called the Hone Heke jug). When they reached the ship in the harbour they saw their house in flames as well as the rest of the town and hundreds of people had nothing but what they stood up in and arrived in Auckland in that plight in March 1845.

Well I must now tell you how we poor folks in Whangarei fared. Nearly all the Maoris about there were friendly but there were some down the river, [in] a large settlement in Matarau that were not. Our friendly natives said we had better leave and go to Auckland, that if the Natives took Kororareka they would not answer for our safety. So my husband said he would go to Auckland and get the Governor to let him have some sort of a vessel and bring it to Whangarei to take us all away. He left at once in some small boat but before he left there were 4 or 5 Chiefs who promised to keep watch over us all and in case of any immediate danger were to let us know. I was to stay with the Mair family until my husband's return with the vessel to take us all away. He had only left a few days when the Native Chiefs came to Mr. Mair and told him that we and all the settlers must get away at once. There were about 50 in all at that time scattered about the settlement and strange to say that day a small craft called the *Trial* with two men on board of her (she was about 12 tons in size) came up the river as far as Graham's town. How it was I can't remember but I think some natives went on board and they were frightened and left the vessel in their boat and the day after that we were all at tea when we heard a frightful yelling. The door was thrown open and the room filled with natives. They all had guns

& spears and the old Chief Tanru rushed about saying Te Horoma Whiena and caught hold of me & threw his blanket round me baby and all for I held tight to my baby. He ran away with me down to the river and put me into his canoe. It was quite dark - you may imagine my feelings better than I can describe them. The old Cannibal had promised my husband that he would take care of me and all the time I was under his blanket he kept jabbering to me words of comfort it seemed but it might have been quite the reverse for all I knew as I did not then understand one word of their language or very little. He and his men took me & some others down the river and put us on board this Craft that the men had left and during the night all the settlers came on board.

Towards morning Mr. Mair came with William Poe, the chief who would not leave Mr. Mair until he saw him safely on board. They came down the river in a boat of Mr. Mair's and when all the settlers were on board, 47 or 50, the Native Chiefs said get away as quickly as possible which we did. We were just packed like sardines in a box. We were three days getting to Kawau Island and it came on to blow. We must all have gone to the bottom of the sea during this time. We had no food and we reached the Kawau in a most pitiable state.

Mr. Leather was living there at that time managing a copper mine. He received us in a most kindly way and did everything to comfort the weak & suffering, turned out of his cottage of two rooms for the females and set his men to work to prepare food for the starving lot. It was here that my husband picked us up in the *British Queen*, a craft of about 30 tons. He had heard that we had been driven away but how he heard I can't remember. My husband thought most likely we might have reached the Kawau and so went in or round that way and thankful enough I was to see him. I was in a very weak state and had it not been for Mrs. John Gorrie I should have died on the way. My poor child was between 8 & 9 months old. None of the people had anything in the shape of clothing but what we had on our back. I had no hat or cloak or outer covering but I was not singular in this respect. As soon as we were sufficiently recovered, which as far as I can remember was a few days, we then left the Kawau for Auckland in the *British Queen*. My husband brought her himself with the help of two men and we were all landed safely in Auckland. My husband had taken a cottage in Parnell and we lived there a short time. Then Mrs. Burrows came to Auckland. All the Missionaries' Wives from the Waimate Mission Station were ordered to Auckland as it was not considered safe for them to remain there with their families. The Bishop took a 4 roomed cottage in Parnell on the beach in the bay. Mrs. Burrows was to go there with her family, and my husband and self were invited to live there also, which we did. Mr. Burrows still remained at the Waimate Mission Station with the other missionary husbands. All the Wives and families of same were to stay in Auckland.

Auckland at that time was in a great state of commotion. Nothing in the shape of business was done. I really do not know how all the people lived. The English Church St Pauls was blockaded & several block houses were erected and guards of soldiers to watch all day and all night around them. Many times false alarms have filled the church with women & children in the middle of the night. After the taking of the Pa, Ruapekapeka, Heke became anxious for peace. All his people were tired of fighting and beginning to feel the want of food. Heke & Rawiti, a Chief that had always helped him, wrote to the Governor asking forgiveness and promising to behave well in the future. Pardon was granted and peace was made in January 1846.

ATTACK ON OKAIHAU

Wartime in Taranaki

Maria and Arthur Atkinson were living at Hurworth, on the outskirts of the New Plymouth settelement, when the land situation in Taranaki became increasingly disturbed in early 1860. By the second half of the year most of the rural settlers had been moved to the comparative safety of the town, but conditions were crowded and soon became insanitary. Gossip and rumour were rife as Maori raiding parties roamed the province, killing settlers and stock and burning homes and buildings.

Maria was of the opinion that the province's troubles could just as well be solved without the help of the government and imported troops, and her letters to relatives often criticise contemporary military leaders and their actions. These examples are again to Margaret Taylor, and to her brother and sister-in-law, Christopher William and Emily Elizabeth Richmond in Auckland. In July 1860 Maria was sent to William's home in Parnell - against her own wishes, but for health and safety reasons. By early the next year she had returned to Taranaki and continued to chronicle events in the province, through her letters, for many years. Mary and Arthur lived in Taranaki for the first 14 years of their marriage, enduring most of the land wars there, before moving to Nelson where Maria raised 4 children, and died in 1914.

In this extract Ar is her husband Arthur and W.S.A., his elder brother William Smith Atkinson.

Letter to Margaret Taylor
Hurworth, 19 Feb 1860
Mr. S.P. King's stone cottage, New Plymouth, 19-26 Feb 1860

I have spent a very busy week in packing our goods at Hurworth and moving down here. There seems little chance of my writing a very intelligible or coherent account of proceedings here, for the hubbub and noise is generally considerable in this small mansion which now accommodates six adults and five children, besides occasional visitors from Hurworth who pop in for a meal or 'shake down' at night. Before public events took their present turn, Lely had arranged to rent this comfortable little cottage of Mr. King's from the first of this month that she might have a place to accommodate William and Em's three girls...There had been so much illness and so many deaths amongst children in Auckland owing to unusual heat and protracted drought that William and Emily were in great alarm for their little ones...This cottage is admirably adapted for the purpose as it is only a few yards from the houses occupied by Mr. and Mrs. S.P. King and the Miss Kings. The four buildings (one is Mr. S.K's office, he is Registrar to the Province) stand in one garden and from a group we have always called Kingston...Lely has taken it for a year, and its first use to us is as a refuge in the expected war. You would hardly suppose we were in town if you could take a peep at us, but we shall be within the lines of sentries and have a special guard close at hand as all the important papers of the Province will be in Mr. King's office.

It just occurs to me that this letter may have put you rather in a way about us all, but you need not be more alarmed than we are and that is not at all, with the exception of Aunt Helen, who seems at times to expect we shall all be murdered. In the first place it is very doubtful whether we shall have any fighting at all, if reinforcements are sent from Auckland by the return of the steamer which passed us going north on the 24th, many people feel certain the Maoris will be overawed; the preparations already being made by the removal of out-settlers to the town, and the erection of strong block houses in one or two places have astonished them a good deal, for they have been such regular spoilt children ever since this settlement was formed that it seems inconceivable to them that they are not to have their own way this time...If we do have any real fighting there can be little doubt which side will have the best of it. If, however...they take to the bush and try to make ravages of property in small skulking parties, they will be able to do much damage and cause a great outlay before they are put down. All the settlers will be compelled to come in before fighting begins, so that no lives need be lost except in fair fight. In their own wars the Maoris fight, or rather shoot for days, with at the end one man perhaps killed or wounded. They have few *good* firearms amongst them and are not good shots like the Red Indians, having had no wild beasts to hunt down, and never living by the chase, there has been little practice for them. They are desperately cautious and seldom come within shot of each other.

My greatest fear is lest some peace in the Villa Franca style should be patched up leaving us no better off than before...There has already been serious loss of time and money which will be severely felt by the poorer class of settlers; but all will be money well invested if this period is indeed the turning point, and the crisis ends in our gaining new blocks of land and thus allow scope for the increase of the place.

You must understand that all the male Hurworthians are members of a Volunteer Rifle Corps (in existence long before the Volunteer movement in England was thought of, so don't suppose we can't originate things out here) and as such may be called on any day to march to the Waitara leaving us poor females all unprotected...

Our household here at present consists of Lely, Helen and the three Auckland children, rightful inhabitants; James and Mary with their little

Anneliz and maid Martha, Edith and myself interlopers...Arthur pays us flying visits and is steadily improving himself as a rifleman. I really think he enjoys the whole affair;...he was evidently meant for less peaceable days and occupations than those he has fallen among.

A settler's homestead near New Plymouth just prior to the war in Taranaki. From S. Hursthouse, New Zealand Britain of the South.

Letter to C.W. and Emily Richmond
New Plymouth, 6 Apr 1860

A hundred times we have longed for you back, dear Will, but you would have either gone mad, or been shot on the day of the battle at Waireka, so perhaps it is as well you are away. Harry is busy by me giving an account of the actual action so I will confine myself to the minor incidents that you can join on to the narrative. You must rest tranquil as to the feeling between the military and civilians; it has never been what might have been expected, thanks in great measure to the relief to the volunteers' discontent which a good fight brought, and to the glow of satisfaction amongst them at having acquitted themselves so gallantly....

There is much more danger of an outbreak from the daily, hourly mismanagement of Gold in such matters as wearing out the men's strength in utterly useless works, and having ridiculous objectless parades at early hours when many are worn out with the night's watch, and feel that crops are wasting and a hundred things being neglected while the old fool is keeping them kicking their heels being inspected. When the news of these murders came into town, Gold was inspecting 600 *un*armed men whose rifles and guns would have had to be scrambled for in all quarters of the town had an alarm been sounded....The utter incapacity and disastrous stupidity of almost all at the head of affairs becomes daily clearer. There does not seem to be an ounce of brains amongst the officers. All our people have done their utmost to make the common soldiers understand that no blame is attached to them for the desertion on the 28th and I believe they understand it themselves.

From Hugh Ronald's report of the state of feeling in the camp at Waitara, however, I fear there is not much British ambition stirred up amongst the troops as a body; he says they are green and unused to action, that they lose nothing, but rather gain from the war's being indefinitely prolonged, they had rather have a year of it with *no* fighting, then sharp work even in a few months....

Thanks to the *Niger* men and our own, the town is for the present quite safe, but in spite of the presence of 1200 armed men the country round is to nearly all intents and purposes a conquered country; the Maoris can go where they like and do as they like and no one dreams that they can be interfered with. Waiting for reinforcements is the continued excuse, but if Wellington and Auckland are threatened we have already more than our share here. I do believe the war here would be soonest ended by sending away *all* the soldiers, women and children so that there would be noting to take care of, and have the *Niger* men and the *Pelorus* men to head up the militia and volunteers. They would soon sweep the settlement clean. Four or five houses were burned in Bell Block last night - the fires were seen from town....

There seems no excuse for Murray's conduct on the 28th; the best is that the whole affair was ill digested from the beginning. The expedition was originally started as an attempt to rescue the Brown family of Omata and I suppose was intended by the authorities to be arranged so as to avoid fighting if possible. Whilst the volunteers and military were falling into their places came messengers post haste to say the Maoris were pouring down in number to meet the troops and attack the town. The alarm guns were fired, the excitement became immense, but no new orders were issued consequent on the changed aspect the movement of the Maoris gave the affair. We all moved to the Marsland Hotel,...soon after the firing began came in Alex King at full gallop. He brought a vague message. This was Hal's message by F. Standish to Murray forwarded to Gold. (We had this from Thos King who heard him give his report to Gold) to the effect that ammunition and reinforcements were wanted...After some delay ammunition carts were dispatched and Capt. Cracroft and his men started off in Col. Murray's tracks. Mr. Pitcairn, spite of his lame arm (which had been in a sling ever since a fall from Platterfort on the night of the

Ratapihipihi attempt) seeing how long the carts would be, volunteered with some others to carry a good deal of ammunition. Judge of his disgust on reaching the troops at finding all the ammunition was for muskets when the rifles were alone then in need of it! He was in a great danger...whilst attempting to join the Volunteers. He was dispatched by Murray just near sundown to order Capt. Cracroft to fall back; luckily he went slowly and was too late, for the gallant *Niger* men had just been offered £10 for the Maori flag and were rushing on the Pa. But for this act our boys might never have seen home again, so you see there Murray did his best to complete his work...

All seem to have been brave and cool but the unlucky four runaways, whose feelings since I don't envy. The brother of the wounded Rawson shot more than one of the chiefs....Young Willie Webster had an exciting little adventure, he was very near one Maori who aimed at him twice, the 3rd time they were so near each other that little Willie fixed his bayonet, prepared to rush if his ball failed, raced the Maori at loading and shot him dead....One man aimed at Ar three times and then Des hit him. Des, Ar and Jim Ronalds were the first to go to young Rawson's help. Hal says he hardly knows how they got him safe across the field to Jury's house the Maori's fire was so hot, they had to set the poor young man down often to load and fire. He is the only wounded man not out of danger. Lieut Blake is going on all right....We offered to take him in here when the others left but I believe the doctors did not wish him to be carried so far. The gallant one-eyed Paul Inch...as soon as he was wounded ground his teeth, rammed down his charge and killed two Maoris right off.

Nearly as bad as Murray's leaving the Volunteers is the fact that it took 4 hours incessant talking from Maclean and Major Herbert and others to induce Gold to send a party to their relief. Maclean considered that if a strong party had held the ground till morning and secured the Maori bodies a most effectual blow would have been struck....

That rifles are most important all agree - the militia officers are longing to get them. Poor Henry, Jas and W.S.A. were not in the battle of Waireka. Henry would have been there had he been a private, he would have pressed himself into the party but his fear that he could not acquit himself as captain and had to be responsible for the lives of others held him back. Ar kept James from going on poor Mary's account...W.S.A. was at his Bell Block post. It is a blow to all three...Charlie was amongst the militia who crossed to the troops and was not in the thickest of the fight. The murdered Shaw was of an Omata family not related to the Halses or Whites. His sister was wife of poor Harry Pasmore, only six months married losing husband and brother in one day on the 28th. Young Sarten was Mrs. Lye's grandson.

The Commissariat displayed the good management and foresight suitable to its duties. All seemed confusion in town, people tearing about late in the afternoon for carts and at last sending them off empty for the wounded. Not an officer...thought of sending a bite or sup to men most of whom had left without dinner, who had been fighting for hours and had a long fatiguing walk home. I was really the first person in town who thought of bread and brandy for them...I attacked Black who thought something should be done but had no orders. He called James from the little back parlour who instantly saw the necessity...and said the bread might if necessary be put down to his account, the red tape boobies hummed and hawed and made difficulties about complicating the accounts and so would have sent nothing because they could not tell whether the food and the brandy would be used by troops or volunteers!...

I expect Eliza and I shall be driven off to Nelson before long. Jane and her boys left in the *Wonga* yesterday, at the same time Miss Hinde, Hammertons, Redheads and lots more. The *Airedale* was too full to take luggage....

Edith likes wartimes, she enjoyed the fires and noise at the Marsland Hotel on the 28th immensely. I wish you could have heard the joy of that night, without the day's anxiety, the deafening cheers and mad excitement in town as the Volunteers came in shouting *Rule Britannia* till hoarse....

Letter to Emily E. Richmond
New Plymouth, 6 May 1860

Winter has come on us all at once this last week, with wind, rain, thunder and lightning. I pity the poor soldiers from Australia who are mostly in tents as the wind has been south-west and cold. We hear very conflicting rumours as to the numbers and intentions of the Waikato party that is on its way down here...The more the merrier all our people think; nevertheless Arthur would have packed me off with Edith, and then W.S.A. would have wished Eliza to go had the *Airedale* remained longer on Thursday (the 3rd). Arthur has no reliance on the so-called defences of the town; with a little pluck and determination a party might come into the middle of it any night, and then though it (i.e. the party) would not get out again probably with more than half its numbers, in the confusion and alarm many Europeans must be sacrificed as people would shoot so wildly that friends would be as dangerous as foes. Neither Eliza or I feel at all timid, we can't persuade ourselves any Maoris are bold enough to venture on attacking the town, they can only know how numerous are the armed men here and will not be aware of the advantages for them the want of all plan and union amongst us would give in a night attack. If anything does happen in the shape of an alarm we shall keep quite quiet in this house where we always have 3 riflemen, generally 4, to guard us. Since Waireka we have always gone to bed in full security and though the Taranakis are said to be again assembling there is no fear from them except for the houses and property at a respectable distance from the town. It is curious that the week preceding Mary's and Lely's departure contained all the greatest excitement and alarm of the campaign, if campaign it can be called. You will hear that the Warea expedition returned in safety, after destroying about £15 worth of Maori property and a hundred pounds worth of Mr. Parris's wheat and oats...In reality the Tataraimaka settlers lost more than the enemy, having the troops on their farms and in their houses a week.

....

May 12...Many people here have been very ill with the sudden change of weather. Severe colds accompanied by diarrhoea and sickness are about....Is it not curious that Harry has never had a wheezy attack since he was in Wellington nearly two years ago.

  Mr. Pitcairn has lived at this village now since the night of the attempted surprise of Ratapihipihi when he had a fall from Platterfoot which rendered his right arm useless for some weeks....It is now too late for his return to England this season, as it would not do for him to go round Cape Horn so late and then reach England in autumn...Hal and James always wish all women and children away and Ar does generally, but W.S.A., who used to take the darkest views, does not believe in the Waikatos attacking the town at night and without notice....

Letter to Emily Richmond
New Plymouth, 20 May 1860

....May 22. Nervous old ladies have been suffering great alarm for two nights...The friendly natives...have kindly got up a little excitement by bringing in reports that the town was to be attacked...Some people sat up on Sunday night, and last night half the troops were under arms all night. Neither Eliza or I can get up a twinge of alarm...At dinner time today we really had a faint hope something was going to happen. Lt. Richardson of the 12th who is stationed near the B[ell] B[lock] house with 55 men, met or saw a party of Maoris at the edge of the bush...They looked at each other and mutually or respectively retired. All or nearly all the troops from town were ordered to move down to the B.B. and the Volunteers and Militia had to be under arms to protect the town. However opposite the Provincial Offices the troops met Mr. Parris who brought news...that the Maoris had all disappeared...The guards round town are doubled tonight, we have Ar on sentry round about this house which is very agreeable except that he pops his head in at my bedroom window in an alarming manner at all sorts of odd hours which I think quite as terrific as hearing a Maori war whoop....

I trust the *Airedale* will appear tomorrow...On her return I hope 'The Coming Man' will be in her to take Gold's place...it seems to me there is not a day to be lost if William's view is the right one that nobody in N. Z. but the Bishop is even listened to at home, for in *that* case in a very few weeks orders must arrive to make peace and beg the Natives' pardon...We have had plenty of opportunities of proving to the Maoris that they can be mastered...if this is not proved to them there will be no enduring life in this Colony for true Britons....

You must take care what letters you let anyone with Taranaki relatives hear or see, because the snobs here are often either secretly or openly military in their leanings, and consider Gold a wary and sagacious leader using laudable caution in his movements, whilst Murray is a maligned innocent, a victim to his rigid attention to his duties. The people who are supporters of the military proceedings always have means of living that are not affected by the present state of things and had no very near friends at Waireka. Old Dr. and Mrs. Wilson, the J.S. Smiths, Mr. McKechny and Fred Carrington are the only ones I can think of just now....

Hurworth is neither burnt nor attacked at present, which is very satisfactory, it is a great comfort that it is so far from town. All the houses within reach are robbed by the soldiers, and there won't be a fowl, duck or turkey alive in the place in another few weeks except in the remote bush regions....

ELIZABETH CALDWELL

Unsettled Days in Golden Bay

Elizabeth Pringle Caldwell, her husband Thomas, and their five children, had already spent ten settled years in the Nelson area before their troubles began. The couple decided to buy a property at Tukurua, on the coastline some 18km northwest of Takaka, when the English gentleman who owned the land decided to return home. Elizabeth writes of the ensuing events in her reminiscences, written in 1890 and copied in the Alexander Turnbull Library. She describes the Tukurua section as 'close to the beach, just at the head of the Bay, commanding a lovely view from Cape Farewell to Separation Point, with the far-distant snowy cone of Mount Egmont in very clear weather'. Taranaki may have seemed 'far-distant', but the outbreak of the land war there in 1860 had repercussions for the Caldwells when they tried to take possession of their land and build a house. The local Maori, previously on friendly terms with the British settlers, became hostile and refused to let further work take place until their claim to the Golden Bay land was sorted out by Commissioner McLean. Subsequently, the family were forced to live in a disused whare, and with Elizabeth being 'inevitably alone with my children', she often feared for their lives.

We now made up our minds to remove to Tukurua by the sea and looked forward to that with great delight. Papa went over to Nelson to see about wood for a new house and to see about the title to the land, but the Maori war broke out in Taranaki and our Maori friends began to look very sullen and silent - old Piraka was very busy casting bullets 'to shoot the white man' he said when the boys questioned him - Korawa returned in a small craft fetching timber for the house and other matters - a cheese press among other etcetera, for he meant to have a dairy farm. They were landed on the Beach at Tukurua and when my people proceeded to level a place for the house and get the studs in, to their astonishment a band of Maoris came along making hostile demonstrations - old Catherine with her hair cut short and standing upright about a foot all over her head, and whenever my people touched a plank, up she bounced, her tongue very far out, war-fashion and relieved them of it at once. They found it impossible to proceed with any work. In such cases the women always head the charge. It turned out that the Maoris had never ceded their title to the land - and never received payment for it.

  As we hitherto had been on friendly terms with the Maoris with whom our children were great favourites, we did not think it prudent and it would have been fruitless to enter into further hostilities, so we waited to see how events would turn, for the news from Taranaki was not reassuring. War had been declared in that Province and smouldering fires seemed gathering, even in our Bay, ready to burst into flame. Of course we reported an account of the attitude the natives had assumed at headquarters, requesting that enquiry be instituted as to the truth of their statements, as they had not molested the first settlers, neither had they any personal enmity towards ourselves. Sir Edward Stafford, who was first Superintendent of the Nelson Province, very wisely and kindly sent the Rev. Mr. Tudor who had been, I think, a missionary among the natives and had great influence among them - to advise them to refrain from joining the Taranaki natives in the rebellion, and also to reassure the settlers of the Bay.

Another important circumstance in the state of affairs was this - Mr. Andrew Duncan who had bought Onekaka from us, had been prospecting widely over the country and had found gold in several places, this, however, had to be kept a dead secret in the present state of native affairs. Thus we were put to the greatest domestic inconvenience and subsequent heavy loss as all our goods were in boxes on the beach, the timber lying useless and worst of all we could get no milk or butter, a serious loss to a young family. My husband went over to Nelson to see if nothing could be done to accelerate a settlement of the dispute but was told that the only plan would be to wait till McLean 'Makarine' could come - he being unquestioned arbitrator in all native affairs. So we had no choice but to wait as patiently as the Maoris for time is nothing to them - they hold the most wearisome endless koreros 'conversaziones' in more polite parlance, squatting comfortably on the ground, in either Town or Country, wherever they happen to be, puffing away at the inevitable pipe, men and women alike - thus they are in no hurry, and the longer they can spin out the conference the better they like it.

But the time passed rather sadly for us. Mr. Duncan's brother having come out from England to join him, it became imperative that I should leave the place to them. I had a tent and there was a large whare on the place that the Messrs Blackbarrows had occupied which could boast of a chimney and as my husband was still detailed in Nelson, I got my boys to remove the furniture and took possession of the domicile - the Maoris grumbled and did not seem friendly but went no further. So though I had been cautioned there seemed no alternative and we placed some boards on the floor which seemed very heavenly comfort. We had plenty of food, and the Maoris did not interfere in any way with our property - some of it valuable though the boxes were lying quite unguarded on the beach. Fortunately the children did not realise the danger of the position and I made no mention of it - kept them comfortable as to food and clothing - the little ones finding great delight in gathering shells on the beach to which they now had near access. At high tides there was an oyster bed uncovered and among those rocks were splendid large mussels. Now, to us, a valuable adjunct - in the matter of diet - some oysters too were to be had, but these were a rarer delicacy, but the want of milk was a serious deprivation. We had a large box of arrowroot which took its place with my baby - now a year old - but it is not very nourishing made with only water. Fortunately there was a lovely little river - as clear as crystal - which came dashing down the far-back hills, so that we had no lack of pure water.

Sometimes at night we used to hear far echoes of the Maori songs and chants, rising and falling on the breeze - and we knew that large war canoes were sent away laden with contributions of bullets and other accessories of war to Taranaki.

Settlers' cottage, Nelson district.

I could scarcely estimate the number of the native population then residing in Massacre Bay. One night however, my eldest son who was an especial favourite with them and who understood their language pretty well, went down about six miles to Puruahoia a well known Pah where Edwin Stanton and his father the old Duke of York were chiefs. Tom counted 200 of them, male and female, the women as talkative as the men, more so indeed they never seemed to doubt their right to the franchise in this parliament. There were long speeches for and against the propriety of joining in the rebellion against the pakeha, and they did not arrive at a settlement, but left it an open question which did not add to our peace of mind, and as we had been told that the Maoris always as a preliminary massacred their best friends, there was considerable reason for anxiety. Being at this time inevitably alone with my children, I never failed to call them round me at night to read prayers, and commit ourselves to the Almighty protecting care of the God of all Comfort and Consolation, so that should we never see the dawn of another morning we should assuredly enter the dawn of Eternal Day.

We kept quite cheerful during the day, my girls were only wee tots, too young to know anything about it, and the boys were very brave and good and obedient. Their work on the farm being stopped they had plenty of time for sport. They used to snare the hakas [?] and were experts in catching fish. In the warm summer nights they would wade out pretty deep in the tide and spear flounders, bringing home goodly baskets of fish then in season. They made long torches of pine wood splintered up and bound together by the ever ready and useful flax. These set alight attracted the fish which were caught by the spear. This art they had learned from the Maoris. But I now come to the most distressing part of my story.

One night after the children were all asleep I lay with my baby beside me in the still moonlight - it was the month of May and very cold, and when going off to sleep there came a violent shock as if I had had a blow on the head with an axe. Not the least unconscious after a few minutes I tried to rise up but found that all down my left side was paralysed. I could not move. This lasted for I could not say how long, but after a time wore off, recurring again at intervals in all, say a dozen times in the twenty four hours. I did not get up but found I could sew occasionally - there was no pain but the horrible thing came on always when I began to feel drowsy, and I dared not sleep. I directed my eldest girl who was six years old to get out from my trunks some black things, as I had mourning for a sister put away. 'What for Mama?'

'To make you a black frock dear' I said.

'Oh you are *so* white Mama, do you think you will die?'

'I am afraid of it my pet,' I said. 'So you would want a black frock for Papa would have to take you back to Scotland, so get me out the stuff.' So as I felt able to sit up I made the frocks to be ready. After a few days my boys had sent word to the doctor a young medico from America who had settled in the Takaka district, 20 miles or so down the Bay. He looked very grave, after some conversation diagnosed the case 'partial paralysis' and 'no wonder' said he 'if your speech leaves you, don't be alarmed - that might come back, but I don't think you can last many days. I hope your husband can come back at once'.

By the time my husband got home I was able to be up and about a little but the mysterious awful affliction kept on. So it became imperative that I should be taken to Nelson for further treatment. A small craft plied between Aorere and Nelson, Aorere being the site of the present town of Collingwood, five miles from our place. Thus I was forced to leave my little ones for a time - to wean my baby, a lovely darling fourteen months old. He could run about nicely and I had made a calico hat for him with a very wide brim, inserting round the edge a fine supplejack to keep off the broiling sun, my stock of straw hats being out. I so well remember giving him his last drink as I sat on the beach before leaving them, his little blue serge coat and big hat which I had put on, the wee white feet bare, and gave him in charge of his eldest brother. I then took a fond farewell of them all with many tears and much anguish of soul.

A young man who was going round on that day to take the census and passed the night there, told me that the baby woke for his usual refreshment about 12 that night, that Tom made him a bowl of arrowroot and sugar, that they both baby and nurse had a good cry, and then had a sleep again. Surely the wind is tempered to the shorn lamb.

My dear friends, the Scotch minister and his kind hospitable wife insisted on my being with them. I had the advice of two skilful doctors who only prescribed rest and nourishment, but it was six weeks before I could return to my family. An old Maori woman, Katherine's mother, Maria, who always said she was 110, and she certainly looked it, but she was a kind old creature - promised me to 'look out' for them, so long as they did not get drowned or burnt, I did not exact much.

On my return I found them all as well as I left them, save that my baby had a cold in his head - he never forgot that parting scene on the beach, and once, when a tall fine young man, startled a gay party at an evening assemblage who were discussing the power of memory and the length back to which it would go. 'I distinctly remember,' said this bold gentleman, 'the day I was weaned.' The ladies blushed and the gentlemen shouted with laughter. No one believed him, but it was quite true as I found on comparing notes some time afterwards.

By this time my family had been removed to a comfortable cottage at Motupipi at the far corner of the Bay where we remained till 'Makarina' had settled the dispute on his visit to Nelson, and it was considered safe for us to take possession of the Tukurua property after two years' weary waiting. Meantime our boxes had been chiefly on the beach - the timber shrunk and warped and all the cattle running wild on the hills. All these losses of time and property were beyond compensation in some ways, though the Government awarded us 300 acres of adjoining land, but we found the land thus awarded utterly barren, incapable of cultivation; however we were glad to be settled and at rest. The Maoris had then all signed allegiance to the Queen.

Whenever it was considered safe, after many months, we set sail in a huge canoe one fine day, away up to the head of the Bay, and took possession of our own land. There was a cottage erected near to the beach - a large kitchen with a spacious chimney, a famous dresser and I had the pleasure of arranging my long shut up dinner set on it, hanging up the teacups on little hooks with great pride and thinking how lovely to be home at last, and so near the sea too, an unspeakable delight to me.

MARIA MORRIS

Captured by Te Kooti

Maria Morris was born in New Zealand but her experience tells of pioneer times and the fate of several immigrant women at the hands of the warriors of Te Kooti. The daughter of an Irish settler and a Maori woman of high rank, Maria was living with her husband Pera Taihuka and a group of other Maori at Matawhero, near Gisborne, when the outlawed chief Te Kooti Rikirangi returned to Poverty Bay in 1868. Te Kooti was a charismatic leader, whose religious thought led to the foundation of the Ringatu Church. He had been banished to the Chatham Islands in 1866 on what he considered unjust grounds, and without trial. He escaped two years later in the company of Hauhau warriors imprisoned there, and took his revenge on those who had campaigned against him in Poverty Bay, killing the Biggs' and Wilsons and several other settlers and Maori, in 'the grey dawn of that terrible morning, November 9', 1868.

Although briefly involved with the Pai Mairire movement, Maria received no favours from Te Kooti. Her husband was shot dead in front of her and she and several others were taken prisoner and marched to Te Kooti's camp at Patutahi. Maria escaped with her sister-in-law, but Te Kooti also evaded capture. He was eventually pardoned by the Government.

The placenames in this account, taken from records in the Alexander Turnbull Library, have been corrected, but some inconsistencies remain in the spelling of personal names.

Just before dark on November 8th Te Kooti and his party marched down from Okauatu to Patutahi, he had about 60 men mounted on horses and a large number of foot soldiers. Many of the mounted troops were dressed in Uniforms taken from the Chatham Islands and were all armed. They found some Natives living at Patutahi and Te Kooti made then tell him where the European and friendly natives were living at Matawhero, Turangonui, Owheta, Muriwai and Pokirikiri. Major Biggs was in Command of The Militia at Poverty Bay where for some time much alarm had been felt owing the intelligence that the Hauhaus were lurking amongst the hills and many of the settlers had moved down to the town of Gisborne for protection. They were not prepared however for Te Kooti's murderous attack in the night. The Hauhaus separated into companies at Patutahi and crept stealthily down the plains and went to the different houses killing all they could find both Europeans and friendly natives. Men, women and little children were murdered in the grey dawn of that terrible morning November 9. It was two o'clock in the morning when the Commander's house was attacked, Major Biggs was sitting up late writing, when the

Hauhaus knocked at his door. He called to his wife who was asleep in bed to escape by the back door but she refused to leave him and they were killed with their little baby.

Another party of Hauhaus went to Captain Wilson's house where he lived with his wife and a large family of children, he defended his house bravely for some time but at last it was set on fire by the Maoris and he was obliged to leave it. The Maoris promised to spare the lives of his family upon condition that he would give his arms to them so relying on this he came out carrying his little boy on his back. Mrs. Wilson and the other children followed. When a little way from the house the Maoris killed them all except the little boy who falling beneath his Father was not noticed. Mrs. Wilson was wounded and left for dead. Several days after the massacre her little boy James was found by some members of the force and he told them that his Mother was still living and lying in an outhouse wounded. This boy was only seven years old and when his father was killed being frightened he kept quiet until the Hauhaus had gone; he then crept away into the scrub and hid himself. The next day he came out and looking about found his mother sadly wounded but alive, she had crawled into the out-house. For seven days she had lived there until help came, her little boy brought her water and found eggs enough to keep them both alive. When found by the Volunteers she was carefully taken to Gisborne and afterwards removed to Napier where she died within a few weeks.

I was living at Matawhero with my husband and others. About 2 am we heard guns fired at Major Biggs', and some of our party got up thinking there was a drunken spree and went to Mr. Cadel's, who kept a general store and sold spirits but finding everything quiet there, they returned home. Soon afterwards they heard gunfire again, and went back to Mr. Cadel's and found his house surrounded by strange men, so they stood still and looked to see what was going on. The Hauhaus saw them and called them to come but, when our party heard them speak in a different dialect they were frightened and ran away. The Hauhaus then fired on them and killed one and wounded another. On reaching home about 5 am they told us that the Hauhaus were coming upon us. We were a large party, and our leading chiefs Wi Pere, Himiona Katipa and others were with us. We rushed out of our houses in our night clothes, and fled in all directions across a field. I heard a voice call out E Maa ma etu (an order to stand) and thinking it was a friendly native who knew my native name E mara, I stood and the man come and took me by the shoulder, when to my surprise I found he was a stranger named Te Whiu - this I found out afterwards while I was a prisoner. Some others captured Piripi Taketake and Harata his wife, a lady of very high rank much loved and respected by all the Europeans and friendly natives. Five of their children were also taken prisoners with Himiona Katipa's wife and 4 others. My husband escaped with his mother and sister, but when he found that I was a prisoner with our child he left there and came back to us. His mother told me afterwards that she tried to persuade him to stay in safety with them for she did not wish him to return, but he replied 'Never mind if Te Kooti does kill me he cannot kill my soul.' The Hauhaus took us all back to our home again and sent a messenger to ask Te Kooti to come down, he was at Mr. Cadel's house with a number of men who were all drinking and helping themselves to new suits of clothes from Mr. Cadel's general store. Te Kooti arrived about 6 am. When Harata (Piripi's wife) saw him riding down she stood up and welcomed him in the Maori style; he had a bottle of brandy in one hand and a long stock whip in the other, and his knee was supported in the stirrup leather as his foot had been wounded in a recent engagement. He did not return our greeting but called the prisoners names out one by one, said 'Harata stand to the left', and she went. Te Kooti then told her husband and children, and my husband to go and stand by her. I thought they were going to be tried for having joined the friendly natives and went and stood by Pera but Te Kooti told me to return to my place by the other prisoners. Then Te Kooti said 'God has told me to kill women and children, now fire on them' and about 60 guns were instantly aimed at them and fired. I heard a fearful scream and on looking back I saw my husband fall close to me; I saw Harata too with her arms pressed closely to her side, and Piripi lying by her by her with a child on his back. One little girl was only wounded and I saw her crawl out from amongst the dead, and one of the men ran up and thrust a bayonet through her back. Te Kooti then ordered his men to load their guns again, and I thought they were going to shoot us too, but Te Kooti simply told them to sing Psalm LXIII and when they had done so he ordered some of his men to take the remainder of the prisoners to their camp at Patutahi leaving the dead to be 'a portion for foxes' (Psalm LXIII) and for the fowls of the air to eat according to the rules of Te Kooti's religion. We had not travelled far before we met my uncle (Napier) who had joined the Hauhaus and had two or three men on foot with him - he spoke to us, and said 'do not turn to the right or to the left but go straight to Patutahi for the Hauhaus are scattered about the country in every direction' 'Where is your sister?' he asked 'She had made her escape' I replied. Then he was greatly distressed for he feared she might yet fall into Te Kooti's hands. He had heard of my husband's death from Te Kooti. So they passed on and we went on our way to Patutahi. As we passed Mr. Cadel's home I saw his body lying in the road in front of his house and a party of about 10 men were drinking and dressing themselves in new suits from his store. We went on past Major Biggs' house and there we saw several men on foot who pointed their guns at us but one of them recognised one of the prisoners a lame man who had escaped from the Chatham Islands and he exclaimed 'they are prisoners we must not shoot them.' That same man had been a prisoner himself at the Chatham Islands, and had remained with Te Kooti.

When we reached a place called Toanga one of the prisoners saw Mrs. Goldsmith's daughter - a girl about 14 years of age - riding towards Major Biggs' house. We called and told her to come to us but she did not hear and rode on. Presently we heard the report of a gun and a few minutes afterwards her horse without a rider galloped up to us. The poor girl was shot near Major Biggs' house as she was trying to reach the Redoubt. Her brother and his wife and child were all killed too during the massacre. One of the prisoners named Hene Kumekume who is now Te Kooti's wife caught the horse and rode it up to Patutahi. Soon after Miss Goldsmith passed us, the lame prisoner who was walking in advance of our guards saw a European riding towards us and immediately made signs to him to go away, he took the hint and made his escape unperceived by the Hauhaus and rode to Wairenga-hika and warned some Europeans, and friendly natives there of their danger and then they all fled to the Hills and got safely away.

We reached the camp at noon and then the Hauhaus built an altar of wood, laid a number of Maori garments and greenstone ornaments on it then put gunpowder underneath the wood and burnt everything as a sacrifice to their God. We spent the night at the camp and the next day one of the natives lent me a horse by stealth and I rode down to Matawhero to bury my husband. On reaching my house I found that Piripi's Father had buried him and his family, and I only saw my husband's body, so I dug a grave close to it with a spade I found in the house then spread a mat at the bottom and rolled the body into it and covered it with mats, and a shawl before I filled up the grave. I then rode back to Patutahi for the Hauhaus had kept my child as a hostage to ensure my return. That night the Hauhaus sallied forth again and burnt and plundered some more of the houses belonging to the Europeans. They had burnt others during the day and the only building left was a little Church which may still be seen at Matawhero. When the Hauhaus returned to the camp the next day I went to hear what they had been doing. We were allowed to walk about the camp and I lost no opportunities of gaining information about their proceedings for I was determined to make my escape as soon as I could and wanted to gain sufficient evidence to hang them all if they should ever be taken prisoners again and here I may say that I have been twice to Wellington to give evidence in the Supreme Court against Hauhaus. I heard that afternoon that they had killed a man named French Bob and his wife and children in the morning.

While I was listening Te Kooti looked up and saw me and said 'Maria don't you have another husband except me.'

'No no,' I replied. 'Is that the reason you killed my husband, because you wanted to marry me?'

'I never will marry you,' he replied. 'Maria if you talk like that I will cut your head off.' My uncle was standing near and said 'Maria go away do not be impudent to him he is a Devil.'

Early the next morning Wi Pere and Himiona Katipa (who had made their escape from the Hauhaus on the morning of the 9th) arrived at Patutahi, with all the friendly natives who had escaped with them, for Te Kooti had sent them a very friendly invitation to come and see him and had assured them that he would not kill them. Wi Pere thought that Te Kooti was one of God's Prophets and trusted him fully. Just before Wi Pere arrived three chiefs Wi Rangiwhaitene, Pane Te Wharau and Natana Tukurangi belonging to a Pah called Owheta came to see Te Kooti without any followers and Natana brought Te Kooti's little boy - a child about 4 years of age - to see his Father. They wished to make peace but Te Kooti took them all prisoners and shut them up in a house and placed a guard over them. When Himeona arrived Te Kooti took him prisoner and shut him up with them then called his men and told them to arm themselves. He then examined Wi Pere's party and seeing Ema Himeona's wife and myself among them he told us to go away from them and said to Wi Pere 'Now Wi you have only two words to say for yourself. Will you stay with me or return to the Government?' Some of Wi's relations immediately made signs to him to stay for they knew that they would all be shot at once if he said he was going back. So Wi replied 'I cannot go back now. I have come to see you' and we all joined Te Kooti with our lips to save our lives but not with our hearts.

The next day we all marched to a place called Okauatu and camped there. Soon after we arrived Te Kooti received an invitation from Paratene Pototi, the leading chief of the friendly natives at Owheta, and other chiefs to go to their Pah for they were anxious to try and make peace, and he went the next day with a large party to Owheta, but before he left he appointed two executioners to kill the four chiefs he had taken prisoners. Waka was ordered to shoot them and Te Waru's son Tepene, who had lost an arm in a fight at Waikato, was told to take a sword and cut the bodies to pieces if Waka did not kill them with the first shot, for the Hauhaus never fired twice upon an enemy. The chiefs did not know they were going to be killed for the Hauhaus told them that they were all going out as scouts and when they had gone a short distance from the camp Himeona Katepa, Wi Rangiwhetere, and Pora Te Wharau were shot and then cut to pieces. I saw the blood stained sword in Tepene's hand when they returned. One of Te Kooti's wives (he had 3 at that time) kept Natana Tukurangi to look after Te Kooti's little boy who was away from his mother and very fretful.

While a portion of Te Kooti's followers were killing the chiefs at the camp of the Hauhaus, those who had gone with Te Kooti were butchering the chiefs at Owheta. They killed two of very high rank that day. Paratene Pototi and Iraia Riki, and several others. My uncle succeeded in warning two old chiefs of their danger and they made their escape from Owheta. Te Kooti took all the people in the Pah prisoners and drove them to the camp at Okauatu after he had killed the chiefs. He was very angry when he heard that his wife had save Natana's life, and immediately ordered his men to kill him, and said 'if my wife offers any opposition you must kill her instead and leave the prisoner'. Shortly afterwards I saw them dragging Natana out to the spot where they had murdered the other chiefs and there they shot him dead. The Hauhaus never buried the bodies of their prisoners and the bodies of the chiefs were all left lying where they had been shot.

When Te Kooti returned from Owheta Wi Pere went to him and asked permission to move the bodies as they were lying in the middle of the road we had to pass and the dogs were licking at their blood which the friendly natives considered a great degradation to their chiefs and we tied all our dogs up but the Hauhaus did not care about it. Te Kooti was very unwilling to grant Wi Pere's request but Wi pleaded long and earnestly and at last Te Kooti said 'You may move the bodies but you must not cover them with earth, just leave them for the fowls of the air to eat.' So Wi and others moved them on one side of the road and when we passed the next day I saw the blood in the place where our chiefs died.

That evening the Hauhaus built another altar and offered a sacrifice to God as they did at Patutahi.

The next day we marched towards Ngatapa and when we reached a place called Makeretu, we camped there for the night. Early the next morning a scout was sent out and just before sunrise the bell was rung for prayers. After two or three psalms had been sung and several prayers said Te Kooti stood up to preach a sermon to his people. He said 'The Secret' that is God had told him in the night that a man and a woman and a child must be killed, and offered as a sacrifice to God. Some time afterwards I heard from some Hauhau prisoners who were taken by the Volunteers that Te Kooti intended to have killed Wi Pere and myself and my child that morning but before his sermon was ended we heard the report of a gun and saw our scout on the hill just above the camp shot dead by a party of friendly natives who had come and attacked the Hauhaus, headed by the native chiefs of Napier Henari Tomoana, and Renata Kawhapo, and Poverty Bay chiefs. Te Kooti's sermon was concluded speedily, his men seized their arms and rushed out to meet their foes - they fought all day without either party gaining any decided advantage   The bullets fell like hail around us and we took refuge under a low hill, and close to the banks of the river which flowed past the camp. Te Kooti did not go out and fight that day, but concealed himself with the women and children under the cover of a low hill. A great many were killed and I saw many wounded brought to Te Kooti during the day, who spat on his fingers, then touched each wound, repeating a prayer as he did so in an unknown tongue. I could not understand it, for it was neither English nor Maori, and sent them to the river to wash.

Just after dark that evening all the prisoners scattered, and stole silently and stealthily one by one from the camp. Katepa's widow Ema and Ririha, Wi Pere's mother and two or three others followed me. We walked for some distance in the shallow part of the river. After a while I looked back and missed my friends Ema and Ririha and found that they had crossed the river and fled to the hills. We heard afterwards that they wandered for many days in the bush living on fern root and berries, at last they made their way to the Bay of Plenty. I continued to follow the river with my sister-in-law and after a while we fell in with Wi Pere, and his family, and several others. We journeyed on together then for some hours, still keeping to the river. When the moon set we left the water and camped for a short time for we were weary. At daylight we fled to the hills. I carried my child on my back all the time. One man carried a bag of flour on his back but we were afraid to cook any of it during the day lest the Hauhaus should see the smoke of our fire. At night we made dampers and cooked them in the ashes for the children. The grown up people had no appetites and scarcely took anything except water.

We were completely lost and wandered about the woods and hills for three days not knowing our way. At last one of the Maoris climbed a high tree on the top of a hill to see if he could recognise any of the hills around us and by that means we found that we were near a well known old Pah called Makohoe. Then we went down the hill through the fern and scrub. There was no road to the river Hihroro [Hihiroroa?] which we followed. We camped by the river the 3rd night and continued to follow it the next day till 3 pm when we came to another river called Paikohu. We crossed it and took a turn towards the Waipawa River and when we came to a place called Koutu we went in the bush and camped there.

After we had given the children some food the next morning our party separated. Wi Pere his wife and children and several others went to William King a chief at the Bay of Plenty. I came down with my sister in law Horeria to a place called Ngakaroa. It was a sheep run belonging to Messrs Poynter and Evans who had made their escape from the Hauhaus.

Eruption at Waimangu, Rotorua District. Auckland Institute and Museum.

Natural Disasters

RHODA COOTE

The 1855 Earthquake in Wellington

Rhoda Coote has already appeared in this book, telling of her journey up the Wanganui River with the Rev. Richard Taylor and others in 1857. She was living in Wellington when a big earthquake struck just after nine o'clock on the evening of January 23, 1855. The main quake and its aftershocks changed the face of the Wellington waterfront, lifting up large areas of swamp around Clyde Quay and raising the shoreline of the harbour by up to three metres. Man-made reclaimations were a major part of the development of Port Nicholson, and despite the obvious unpleasant aspects of the 1855 quake, it gave the reclaimers of the future a head-start in redefining the waterfront area.

The sole fatality of the 1855 earthquake was Baron Charles von Alzdorf, who arrived in Wellington in 1840 and became an important businessman in the growing town. He soon owned his own wharf and hotels. Although an earlier earthquake, in 1848, had cracked the walls of one of his buildings he did not heed the warnings of nature and built a two-storied hotel - which collapsed and killed him during the shake of 1855.

In January, 1855 we experienced a severe earthquake, which was a great shock to our appreciation of New Zealand and truly alarming. On *January 23rd* after a very windy and boisterous day, about 9 o'clock in the evening we were startled by a rumbling noise, followed instantly by a tremendous shaking of everything about us. Floor upheaving, tables and chairs rocking and everything breakable crashing. The first shock lasted several minutes they say, and threw down every chimney in Wellington as well as many buildings and did a great deal of damage in the town. We were in a low wooden house close under the hill, so it only threw down our chimney and broke our lamps and most of our glass, but so severe were the shocks that we left the house and stayed outside a great part of the night, though it was raining slightly. The animals were greatly frightened, horses galloped about and the fowls began cackling, and our poor servant Eliza came in to us and we all stayed out for several hours. A party of soldiers came over from the barracks to see if we wanted help and Colonel MacCleverty kindly came to ask after us. The shocks continued more or less violent, but none like the first, till between 3 and 4 o'clock, and then became less frequent, and morning broke to gladden our hearts but to reveal a miserable picture. The first thing we noticed was the extreme lowness of the tide; the sand extended far beyond its usual limits, and then all at once it was covered again by the sea, this advancing and receding of the tide took place three times in twenty minutes, and eventually left the harbour raised about three feet. The Beach where all the shops are situated was a miserable picture, few houses uninjured whilst many were perfect wrecks, and the contents of many of the shops were floating about on the water or thrown up on the shore. But only one life was lost and that was Baron Dalzdorf [von Alzdorf] of the hotel, and he was in a very delicate state and the shock may have affected his heart, not but which the wall of the room he was in fell. The Cliffords' house was left with only one room safe, and they went to the MacClevertys' - the Featherstons' was also very shaky and Mrs. Featherston and the baby came to us, but the Dr. would not move. Government House and the Bank, only just finished were much damaged, and all through the town scarcely any escaped. From the country strange stories came of the ground opening and engulfing cows etc., but I believe imagination was very active in originating most of the mischief reported, but it was quite terrible enough, and for days the earth continued to vibrate every now and then and we did not dare undress and go to bed for three nights. Then by degrees the shocks became very light and less frequent and we resumed our usual mode of life.

Sunday 28th. The effect of the earthquake was still so great on the nerves of the good people of Wellington that the Service this morning was held outside the Church, the Clergyman thinking it right to be prepared for what might happen, which I thought a very bad example to set to his Congregation, but we had a very good sermon, it seems, with a short service. It was the same in the afternoon, the people were all outside the church - happily it was fine. I have not mentioned that finding houses so scarce and extravagant in price, Henry sent home for one soon after we arrived, and just about this time we heard of the arrival of the ship the *Royal Stuart*, in which it was, first at Canterbury and now on *January 29th* it reached Wellington and was pronounced to be of all kinds the most suited to stand the shock of earthquakes, wooden walls with iron posts. Strange indeed that it should have come at such an opportune time. It was some time before we could get either plan or model of it so that days elapsed without anything being done, and now alas a very disagreeable quarrel arose between the Provincial Government and Military Authorities about some tents required for the people rendered houseless by the earthquake, which led to a most uncalled for attack of the former on Colonel MacCleverty. This became so warm that the cause of it all was forgotten, making this time most trying in every way to the society of the place, which never quite recovered the moral shock though the physical one soon passed off.

The Great Snow of 1867

The heavy snow of the winter of 1867 was disastrous for many Canterbury runs. While five days of steady snow weakened the vast flocks, it was the warm wind and heavy rain of the ensuing thaw that caused most of the stock fatalities, as paddocks flooded and sheep drowned. The lambing season had just begun and Lady Mary Anne Barker reports that 3000 lambs died as a result of the storm.

A more detailed version of this snowstorm story appears in Lady Barker's Station Life *but this excerpt is taken from her last book,* Colonial Memories, *published in 1904. This was her only book to be published under the name of Lady Broome. In it she recounts her reminiscenes of life in colonial settlements around the world, including 'Old New Zealand', Western Australia and the Caribbean. Her absent husband Frederick is again referred to as F.*

I well remember that Monday morning and the strange restlessness which seemed to extend to the sheep, for they must have felt the coming trouble long before we thought of calamity. The weather during the last week of July had been quite beautiful, our regular winter weather, and we had taken advantage of it to send the dray down to Christchurch for supplies. My store-room was all but empty, and the tea-chest, flour and sugar bags, held hardly half-a-week's consumption, so the drayman was charged not to linger, but to turn round and come back directly he got his load. When speaking of supplies it must be borne in mind that tinned provisions were almost unknown in those days, and certainly never found their way to a New Zealand sheep station. F. had also taken advantage of the beautiful open weather to ride down to Christchurch about wool matters, so I expected to be quite alone with a young man who was learning sheep-farming under F.'s auspices, and my two servants.

But F. had hardly started before a cousin rode up the track and, hearing that I was feeling somewhat depressed and lonely, very kindly volunteered to stay, and before the afternoon was over a neighbouring young squatter also appeared, and asked (as was quite a common thing in that hotel-less district) for shelter for the night. Nothing could have been more unexpected - except that one's station guests were always unexpected - than these two visitors, but it proved a fortunate chance for me that they appeared just then.

The weather was certainly curious, and we all noticed that the sound of the sheep's bleat never ceased. Now the odd thing at a sheep station used

The Canterbury Plains looking north from the Port Hills above Lyttelton, including the Bridle Track negotiated by the first settlers. From Canterbury Old and New 1850-1900

to be that you hardly ever saw a sheep, and still more seldom heard one, except perhaps in the early morning, when they were coming down from their high camping-grounds. And sheep always 'travel' head to wind, but the sheep that afternoon kept moving in exactly the contrary direction. Still I was not in the least uneasy about the weather, except as it might affect the comfort of F.'s seventy-five mile ride to town, and I knew he would be under comfortable shelter at a friend's half-way house that night. So we gaily and lavishly partook of our supper-dinner, had an absurd game of whist, and went to bed as usual.

It was no surprise to me to see snow falling steadily next morning, but it was disagreeable to find there was very little mutton in the house, and that it was quite likely the shepherd would wait for the weather to clear before starting across the hills and swamps between us and the little homestead where the woolshed stood, and from whence the business of the station was carried on.

The three gentlemen lounged about all day and smoked a good deal. They told me afterwards how bitterly they regretted not having made some preparation in the way of at least bringing in fuel, or putting extra food out for the fowls, etc. But each said to the other every five minutes, 'Oh, you know snow in New Zealand *never* lasts,' though their experience was only a very few years old. It was short commons that second day, and I thought sadly that the dray would have only reached Christchurch that evening! We all felt depressed, and, as no one had any use for depression up that valley, the sensation was quite new to us.

It was not until we met on the third morning, however, that we at all acknowledged our fears. By this time, the snow was at least four feet deep in the shallowest places, and still continued to fall steadily. It was impossible to see even where the fowl-house and pig-sties stood, on the weather side of the house. All the great logs of wood lying about waiting to be cut up were hidden, so was the little shed full of coal. A smooth high slope, like a hillock, stretched out from the outer kitchen door, which could not be opened that morning, out into the floating whiteness. All our windows were nearly blocked up and became quite so by the evening, and no door except one, which opened inwards, could be used. And there was literally no food in the house. The tea we had at breakfast was merely coloured hot water, and we each had a couple of picnic biscuits. For dinner there was a little rice and salt. Imagine six people to be fed every day, and an empty larder and store-room!

The day after that my maids declined to get up, declaring they preferred to 'die warm'; so I took them in a sardine each, a few ratafia biscuits, and a spoonful of apricot jam. These were our own rations for that day. We had by that time broken up every box for fuel, and only lighted a fire in the kitchen, where also a solitary candle burned.

'Be very careful of the dips,' said one of my guests, 'for I have heard of people eating them.'

'I hear the cat mewing under the house,' said another; 'we'll try and get hold of her.'

'I wonder if those are the cows?' asked a third, pointing to three formless heaps high above the stockyard rails, but within them.

By Friday morning the maids, still in bed, were asking tearfully, 'And oh! when do you think we'll be found, mum?' Whereas my anxiety was to find something to feed them with! We shook out a heap of discarded flour-bags and got, to our joy, quite a plateful of flour, and a careful smoothing out of the lead lining of old tea-chests yielded a few leaves, so we had girdle-cakes and tea that day. I was very unhappy about the dogs: the horses were out on the run as usual, so it was no use thinking of them.

On Saturday there was literally nothing at all in the house (which was quite dark, remember), and my three starving men roped themselves together and struggled out, tunnelling through the snow, in the direction where they thought the fowl-house must lie. After a couple of hours' hard work they hit upon its roof, tore off some of the wooden shingles, and captured a few bundles of feathers, which were what my poor dear hens were reduced to. However, there was a joyful struggle back, and after some hasty preparation the fowls were put into a saucepan with a lump of snow, for there was no water to be got anywhere, and a sort of stew resulted, of which we thankfully partook. This heartened up the gentlemen to make another sally to the stockyard in search of the cows. The clever creatures had kept moving round and round as the snow fell, so as to make a a sort of wider tomb for themselves, and they were alive, though mere bundles of skin and bone. They were dragged by ropes to the stable and there fed with oaten hay. It was no question of milking the poor things, for they were quite dry.

Next day the dogs were dug out, but only one young and strong one survived. Two more were alive, but died soon after.

On Sunday it had ceased snowing and the wind showed signs of changing. I struggled a yard or two out of the house, as it was such a blessing to get into daylight again. My view was of course much circumscribed, as I could only see up and down the 'flat', as the valley was called. But it all looked quite different; not a fence or familiar landmark to be seen on any side. If I could have been wafted to the top of the mountain from which we saw the sun rise the summer before, what a white world should I have beheld! And if I could have soared still higher and looked over the whole of the vast Canterbury Plains, I should have been gazing at the smooth winding-sheet of half a million of sheep, for that was found, later, to be the loss in that Province alone.

Yet, as we afterwards came to know, it was not really the fall of snow, tremendous as it had been, which cost the Province nearly all its stock. As I have said, the wind changed to the north-west - the warm quarter - on Sunday night, and it rained heavily as well as blowing half a gale. On Monday morning the snow was off the roof and it was possible to clear some of the windows. An early excursion was also made to the styes and a very thin pig was killed, an, as a bag of Indian meal for fattening poultry had been found in the stable loft, a sort of cake could be made. So we were no longer starving, and the maids got up!

Twenty-four hours of this warm rain and wind was what did all the mischief to the poor sheep. By Monday night every creek within sight had overflowed its banks, and was running - a dirty yellow stream - over the fast-melting snowfields. The rapid thaw and the flooded creeks made locomotion more difficult than ever, but the three gentlemen set to work at once to try to release the imprisoned sheep. There was but one dog to work with, and he was so weak he could hardly move, but the poor sheep were still weaker. Contrary to their custom they had mostly sought refuge beneath the projecting banks of the creeks, and would have been safe enough there if there had not the sudden thaw let the water in on them before they could struggle up, so they were nearly all drowned. It was most pathetic to discover how in some places the mothers had tried to save the lambs by standing over them in a leaning attitude so as to make a shelter. The lambing season had just begun, and on our own run, which was but a small one, we lost three thousand lambs. Several were brought in to me to try and save, but I had no cow's milk to give them, and warm meal and water did not prove enough to keep the poor little starving creatures alive. It was heart-breaking work, and when F. returned it was to find the fences tapestried with the skins of a thousand sheep.

As soon as we could move about on horseback we rode all over the run and found that the sheep had evidently fared better when they had kept on higher ground. It was curious to see the tops of the little Ti-ti palms, some ten or twelve feet high, entirely nibbled off where the sheep had clustered round them, and, as the snow fell, mounted higher and higher until they could reach the green leaves. In those days all the flocks were pure or half-bred merino; active, hardy little black-faced sheep, tasting like Welsh mutton, and delicious eating. On these excursions we often came across dead wild-pigs, boars cased in hides an inch thick, which had perished through sheer stress of weather. It was wonderful to think that thin-skinned animals, with only a few month's growth of fine merino wool on their backs, could have survived.

During the long bright summer which followed, we used to often ask each other if it could be true that hills had apparently been levelled and valleys filled up by the heaviest snowstorm ever known. But when we looked at the Ti-ti palms with their topmost leaves gnawed to the stump, we realised that the sheep must have been standing on eight or nine feet of snow to reach them. When the survivors came to be shorn, it was plainly to be seen by the sort of 'nick' in the fleece, where their three weeks' imprisonment had evidently checked the growth of the wool. Many of the hardiest wethers must have been without food for that time, as the pasturage was under either snow or flooded.

AMY PATERSON

The Tarawera Eruption

The sudden eruption of Mount Tarawera in 1886 both mystified and terrified the occupants of the Rotorua district, many of whom did not know what was going on until hours after the eruption began. At the time of the eruption the Robinson family, including 18-year-old Amy, lived at Awahou, some 11 km out of Rotorua on the main road to Tauranga. From a distance of about 30 km from the exploding mountain, Amy Robinson had a grandstand view of the most spectacular volcanic eruption witnessed by Europeans in New Zealand.

Tarawera Mountain lies to the north-west of Lake Rotorua, and at the foot of this mountain was a small lake called Rotomahana. On each side of this small lake were two terrace formations. On the south side were the white terraces with a boiling cauldron at the top, which at times overflowed and covered this terrace formation with silicated water, covering the whole formation as it flowed down to the bottom into this little lake. Across the lake, where you had to go in a boat for about half a mile, was another terrace formation on a smaller scale, though steeper, which had a pink appearance, and also a boiling cauldron at the top. Like the white terraces they overflowed, filling the large basins with hot water. These Terraces, as well as wonderful, were beautiful, and said to be the largest of their kind in the world.

On the 10th June, 1886, I was living with my parents, some twenty miles as the crow flies from Tarawera. We heard a great noise at 1 a.m., just like a storm brewing, expecting any minute to feel the house shake with the wind; but it kept on and on, and we could not sleep for the noise. We heard our father come into the room next to our bedroom, so we called out, 'What's the matter?' 'Oh!' he said, 'There's an eruption somewhere and I'm going over to see if our old neighbour is safe.'

My mother, sisters and I got up and dressed ourselves, this rumbling noise which was louder than thunder still going on, and the house in a tremble all the time. After the moon had set it was very dark, and on looking out of the door, an awful but grand sight met our gaze; a dark cloud in the western sky; lightning and electricity flashing all through it; red hot stones flying in the air and meeting others coming down, which smashed together and fell into pieces through the dark cloud. The noise was deafening all the time, but there was an awesome feeling about it, and we thought every moment was our last, as even at this time we did not know where it was all happening. However, some of the family went up a hill in front of the house, and through the lightning and electricity flashes they could see Rotorua below it; therefore they concluded that it must be near Rotomahana.

About four o'clock in the morning we heard voices on the road, so we called out 'Who is there?' but the noise was too great for them to hear. Going out to them we found men, women and children, with nothing but their night clothes on and blankets thrown around them. On hearing the roar and noise and seeing flashes of fire (as they thought) jumped to the conclusion that Sulphur Point, which was a mass of bubbling water and sulphur, was on fire. They jumped out of bed, grabbed a blanket and ran along the street, calling out 'Rotorua is gone and Ohinemutu is going. Put as much land as you can between you and it.' They never stopped to look round till they got to where we were living, some 7 miles from Rotorua, as they were afraid of being caught in it. As it was bitterly cold, we had to take them in and make good fires, and a cup of hot tea. We kept going outside to see the wonderful sight, for fear we missed anything; but we could have enjoyed the awesome sight had we felt we were safe, and not felt that we may be swallowed up at any moment, yet did not know by what.

The night grew darker, so the electricity in the air showed up more plainly every time it flashed through this dark cloud. Still more and more people kept on coming, as we were on the main road, which was in those days the only exit from Rotorua to Tauranga. Eventually we had to put a fire on in the schoolroom (native school) to accommodate all the people. It was well on in the day before the sun got over the dark cloud of mud and ashes from the eruption, and how thankful we were to see the sun, as we began to despair of ever seeing it again.

By this time we were getting all sorts of reports of what was going on, that we did not really know what was happening, as there were no telephones or motor cars in those days. This dark cloud approaching us like a raincloud turned out to be a cloud of sulphurous dust from the eruption, which poured over us for about two hours, but fortunately for us the wind changed and blew it away out to sea in the Bay of Plenty, leaving the whole place covered with a white ash like cement over everything.

When daylight came the people who had arrived first wished they had their clothes on, so some of the men said they would walk back to Rotorua and get some, but were turned back by this sulphurous cloud of steam, choking them. Later on, buggies kept arriving, filled with frightened-looking people, so the men then returned with them to get some clothes. We had to keep these people for a few days till they calmed down, and were able to return to Rotorua.

Village, buried in the ash of Mount Tarawera. Auckland Institute and Museum.

When we got the real truth of things, we found out that it was an eruption of the Tarawera Mountain which had the whole end blown out, and destroying those beautiful terraces, the beauty of which could never be explained, but one had to see them to know what they were like. I had only been twice over them, as I thought they would always be there to see.

The little village of Te Wairoa, only nine miles from Tarawera, had a few inhabitants, mainly a Hotel where tourists had to stay one night before going out to see these terraces. It was completely buried, the weight of mud and ashes broke all the buildings down, and the inmates when they saw this happening rushed out of the Hotel and houses, and took shelter in the Maori whares; the roofs of these places coming right to the ground, therefore did not cave in with the weight. The native schoolteacher, Mr. Haszard and family, and a nephew, stayed in the schoolhouse thinking they were safe, but the roof caved in and fell on them, killing Mr. Haszard, three of the family and the nephew. Mrs. Haszard and the two daughters were saved by being near the walls, when the roof fell into the middle of the room. There it made an archway where they were standing. The two girls escaped through a window, but Mrs. Haszard, who was sitting in an armchair, was pinned in it by a beam across her legs and one at the back of her chair. She had a rug over her and a small child on her knee who got smothered in her arms. Here Mrs. Haszard was pinned for 18 hours. When the rescuers came to try and find them, after they removed the timber and mud, they spoke to her and she said 'If you can break the legs of the chair and let it down, I can get out,' so they worked away in the mud and debris and at last released her. She handed them the child saying 'It is dead,' then told them where all the others were lying dead in the room. When they got Mrs. Haszard out, she with the two girls were taken into Rotorua. It was a terrible journey as much of the road was blocked through the bush country; trees were flung across the road in several places, and roads had to be cut round them. In some places in the open, great cracks had opened in the ground, so they had to be carefully negotiated to get the buggy across. Most of the bodies had to be carried out on stretchers and taken to Rotorua for burial. It was a sad sight the next Sunday morning to see those six coffins being taken to their last resting-place.

Being winter time there was only one tourist in the Hotel that night, a good Christian young man from overseas who gathered the servants and others who had come to the shelter thinking it was the safest place, and had a short prayer committing all to God's care. They then left the building and this young man, Mr. Bainbridge, stood aside to see all the females out of the door. As the last one left, just as he moved the verandah fell with the weight of the mud and ashes, and he was caught under it. The others did not know he was missing for some hours after, as each one made a rush for the Maori houses, when flashes of lightning lighted up the place, and they could see where to go. As the mud and ashes were still falling about them and the terrible noise was going on all the time, they could not hear one another speak.

There was a small settlement of Maoris, many of whom used to guide the tourists around the Terraces, as it was not safe for any one to go alone because there were hot springs and boiling mud holes all about. These Maoris were all buried.

The Maoris from Te Wairoa could not stay on there, so one of the tribes in Rotorua offered them a piece of ground to settle on near Rotorua. One old Maori man refused to leave, telling his people this was a judgment on them all for their sin and wickedness. He had to be forced away, and was put in hospital in Rotorua, where he only lived a short time.

J.M. BUCHANAN

Fatal Flood in the Bush

J. M. Buchanan was one of more than 70 contributors to Tales of Pioneer Women, *put together for the centenary of New Zealand by the Women's Institutes of New Zealand in 1940. The book is a collection of colonial tales sent in by members. While many of the stories in the book are written by the descendants of early settlers from around the country, Mrs. Buchanan's tale of a flood is a first-hand account of a truly traumatic experience for a woman alone in the bush. The Paturau River area is in the uppermost reaches of North Westland and then, as now, was sparsely populated and accessible only by a long and round-about route from Collingwood, in Golden Bay.*

It was my good fortune to live for several years close to a very beautiful West Coast river, the Paturau, usually an ideal trout stream, but occasionally a restless giant before whom great forest trees sink with a crash of broken boughs and are borne away rolling along in midstream, or hurled against the banks, aiding in the destruction of their fellows.

One such flood occurred just after I had come out into the wilds to join my husband, who was in charge of a large tract of country owned by an English company, and lying to the south of Westhaven, a great landlocked sheet of water near the northern extremity of the South Island.

At that time, February 1897, the country was quite undeveloped, except for some rather disappointing quartz mines; it consisted of thick bush alternating with open pakihi land, and some rough steep country.

I first saw the river one summer evening when, after a rough ride of nearly thirty miles we reach its bush-fringed banks and our horses slipped and scrambled down the boulder-strewn furrow that led to the ford. Out in the river we stopped to let our horses drink, and to enjoy the loveliness round us. Leaving the ford we passed through a belt of beautiful bush and came out on to the clearing where stood the cottage.

My husband had brought a horse for me to our little seaport, Collingwood, as we - and our goods - could only reach the cottage on horseback. Most of the journey had been along the shore of the Inlet (as Westhaven was called) and could be attempted only within the four hours when the tide was lowest. There were no roads; we followed narrow, boggy tracks, where there was a bottom if you went deep enough - and corduroy where the bottom was undiscoverable. Along these tracks a string of pack-horses came past the cottage two or three times a week, taking stores of all descriptions to the mines, and also our very precious mail-bags.

In a small valise strapped to my saddle I brought out a change of clothing and anything absolutely necessary; my luggage, sewing machine, etc., would follow by the packer in a few days.

The day after my arrival at the cottage, my husband proposed that we should go and see the mines, but before we got half way, a thick wet mist caused us to turn and postpone our trip (as far as I was concerned) till brighter weather.

The following day there were heavy showers, but my husband could not delay his visit. He was reluctant to leave me thus, quite alone, but I assured him that I would be quite happy tidying up the cottage; and when I say that I was the first woman to enter it, housekeepers will understand that there was ample scope for my energies. My husband had been hitherto at the mercy of a man-cook of the backblocks variety.

So busy was I, that I scarcely noticed that the rain had become heavy and continuous, till I went out on the verandah to speak to two men returning to the mines after a brief visit to their homes on the other side of the ranges. They had, in the usual kindly up-country fashion, called at the post office for our letters and I was delighted to get quite a budget. Behind them came the packer with our goods. He hurried on with the others towards the mines, fearing that the river might be 'up' before he could get back.

Already great pools of water were showing amongst the logs and stumps of the felled bush in front of the cottage, but this was to be expected in such heavy rain. To make the time pass quickly and bring nearer the hour of my husband's return - and afternoon tea - I began a letter to our son telling of our experiences so far, and saying that I had certainly expected the proverbial rain of the West Coast - 'but this is a deluge.'

Glancing out of the window, I saw a small log rolling along in one of the big pools. This, thought I, means a current and requires investigation. So I arrayed myself in a waterproof poncho and felt prepared for anything. It was a shock, on opening the cottage door, to see much larger logs floating by in the yellow flood that was now all round me. One step off the verandah, and I was in it up to my knees, but I struggled across the roadway to a fence that ran along the opposite side. With my feet on one of the lower wires, and clinging tightly to the top one, I sidled along, sometimes slipping off with a horrible splash but never losing my hold, till at last I reached a steep terrace - evidently an old riverbank, and I was soon high above the waste of waters.

So sure was I that the cottage would be swept away, that my one thought was to get up to the mines, and I set off along the track in that direction. I soon found it turning to the bush along the edge of a heavily flooded stream, whose waters were rapidly encroaching on the corduroy. Soon I could go no further. And still the rain was coming down in torrents and the air was full of a roaring sound - the raging of the river as I then thought - though it was only the echo of the surf breaking on the West Coast beyond a narrow range of hills.

Clambering up the steep bank above the track, I sheltered for a time under a tree-fern, and began to realise that I was indeed alone. Before me the bush stretched away towards an unseen lonely shore; behind rose the mountains, while the nearest habitations were the store on the shore of the Inlet, five miles away beyond the river, and the huts at the mines, away up in the hills. By this time I was sure I had been cut off from them by the waters that had stopped my progress in that direction. Late afternoon was fading into evening, and through the monotone of incessant raindrops on the leaves, weird, unexplained noises thrilled me. It might only be the rustling of half-drowned ferns, or a tiny splash as a low-growing branch swept against the current, but they whispered and sighed till my heart was throbbing.

Stern common sense came to the rescue, and realising that my best chance in every way was to be strictly practical, I set to work to counteract the chills that, in spite of the warm humid air, were now making me tremble. I took off a boot and a stocking (which, thanks to my being still in travelling trim, was fortunately a thick woollen one), and having wrung it as dry as possible, I rubbed my foot with it so vigorously, that, by the time the process was repeated with the other foot, the chills had vanished.

I now knew that I must spend the night in the bush; but a sense of thankfulness that I had escaped from the flooded river so filled my mind that it left very little room for fear. But I saw that it would not do to remain where I stood - where if I were to slip I should fall onto the hard corduroy. I, therefore, went a little further up the hillside, clinging to the dripping fern fronds and creeping plants, till I found an old fallen tree beside whose trunk I could get a little shelter through the hours of darkness that was fast closing round me. I now felt the benefit of my poncho, for it spread out underneath and over me, and not only did it keep the rain out to a certain extent, but it conserved the warmth I had gained by the exertion of climbing up the hill.

Then I laid me down in peace, and slept. I was indeed kept in safety and knew that I was protected.

When I next became aware of my surroundings, I realised that I had been asleep for hours and that a few more would bring daylight, and perhaps sunshine, for the storm was over.

Lying there on Nature's very heart, one seemed to grow akin to all her creatures. There was no sound of life, but I was conscious that near me were the birds, fluffy little balls, waiting as I was, for the day. Gently the velvet blackness of the night faded, and in the greyness things round me took form. Above the dark trees a star still burned in the clear, cold sky. Slowly it paled before the growing light; colour came to earth and with it the day.

Hope came too, and the thought of our little home. I knew that there lay my only chance of obtaining the rest and food I sorely needed. So down through the shining ferns and dripping undergrowth, I made my way towards the track and the clearing. I must have looked a veritable scarecrow, my clothes stained with the soft brown bush soil and the green of bruised ferns, and my hair lay on my neck, a wet tangle, full of twigs and earth. When I reached the clearing I felt as if I had been dreaming. The yellow flood whose horror had haunted me, was gone, and there stood the cottage in the calm brightness of early morning.

Then I saw my old friend the fence, all hung with drift; and the bridge that should have spanned our little creek was now lying on a tangle of logs in the paddock. Soon I reached the cottage, and pushed open the door.

Over the floor and everything on it, was spread a soft wet silt, as unbroken as a tideswept stretch of beach, till I stepped into the room; and then, deep in my footprints patches of the carpet could be seen. All through the house for nearly two feet above the floor, this horrible mud lay thickly. Above that, all was as I had left it, and the contrast was most fantastic. There, on the writing table lay my letter - the last words 'this is a deluge' - and in my room my watch hung ticking on its tiny stand.

I now began to feel very faint; a cup of tea and a scone had done duty for lunch the day before. The bread crock was brimming over with dirty water and silt was everywhere, even in the oven. Fortunately I found some dry wood and soon had some water boiling. Feeling very like Robinson Crusoe I cut open a sodden bag of oatmeal and found the centre of it quite dry - this I made into a kind of gruel - my one desire to get something hot to drink that would also be nourishing.

Shivering in my saturated clothes I collected all the dry blankets I could find, and piling them on my bed made a cosy nest in which I was soon fast asleep.

But, ugh! the waking - warm and dry, but with one's bedroom floor a sea of mud.

Fortunately my valise had been put on a little table beyond the reach of the water, so I had some dry clothes, and by making stepping-stones in the mud with towels, I was able to reach the only dry foot-gear in the house - a pair of rubber fishing boots that luckily were hanging up.

The rivers fell as rapidly as they rose and so in the bright sunshine ended my night in the bush.

Kind was the sympathy and many the offers of help showered on us, but there was one whose need of sympathy was far greater than ours. The man who had so kindly brought out our mail had left a bright little home that morning. It stood near a river that flowed down the other side of our hills. About dusk a boy in the neighbourhood saw that the cottage was being surrounded by water and went to the rescue of its helpless occupants. Gladly the woman went with him, she carrying the baby, one child clinging to her skirts, while the boy took charge of two smaller children. They had to walk along a bush tramway which, being raised above the surrounding country, was still beyond the reach of the floods. Here and there, openings had been left in the embankment to allow the water to escape from the hills behind. Hampered by the children and made giddy by the swollen water, the poor mother stumbled and fell on the rough slabs that bridged one of these channels. Her baby slipped from her arms and in a moment was swept out of sight. Lifting the two elder children into the rough loft of a small stable that stood near, and bidding them wait till he returned, the boy led the distracted mother to the house for which they had been making, carrying with him one of the little ones.

Kindly neighbours took them in while he returned for the other two children, but when they were on their way to join their mother the embankment, undermined by the rapidly rising waters, gave way both before and behind them. A small tree was now their only refuge, and into this he persuaded the children to climb. Thinking that his weight might be too much for the slender branches, the brave boy spent most of the night standing in the water and talking to the children in order to keep them awake; for he feared that they might go to sleep, relax their hold, fall off, and be drowned. For this night's work he was rewarded with well-earned medal from the Royal Humane Society.

Next pages:
'Three on a log' Karekare-Piha area, A.P. Godber Collection, Alexander Turnbull Library.

Different Paths

Charlotte Bronte's Friends

A lifelong friend of Charlotte Bronte, and immortalised as the character Rose Yorke in Bronte's 1849 novel Shirley, *Mary Taylor had set her determined mind on emigration to New Zealand as early as 1841. In fact, she did not make the trip to Wellington until 1845, two years after her brother William Waring Taylor. Little is known of her early years in the colony but in 1850 she opened a shop at the corner of Cuba and Dixon streets with her cousin Ellen, who had arrived the year before. The venture was a success, and despite Ellen's death of consumption in 1851, Mary continued to run the business for a further eight years. Mary firmly believed that it was the 'first duty' of women as well as men to earn a living, and on her return to England in 1860 she wrote several articles espousing this and other 'feminist' views as well as a novel of her own. She never married, and died in 1893.*

Mary's correspondence has been published in Mary Taylor, Friend of Charlotte Bronte, *edited by Joan Stevens, but these letters by Mary and Ellen to Charlotte Bronte come from the Alexander Turnbull Library collection.*

Wellington, April 5th, 1850.
Dear Charlotte,

....My own concerns have advanced rapidly. As much in this last 6 months as in the 4 years before. Ellen has come out with just the same wish to earn her living as I have and just the same objection to sedentary employment. We both enter heart and soul into the project of keeping a shop and actually hope to make £300 or £400 a year by it. John and Joe have echoed her and me both with gifts and loans so that we begin with as large a capital as probably any in Wellington. We hope to have together fm £600 to £800. Our first step was to take some land (a st. corner) and build a house 28 ft by 26. This is just in the heart of the town (*as laid out*) nevertheless until our house was built you could not see a st. at all, and the usual cart-road goes just thro' the middle of it. Since we leased our bit 3 more people have taken the rest and one man has built a house and got into it.

It is just now blowing a cold south easter. I am sitting upstairs in a room with 2 windows looking to the east; by a glowing fire. In one room behind are 6 pieces [of] paper hangings to be hung tomorrow; it is our best room. In the other some crockery to be sold - when the house is finished. Our back room downstairs is top full of groceries, to be sold when the house is finished but alas in each of the other 2 rooms is a carpenter's bench and there are 6 doorways wanting doors. Our new house delights us with its roomy comfort and now let me tell you what roomy comfort is. First understand it is made of boards overlapping, nailed to upright posts - our uprights are 2 and a half inches by 3, and the level piece at the bottom is of blue gum a very hard heavy lasting wood fm Hobart town. Inside the house is lined with boards - but without overlapping. In the shop and kitchen these boards are planed and grooved together, in our bedroom they will be stretched with calico and papered and for the present the other three rooms will be unfinished. The rooms upstairs are only 2 ft high at the eaves. The best is 19ft by 12. We think it handsome. - Now for what we are to do. First remember that we have by far the best house on our acre and the best but one in our 2 streets. The shop will be *among* the first in town and the situation too. I can scarcely tell you how I have learnt something of most of the people whom I shall have to buy of. Waring has dealt with them and I have lived in the same small town with them these 4 or 5 years. I know too the extent to which Waring sells on credit and how glad any of these people would be to sell for money. Of most things too I know pretty well the prices I can get for them and what I ought to give. Waring gives us his opinion too and many things we can get fm him and know the prices at home too. Is this interesting? Well if it isn't here's some gossip. We have got a mechanics' institute and as it is the only place of (respectable) amusement in the town we encourage it with all our hearts - i.e. encourage everything abt it but the objects it was instituted for. One of these not-objects is dancing. So we are going to open the new Hall with a dance by and by, one half the members sulking at it and the other half just carrying their point by dint of cunning. My share of the business is to find young ladies for these young gentlemen - of course all the dancers are young and I hope to get 6 or 7 who will be glad to avail themselves of the bachelors' tickets. I cannot tell you with what zeal I labour to spite the 'uneasy virtues' that are always saying something against 'promiscuous dancing' - what a phrase. With many of them the objection is not to the character of the company but to their station. Of course we think our character much above our station. I don't approve of being so slighted. Besides we have and can have a pretty even number of ladies and gentlemen which is not easy to get any where else. So we crow over them and won't have them - as we don't want them. I have got into all this heap of social trickery since Ellen came, never having troubled my head before abt the comparative numbers of young ladies and young gentlemen. To Ellen it is quite new to be of such importance by mere fact of her femininity. She thought she was coming woefully down in the world when she came out before. And the class are not in *education* inferior though they are in money. They are decent well to do people. 1 grocer 1 draper 2 parsons 2 clerks 2 lawyers and 3 or four nondescripts. All these but one have families to 'take tea with'; and there are a lot more single men to flirt with.

For the last 3 months we have been out every Sunday sketching. We seldom succeed in making the slightest resemblance to the thing we sit down to but it is wonderfully interesting. Next year we hope to send a lot home. Mrs. Taylor has got another little girl. Miss Knox, the third sister is going to follow Mrs. Cowper's example and marry a rich old man of disgraceful character. She is just abt 17 and her intended (Capt. Rhodes) has just put her to school. Waring has a good trade and fair health so has Mrs. Taylor and the children - the health, not the trade. My cattle are nearly all in existence yet and instead of gaining I shall lose by them in consequence of keeping them so long. Meat sells for 5d. a lb. and I shall not get 3d. I should be ill off, but that Joe and John have given me the money which at first they lent me. With the increase I shall probably escape loss. With all this my novel stands still - it might have done so if I had had nothing to do, for it is not want of time but want of freedom of mind that makes me unable to direct my attention to it. Meantime it grows in my head, for I never give up the idea. I have written abt a volume I suppose....

MARY TAYLOR

Wellington, New Zealand
April 25th, 1850

Dear Charlotte, - I have set up shop! I am delighted with it as a whole - that is it is as pleasant, or as little disagreeable as you can expect an employment to be that you earn your living by. The best of it is that your labour has some return and you are not forced to work on hopelessly without result. Du reste - it is very odd - I keep looking at myself with one eye while I'm using the other and I sometime find myself in very queer positions. Yesterday, I went along the shore past two wharves and several warehouses on a st. where I have never been before during all the 5 years I have been in Wellington. I opened the door of a long place filled with packages with a passage up the middle and a row of high windows on one side. At the far end of the room a man was writing at a desk beneath a window. I walked all the length of the room very slowly, for what I had come for had completely gone out of my head. Fortunately the man never heard me until I had recollected it. Then he got up and I asked him for some stone blue, saltpetre, tea, pickles, salt etc. He was very civil; I bought some things and asked for a note of them. He went to his desk again and I looked at some newspapers lying near. On the top was a circular from

Smith & Elder, containing notices of the most important new works. The first and longest was given to *Shirley* a book I had seen mentioned in the *Manchester Examiner* as written by Currer Bell [nom de plume used by Charlotte Bronte]. I blushed all over; the man got up, folding the note. I pulled it out of his hand and set off to the door - looking odder than ever for a partner had come in and was watching. The clerk said something about sending them and I said something too, I hope it was not very silly - I took my departure.

I have seen some extracts from *Shirley* in which you talk of women working. And this first duty, this great necessity you seem to think that some women may indulge in - if they give up marriage and don't make themselves too disagreeable to the opposite sex. You are a coward and a traitor. A woman who works is by that alone better than one who does not and a woman who does not happen to be rich and who *still* earns no money and does not wish to do so, is guilty of a great fault - almost a crime - a dereliction of duty which leads rapidly and almost certainly to all manner of degradation. It is very wrong of you to *plead* for toleration for workers on the ground of their being in peculiar circumstances and few in number or singular in disposition. Work or degradation is the lot of all except the very small number born to wealth.

For the last month I have really had a good excuse for not writing any more book. I have worked hard at something else. We have been moving, cleaning, shopkeeping until I was really tired every night - a wonder for me. It does me good, and I had much rather be tired than *ennuyée* ....

PAG [Mary Taylor]

Wellington, N.Z.
August, 1850.

My dear Miss Bronte, - I shall tell you everything I can think of, since you said in one of your letters to Pag that you wished me to write to you. I have been here a year. It seems a much shorter time, and yet I have thought more and done more than I ever did in my life before. When we arrived, Henry and I were in such a hurry to leave the ship that we didn't wait to be fetched, but got into the first boat that came alongside. When we landed we inquired where Waring lived, but hadn't walked far before we met him. I had never seen him before, but he guessed we were the cousins he expected, so caught us and took us along with him. Mary soon joined us, and we went home together. At first I thought Mary was not the least altered, but when I had seen her for about a week I thought she looked rather older. The first night Mary and I sat up till 2 a.m. talking. Next day we went to tea to the Knoxes, Waring's new relations; you have no doubt heard of them. The Doctor is an idle fool and his wife not very much better; he might earn his living if he would, but he won't. In a few days we began to talk about doing something; it seemed the only thing for Henry to do was to buy sheep and go and keep them in the country. He went to look at Rangitike [Rangitikei], a large district bought of the natives, it is somewhere on the West Coast between here and Taranaki; he came back and said it was too wet for sheep, but he thought he would have to go there. In November he went to Sydney to buy the sheep, but he found freights too high there, so he settled to wait a bit; and he is waiting yet, that is, he hasn't come back, and we haven't heard a word of or from him for five months. He must have gone into the bush, but if he has he ought to have told us. I wish he'd come back. Mary and I settled we would do something together, and we talked for a fortnight before we decided whether we would have a school or shop; it ended in favour of the shop. Waring thought we had better be quiet, and I believe he still thinks we are doing it for amusement; but he never refuses to help us. He is teaching us book-keeping, and he buys things for us now and then. Mary gets as fierce as a dragon and goes to all the wholesale stores and looks at things, gets patterns, samples, etc., and asks prices, and then comes home, and we talk it over; and then she goes again and buys what we want. She says the people are always civil to her. Our keeping shop astonishes everybody here; I believe they think we do it for fun. Some think we shall make nothing of it, or that we shall get tired; and all laugh at us. Before I left home I used to be afraid of being laughed at, but now it has very little effect on me.

Mary and I are settled together now; I can't do without Mary and she couldn't get on by herself. I built the house we live in, and we made the plan ourselves, so it suits us. We take it in turns to serve in the shop, and keep the accounts, and do the housework - I mean, Mary takes the shop for a week and I the kitchen, and then we change. I think we shall do very well if no more severe earthquakes come, and if we can prevent fire. When a wooden house takes fire it doesn't stop; and we have got an oil cask about as high as I am, that would help it. If some sparks go out at the chimney-top the shingles are in danger. The last earthquake but one about a fortnight ago threw down two medicine bottles that were standing on the table and made other things jingle, but did no damage. If we have nothing worse than that I don't care, but I don't want the chimney to come down - it would cost £10 to build it up again. Mary is making me stop because it is nearly 9 p.m. and we are going to Waring's to supper. Good-bye. - Yours truly,

ELLEN TAYLOR

Little Biddy of the Buller

Being unable to read or write was the handicap of many working-class settlers, so that records of earlier times tend to reflect the interests of the more privileged. The fascinating lives of pioneer servants and workers live on in some family traditions, as oral records, but much of the fascinating detail is lost. Look at early pictures of the goldfields, for example, and there is evidence of women taking an active part in the gold rushes, including working as publicans and entertainers. Yet there is little record of life there from a woman's perspective. Bridget Goodwin could not write her own story for she was one of the illiterate. Her revealing description of goldfields' conditions, however, prompts the inclusion of this story, based on an interview late last century. It appeared in Tales of the Golden West *by W. H. Hindmarsh, writing under the nom de plume 'Waratah'.*

It was a party of three, two men and Biddy. They clubbed together upon communal principles, and for weal and woe worked the Buller River beaches for gold. It was a queer combination - 'two's company, three's none' - as the saying is, but the rule in this instance was a decided exception.

> *For they lived and loved together*
> *Through many a changing year,*

occupying the same hut, and having all things in common, and saw nothing wrong in it.

'Little Biddy' was the name she was popularly known by, until age and infirmity warranted her being called 'Old Biddy.' The after part of her name was - but it doesn't matter - it was shrouded in mystery. It might have been her maiden name of long ago, or assumed, out of compliment to Mrs. Grundy, as representing her connection, with one or other of her male partners, but it is almost certain that she never went through the formality, as we understand it, of looking up the Registrar of Marriages, for his blue paper certificate, or interviewing the parson or his clerk for her marriage lines.

This party of three came overland from Nelson to the Golden West, somewhere in the middle sixties, and struck the head waters of the Buller, and fossicked for gold for many years, between Hope and Inangahua Junction, working like human dredging machines, scooping up, cradling, and panning off the golden sand from the river bed and its streams, with varying success. The party of three originally came over from the

Victorian diggings to the Nelson district, and put in time at the Collingwood and Tadmore rushes, bossed, all along the line by Little Biddy, who kept her first and second mate well in hand, and personally engineered the gold-seeking business.

Biddy was a little morsel of a woman, four feet nothing in height, under seven stone in weight, slight in figure, but well formed, looking from a distance as if she were but a child of fourteen; but face to face with her interviewer, the furrows and wrinkles on her sunburnt features, the colour of parchment, the iron grey hair, the washed out expression of her far away blue eyes, were evidence, so plainly visible, of the daily struggle for existence this little woman had passed through in the open, seeking for gold, precious gold, under circumstances of extraordinary hardships.

'She was a good genuine-hearted little soul, and would never see anyone want a meal, or a drink of tea, keeping herself and her hut always clean and tidy,' says one of her admiring friends who, journeying to and fro, inspecting telegraph wires, often called to see Biddy when she was located in her hut at the Iron Bridge across the Buller, not far from the Lyell township.

Infirmities of age and other things attacked Biddy's first mate, and she brought him in to the hospital at Quartzopolis, where he died and was buried, and the little woman wept sorely at losing this rough companionship; and often, in later years, the memory of him, and his kindness, would bring the tears into her washed-out blue eyes. She returned to her hut at the Iron Bridge to live with and work for, her second mate 'Old Bill', as she called him; but she was not so fulsome in her praise of him as she was of her first mate, for he began to loaf round, and let her do all the work of getting gold to pay for the daily tucker. 'Old Bill', however, broke down at last, and poor little Biddy had to take him to the hospital, where he soon crossed the border and followed the first mate to the cemetery.

The little woman was now bereft, and in a manner helpless: but her independence of character came to the front, and, declining to live 'sumptuously every day' at the hospital, secured a two-roomed habitation in Quartzopolis, retired from gold-seeking business, and joined the noble army of martyrs, in that case made and provided by virtue of the 'Old Age Pensions Act;' and Biddy, for some years, received the munificent sum of one shilling a day, and monthly expressed her thanks with many others, in the formula, 'Seddon - and the Lord's name be praised.'

Biddy took up her residence and lived by herself in the two-roomed tenement, the rent of which was guaranteed by the 'Lady Chairman' of the benevolents, and the closing years of her long, long life, were made pleasant by the visitation of the local Anglican Vicar, or his curate, with a numerous assortment of lady friends who seldom came empty-handed; and when Biddy went to the Parish Church in fine weather she appeared in cast-off garments, cut down by some of the 'lady benevolents,' to suit her little figure, and it was noticeable that her garments and head gear were somewhat of a mixture of the fashions prevailing in days gone by.

Lyell Township in the Buller Gorge, 1880s. Auckland Institute and Museum.

It must be admitted that Biddy smoked - and strong tobacco at that - but in the presence of her pastor, or the lady chairman, she denied the soft impeachment that she smoked and always hid her pipe at their approach. But one young lady visitor, knowing little Biddy's infirmity, conveyed plugs of tobacco to her surreptitiously and under strict secrecy, and so her enjoyment of the fragrant weed was not stinted. It is a pity that the education of the little woman had been neglected as a child, for she could have employed her hours of idleness in reading religious works, or some of the many book of fiction, procurable at the circulating library.

Biddy's confessions to her one and only lady confessor (the tobacco conspirator) were somewhat of a startling nature, and much of it given under the seal of secrecy must pass for ever into oblivion; although it is sincerely to be hoped that she has long since received absolution for the sins and errors of her life on earth.

Sitting by the open fireplace of her residence in Quartzopolis, her kettle singing merry tunes above the hot fire, which she always kept going to keep her old bones warm, Biddy confessed to some reminiscences of her past life, just prefacing her remarks with the request, 'You wouldn't mind me smoking, Miss?' 'Certainly not, I rather like it, Biddy,' was the reply of the lady confessor.

Filling and lighting her pipe and blowing a cloud up the chimney, where it joined the smoke from the fire, ascending heavenwards by way of incense, Biddy, under the soothing influence of the fragrant weed, commenced the following general confession:-

'I was born in Ireland, Miss, but when and where I cannot say. My education as a child was neglected, for I can't read or write. I'm a believer in the Church of England, and I like the parson you've got in this place. He reads to me and does his best for me.'

Here, Biddy, puffing at her pipe, and sending clouds up the chimney, became confidential as to her arrival in Australia, and continued:

'My first recollection of looking for gold was at Bendigo, and one night, Miss, there was a terrific storm, uprooting great trees, and in the morning, nuggets of gold were clinging to the roots of the trees, and I seen hundreds of people, men, women and even children panning off the ground all round, as quickly as they could. It kept 'em at work for some time. It was wonderful, Miss!' ejaculated Biddy, with an extra draw or two at the pipe. Presently continuing her narrative: 'I came over to New Zealand in the sixties, with my two mates, from Ballarat, and landed in Nelson, working at some diggings not far off, and then we tramped overland to the head of the Buller River, and commenced fossicking in the streams and river beds above the Hope Junction and the Murchison. I seen rich patches from time to time, and we worked at them, with pick, shovel, and cradle, coming down by degrees to the Junction of the Inangahua. This was before you, Miss, or Quartzopolis was ever thought of.'

Here Biddy took a rest, and a strong whiff at her pipe, so as to collect her thoughts.

'It was a hard, rough life for a woman,' continued Biddy, 'I seen us working all day long, up to our hips in water, Miss, and in all sorts of weather, but me and my mates stuck together, and we managed to make sufficient for tucker, and something over, and we would go to the Lyell, and sell our gold to the banker there.'

'Were you able to put some of the money by for the future, Biddy?' timidly asks the lady confessor.

'Miss, I won't deceive you,' replied Biddy, 'after buying tucker, we knocked down the rest of the money on a long booze, and when it was all spent we would stir ourselves up a bit, swag our tucker on our backs, and return to our hut, and to our claim, and began fossicking about for more gold. When my first man died in the hospital, I cried very much at losing him, and even now, when I think of him, the tears come to my eyes.'

Little Biddy of the Buller. Alexander Turnbull Library.

Here poor Biddy paused in her confessions, laid aside her pipe, and after a while wiped her eyes, relighted her pipe, and drawing energetically at it regained courage, and went on.

'"Old Bill" - he was my second mate, Miss - was quite another sort - hard to get on with, and had a funny complaint, for when he raised his head to look up, Miss, he would get giddy, fall over, and go out of his mind for a bit. I think prospecting and working on the beaches, and looking down so much for the gold, must have caused it. Our hut was near where the Iron bridge crosses the Buller to go to the Lyell, and one day I seen "Old Bill" cutting down a small tree for firewood, and not looking up to see where it would fall; the top branches fell among the telegraph wires, and mixed 'em all up, and when the inspector found it out he came and frightened us, saying it was a case of going to jail. I asked him to let us off, as it wasn't done intentional, and told him of "Old Bill's" infirmity. The inspector let us off, saying he forgave us, and I got him a nice cup of tea.'

Biddy took another rest, and then went on: '"Old Bill" got sick and loafed round, so I had to go and fossick about for gold by myself, buying tucker, and humping it on my back from the Lyell to my hut till I got so bad with rheumatics, and "Old Bill" getting worse, we went to the hospital at Quartzopolis, where he died and was buried, and I wasn't sorry a bit, Miss, for I felt my days were numbered.'

Here Biddy ended her confessions, and the young lady confessor, bidding her a cheery goodbye, left her to her pipe and her thoughts of long ago.

On the occasion of the Queen's Diamond Jubilee in 1897, Little Biddy was visited by many of her lady friends, bringing with them supplies of delicacies and creature comforts; and amongst the good things, a bottle of port wine, found its way into Biddy's larder, with strict injunction to drink the Queen's health by two or three teaspoonfuls at a time. One young lady visitor, however, supplemented the gifts with a 'wee-drap' of Scotch, of which Biddy was particularly fond, and so they left her to the full enjoyment of the banquet, in honour of Queen Victoria.

Later in the day, the parson made one of his usual visitations, first cutting and splitting up a good stock of firewood for poor Biddy. His reverence was an expert at the axe, and could wield it, with as much force and power, as he could a sermon. Not seeing Biddy about, he went inside the hut, and, to his dismay, found the poor creature in the last stages of passing away; hastily flying off on his bike, he brought the doctor to see poor Biddy, lying in her last extremity, and upon a close examination, the medico startled the parson by laughing heartily at the situation, for it turned out that Little Biddy was dead - drunk. They wrapped her up tenderly and left her to sleep it off, and on the morrow she was very penitent, but contributions of wine and whisky for 'Old Biddy' were peremptorily stopped.

Two years after the Queen's Diamond Jubilee, the end came that comes to us all, sooner or later; and Little Biddy of the Buller, after a sojourn of many years in this vale of tears, slept the sleep of death, and was laid to rest in the quiet graveyard of the new cemetery, there to await the consummation of all things.

The following is an extract from the very brief record in the register of deaths in the Parish Church, Quartzopolis:

No. 126

BRIDGET GOODWIN.

Died 19-10-99.

Buried 20-10-99.

Age 86.

CAROLINE NGOUNGOU

'My Life Among the Maoris'

Caroline 'Queenie' Perrett was 60 years old before she discovered her 'real' name, or indeed that she had another name apart from that which she was called by her husband and friends. She had no memories other than the life she had spent with a tribe of itinerant Maori on the gumfields of Northland, and of married life in Whakatane up to 1926. So naturally she was cynical when a woman, struck by Caroline's strong resemblance to her own mother, stopped her on the street one day and questioned her origins.

The discovery of two distinguishing burn marks - one of which even Caroline herself did not know existed - established that she was in fact Caroline Perrett, who had gone missing as a girl from Lepperton in Taranaki, 52 years earlier. Caroline's father, William Perrett, was a small farmer and surveyor who had successfully tendered to shift a Maori burial ground to make way for the construction of a railway line. Despite warnings from the local, friendly Maori that the land was tapu and misfortune would befall him, William carried out the work and in 1874 their prophesies became fact. Eight-year-old Caroline was sent out to bring in the family's cows from a nearby clearing and was never seen again, despite the efforts of 150 people in a search party. The last sighting of her was made by a local bushman, who said he saw her standing on a log surrounded by Maori, who then disappeared into the bush with the child. The only other news of Caroline's whereabouts received by her family came some years later, when a young surveyor reported seeing a white child with a group of Maori in the Kaipara. He had tried to speak to the girl, but she had appeared frightened, and ran off.

Caroline's mother died shortly after her disappearance and her father some years later, neither ever again seeing their daughter. But the memory of her abduction was kept alive by her brothers and sister, culminating in her 'discovery' by Caroline's niece Mrs. Hayward, the daughter of Mary Ann Kay (née Perrett), in 1926.

Once the story of her 'life among the Maoris' hit the newspapers of the day, Caroline became a celebrity, 'one of the most romantic figures in the Dominion today', and her story became distorted to include melodramatic touches such as her marriage to a Maori chief and memories of 'bloodthirsty [Maori] warriors coming back from the wars against the Pakehas'. To set the story straight, Caroline told her story to journalist J. R. Sheehan of the Sun *newspaper in Auckland, where it appeared as a full-page feature on July 27, 1929. Her comment? 'I don't know why they make such a fuss about it.'*

I have no recollection whatever of my early life in Lepperton. Neither is it true, as has been read to me from the newspapers, that I can remember being taken across the sea in a great canoe by the Maoris. My first conscious memories begin from the time when, as a small girl, I was digging gum with a band of wandering Maoris in the Kaipara district, north of Auckland.

I could not speak Maori then, so it must have been shortly after I was kidnapped. The Maoris were very unkind to me at the time, though I was never struck or beaten. They simply ignored me, and had it not been for the kindness of one or two of the womenfolk life would have been miserable indeed.

Their method of teaching me the language was very simple. Pointing to some article on the ground they would order me to pick it up, and in a very short time I was able to speak Maori as fluently as any of the tribe.

It was then I discovered that the Maoris with whom I worked belonged to no special tribe, but were drawn from all over the Waikato and Wanganui districts and banded together for the common purpose of digging for gum. They were split up into about 40 camps scattered all over the Kaipara district.

We lived in raupo whares and the life was hard and comfortless. Every morning, at daybreak, I used to go out with a spade and spear and dig until sunset. All the children worked just as hard as their parents and though it may seem hard to Europeans we thought nothing of it. In the evening we sat in the camp and scraped the gum. The dust and scrapings we flung on the fire which blazed up and lit the darkness. There were no candles at all.

There was plenty of gum in those days - great lumps of it and it was easy to find. When we had enough we took it down to the store and sold it. What the name of the settlement was I never found out, but there was actually no township - only a shop or two. Our camp was ten miles from this place, and when I was only a child, I used to walk this distance with about 60lb of gum in a sack. It was backbreaking work, but I did it for years, and it doesn't seem to have done me much harm, because I am still hale, hearty and working hard at 63 years of age.

After selling the gum we would each carry a 56lb bag of flour back to the camp.

As to clothes, I got just enough to keep me covered and no more. Print dresses, bought ready-made, were what I usually wore. Boots I never saw at all. My feet were as hard as iron and nothing could hurt them. About £1 was allowed me each time I sold my gum. The balance, in accordance with Maori custom, went toward the camp food.

The storekeeper to whom I sold my gum never passed any remark about my white colour. Perhaps he was an Austrian or a Dalmatian, but newly-arrived in the country, and thought I was an albino Maori - a freak of nature. I do not know. In any case I did not stop to consider I was different

Gum diggers probe for kauri gum in Northland. Auckland Institute and Museum.

from the Maoris to whom I belonged. I saw my face in the river often, but it did not seem strange that I was of a lighter colour. That seems difficult to explain, but nevertheless it is a fact.

I remember a Pakeha speaking to me one day when I was a young girl and he offered me some biscuits. Of course, what he said was meaningless to me. Since the mystery has been cleared up I have been told his name was Coxhead, a young surveyor. He had heard of a white child being kidnapped from Lepperton and he thought I might be the missing girl. This was what he told my sister, Mrs. Kay, of Lower Hutt, some years afterward.

The Maoris were very annoyed about my talking to the young surveyor and called me away. 'Never speak to the Pakehas at all,' they said.

As I grew to young womanhood among the Maoris, the feeling against me grew less and what remained of it was more conspicuous among the men. The women were very good to me and the children played with me just as though I were one of themselves. They never asked me why I was white, nor did I at any time hear any curiosity expressed or any reference as to my origin. Neither was I curious, because I accepted the fact that I was a Maori.

At night, sitting around the camp fire scraping the gum, my Maori brethren sang and laughed and told old legends that had been passed down from father to son for hundreds and perhaps thousands of years. They were a merry lot when work was finished.

Food was plentiful. We did not need the European butcher shop then. Tunas, kereru (wild pigeon), and pigs gave us all we wanted in the way of meat. The pigs we caught with our dogs. And fat! Nowadays we have to feed the ordinary pig up such a lot to get him fat and there is little fat on the wild pig. But in those days the wild pig was very fat and good, and we enjoyed him very much. And the little pihipihis, the little bright-eyed silly birds - we caught them too. First, one would be caught in a snare and kept alive. He would call to his mates, who would flock around in scores to see what was the matter. Before they knew what was wrong a Maori would rise up from behind and sweep them to the ground with a big stick. Then he would put them in a bag and wait until some more of the foolish little birds came along. When enough were caught they were preserved in fat until such time as they were wanted.

We had a very crude way of making bread. We mixed the flour and water together until a hard, sticky mass was formed. It would then be pulled into a long roll and a stick was pushed through the centre of it and set in front of the fire. The stick was slowly turned until the bread was properly baked. Just flour and water and baking soda, but it was wonderful bread! I liked it better than I like European bread now. And the big, sweet tunas we used to catch were the finest I have tasted. Perhaps it was because we worked so hard that I thought they were so good. There is no sauce like the sauce of hunger.

We shifted our camps from place to place as we searched for gum. As to education, I didn't know what it was. There were no schools in that life, and I had never heard of them at all. The education I got was the education of the out-of-doors, and though perhaps pakeha children could read and write and add up figures, I could have shown them a lot about real life - a life where to live was to work, and to work hard. I have never learned to read and write and I have never missed it. I didn't know whether it would be a benefit to me, but where I have lived it has never been necessary, anyway.

On Sundays there was no work in the camp. That was the one day we could relax. We observed the same Sunday as the Christian world, because that was the one day we could not sell gum at the store. That is how we came to fix on that particular day. We would lie round and eat and talk and laugh and make merry generally. Yes, Sunday was a day to look forward to.

And at Christmas we had a big feast and celebration. Though there was no Christmas pudding there was plenty of everything the Maoris liked and we ate just as much as the Europeans do nowadays, though perhaps we did not feel quite as sick afterward. I don't remember ever seeing any liquor in the camps. Sometimes Maoris would go away and get drunk, but that was very rare.

My memory is very indistinct, because I have worked hard and passed through great troubles, so I must be excused if there are things I cannot tell. What religion we had I cannot say now, because it is so long ago I do not think we had any. We were just a tribe of nomads and all we thought of was work and eating, for they are very necessary things, too.

I used to go down to the river with all the women and children and do the washing. Soap, of course, we had in plenty. We bought it from the store in great bars. At the riverside we would chatter and laugh and sing, just the same as other women.

My hair was cut short just like a boy's, and my skin was tanned by exposure to the weather as the years went on. I saw many pakeha men who never suspected I was not a Maori, but I never saw a pakeha woman. In fact, it was not until after my second marriage that I first saw one, and I remember how frightened I was. But I saw little of pakehas generally until I came down to live here at Whakatane.

Every little while we would go down to Mahurangi Heads to rest at the pa, near Waiwera and Warkworth. There used to be hot springs there where we bathed. I have been told since that they are all fenced in and are good hot springs. After spending a time at the pa resting after our labour and enjoying ourselves, back to the gumfields we would go to work as hard as before.

It was here on the Kaipara gumfields that I was first married. I was only about fifteen when my husband took me. I had known him and worked with him for years, and he was a big, fine-looking Maori. Some of the papers have said he was a Maori chief, but that is not true. He was just a nomad Maori, digging gum as we all were doing. His name was Ewa Ngaru, and he was much older than I was, though I cannot say what his age was. He had come up from Tauranga a long time before.

We were married according to Maori custom and went on with our work side by side on the gumfields. He was a very good husband to me. I kept on working right up until the time my baby girl was born. After the birth, my husband's mother looked after the baby and I went back to the gumfields.

My first baby grew up fine and strong and healthy, and was married many years ago. Her name is Mrs. Ngaruna Mikaere, and she lives near Coromandel. She has had 13 children of her own, of whom 10 are now living.

Shortly after the birth of the baby my husband's health began to fail and he grew weaker and weaker as time went on until he could work no more. His trouble was consumption. It was very sad and pitiful and 18 months after the baby was born he died of the disease, leaving me a young widow of about 18 years of age. A great tangi was held for him, and his body was kept for two days before he was put into a rough wooden box and buried. I was heartbroken and my hair was cut off close to the scalp as a special sign of deep mourning. The custom is kept up among the older people today, though the younger Maoris are letting all the old customs go. The cutting was done by the women of the camp, who consoled me in my great loss.

Soon after his death I was stricken with typhoid fever and for eight weeks I was very close to death. I went down to nothing but skin and bone and all my hair fell out, leaving me quite bald. I must have looked a strange sight. My Maoris friends were very good to me then and all the old feeling against me had completely passed away. They waited on me and did everything they possibly could to bring me back to health, even though they were so busy themselves. It is hard to say how I caught the disease, as it was not common among the Maoris with whom I lived. Most likely it was drinking from some small stream on the fields. My Maori friends kept putting cold water on my head to keep me cool, for I was parched and burning, and felt that I was on fire.

However, though it was a hard struggle, I eventually battled through, but it took me months to regain my proper strength and condition. But I will never forget my old Maori friends for their great kindness then. It is burnt into my mind in fire.

Though I never made fancy mats or did any of the finer work, I used to make any number of potato kits with the rest of the women. I liked that work, too. They were happy days, indeed, when we sat together and talked and laughed. Alas! Most of my friends have gone from this world and I have seen none of my old acquaintances from the Kaipara gumfields for over forty years.

One habit I could never take up was that of smoking. The Maoris, both men and women, were always puffing away at their clay pipes, but I could not acquire the habit, though I tried once or twice. The torori, or Maori tobacco, was terrible stuff and burned my tongue. It was made from the proper tobacco plant, but had none of the usual ingredients of the prepared tobacco and was very bitter. Perhaps it was my forgotten white blood that rebelled against the habit. The rest of the camp thought it was strange that I did not like it.

I was still on the Kaipara fields when I met Ngoungou, my present husband. I suppose I would be about twenty at that time.

Ngoungou came from Wairoa and was a big, fine-looking young Maori. He had come up from the South with his grandfather to pay a visit to some relatives and it was then he first saw me and wanted me to be his wife. On his way up to Kaipara, Ngoungou was in Te Puke on the night of the great eruption of Tarawera in 1886 and could see far-off the glare of the great mountain that slew so many, both Maori and pakeha. Then he came up to Tauranga and took a boat up to Auckland, before travelling on to the Kaipara district.

I fell in love with Ngoungou, for he was a very fine-looking Maori indeed and he took me to be his wife according to Maori custom. There was feasting to celebrate our union. It was agreed I should go down to Whakatane with my husband, but first we were to have three months' holiday. So, after about 12 years on the fields I left my Maori friends behind me for ever and turned southward, never more to see Kaipara. My little daughter was left with the tribe.

With us we took the dead body of my first husband's brother, which was to be taken back to his home in Tauranga. From Mahurangi we came down to Tauranga by boat - quite a big voyage in those days. On arrival at Tauranga a big tangi was held to do honour to the body of my brother-in-law, Pikake Ngaranui, and then we went on to Karikari, where we stayed for nearly two months. From Karikari we came down to Te Puke, which was practically nothing in those days. There was only one hotel and the population there was all Maori. We stayed there six or seven weeks before coming down through Whakatane to Poroporo, where I have lived ever since, about 43 years.

Here, all the children of my second marriage were born, Maui, my eldest son, being born shortly after we arrived here. Whakatane was a very small place at that time, containing only about four shops. It was very wild and desolate and, of course, Maoris were swarming in the district. The ship from Auckland used to anchor alongside the Pohutaroa Rock, which now stands back quite a distance from the water. Where the hotels are now was the seashore.

Many a time I have seen pakeha sailors from the boats roll a keg of liquor along the waterfront, and have a big haurangi there. Sometimes it used to end in a fierce brawl with blood and skin flying. Now, the place is quite civilised, but in those days it was no place for a weakling.

My husband and his family owned a 60-acre farm out here at Poroporo, where we still live. In those days it was all swamp, though it has long since been drained. We lived down on the banks of the Whakatane River in raupo houses. They were quite warm and snug, and I think in every way equal to the European houses as far as comfort is concerned. Often yet, I think lovingly of those old Maori huts and wish I was back in them again.

The white people around the district took no notice of me and never, to my knowledge, asked any questions as to the whys and wherefores of my life among the Maoris. They just accepted the fact as part of the general scheme of things. In deference to the wishes of my husband's family, who belonged to the Church of England, my husband and I decided to get married according to the English law, though we were actually just as truly married by Maori custom. But a hitch arose. The Maori girls around this district were very jealous about my marriage to Ngoungou, and there was a good deal of bad feeling shown about the whole affair. The Maori minister of the Church of England refused to perform the Christian ceremony for us, influenced, no doubt, by the attitude of the rest of his race here. In any case, he gave no definite reasons. We were determined to get legally married in some way, so we approached the Catholic priest and told him we would turn Catholic if he married us. He agreed and Ngoungou and I were duly married after we had been living together in Maori fashion for over a year.

There was a surprising change in attitude of the local Maoris after the ceremony. Where, before, they had been making life miserable for us, taunting us and being rude to us generally, they swerved completely around after the ceremony and were as good as they had been toward us before.

Another surprising thing for which I could not account was my strong objection to being tattooed. When I was quite a young girl tattooing was all the fashion and was considered to enhance the beauty of the young woman. The work, which was very painful, was always done by a specialist in that line. The flesh was cut into by a piece of sharp metal tapped by a block of wood, and the dyes, which were made by the Maoris themselves, were affixed. They would bleed copiously after the operation which took a long time to complete, but they were forbidden to wash the blood away. They were also warned against looking into water as it was said if they did so the colours would not stick. It is a custom that is almost dead now, but in those days a Maori was not considered to be fashionable unless he or she bore some pattern of the tattooist's art on face or body. Though I was often pressed to be tattooed I refused vigorously. Why, I do not know, but the idea repelled me.

I have no recollections of any of the Maori wars. Perhaps I have heard the men speaking of them, I could not say now. My memory is so bad: and then again a Maori woman has plenty to do looking after her husband and her work without troubling about such things as wars. Not as far as I can remember have I ever heard Maoris say much against the white man. No threats or rebellious talk - not even away up on the gumfields, where there was a collection of men and women of practically every tribe in New Zealand. The Maoris treat their women well and I do not know if I would have been any happier living as a European. Sometimes the Maori gets very angry and scolds his wife soundly, but it is unusual for him to strike her. Nor do the Maori men fight much among themselves, though they often get angry and talk a good deal.

Sketch of Caroline Ngoungou on the gumfields from the newspaper account of her adventure. The Sun, *Auckland, July 27, 1929.*

One of the great events of my life was when I first wore boots. That was when I came down to Tauranga with Ngoungou. They were lace-up boots and I was very proud of them, though I seemed to be tied up and could hardly walk. You must live for years without boots to understand how I felt. The way I staggered along the streets must have amused the people.

It was in Tauranga, too, that I first saw a pakeha woman and I was very frightened of her. She was a pretty woman I thought, but she did not look hardy and healthy as I was. She had pink and white cheeks and a very clear skin and such beautiful clothes on, I remember. She thought I was a great curiosity, dressed as I was in the roughest of garments. I felt so bashful I did not know what to do and ran to my Maori friends again for comfort. But the lady passed on and forgot me very soon, I suppose.

Soon after I settled down with my husband at Poroporo, I came into contact with a number of pakehas and sometimes I used to go out and work for the pakeha women. It was amazing how quickly I picked up the English language. The words and the meaning of what they said to me came to me quite naturally and it was not very long before I was able to speak English as well as most people. People, in later years, asked me where I had come from but I could not say. I said I was a Maori and had always lived with the Maoris and that was all I knew about it. I have been in the same place here for 43 years and I have never been down even as far as Opotiki. I would like to see Auckland. People tell me it is a great town, very much bigger than Whakatane, but I don't suppose I will ever see it before I die.

I saw the great rebel chief Te Kooti on several occasions after he was pardoned by the Government. He was not a very big man and had a white beard. He seemed very nice, but I was frightened of him.

Five of my children by my second marriage are alive. Ra, who is unmarried, lives at Thames; Pene, who has 10 children, is at Whakarewarewa; Maui has a family of five and lives here at Poroporo; Timi, who is single and my daughter Naha, who has two children, are here also.

The way I was discovered to be Caroline Perrett was remarkable. It did not happen in Taneatua as has been stated in the papers, but down in Whakatane one Saturday afternoon.

At Taneatua, only about nine miles away from Whakatane, lives Mrs. F.J. Hayward, a daughter of Mrs. Kay, of Lower Hutt. Mrs. Kay has since been proved to be my sister, and therefore Mrs. Hayward is my niece, although I knew nothing about it at this time.

Saturday afternoon is a busy day in Whakatane. Pakehas and Maoris from all over the surrounding districts flock in to do their shopping in the town. The Saturday I am referring to was about three years ago.

I was walking down the main street when Mrs. Hayward came up to me and said:- 'You are a white woman. What are you doing with the Maoris?'

I told her I knew I was white-skinned, but had always lived among the Maoris, and had no idea whence I came.

'You look very much like my own mother,' said Mrs. Hayward. 'She lost a sister, who was supposed to have been kidnapped by the Maoris many years ago. She said she would always know her lost sister, because she had a white mark on her neck, caused by a burn. Have you a scar on your throat?'

I thought that was peculiar, because I had just the mark she spoke of; but still, I could not believe it, and told Mrs. Hayward so. She said she was sure I was her missing aunt, both because of the scar and the family likeness, and she would write to her relatives to verify her facts.

When I got home I told my daughter Naha what had happened, but Naha

Caroline Ngoungou photographed by The Sun *newspaper in 1929.*

said it was nonsense. 'Don't take any notice of it,' she said. But Mrs. Hayward wrote away, and found that the mark was as she thought, and she was sure I was her [Mrs. Kay's] long-lost sister. Shortly afterwards, one of my brothers came up from Taranaki to make sure it was true.

'I am convinced you are,' he said after he had seen me; 'but to make it doubly sure, if you are really Caroline, you should have another mark below your left breast. Caroline was burnt both there and on the neck when she fell across the bars of the fireplace as a little girl.'

That was news to me, because none of my family knew, nor did I know myself. A close examination, however, proved that the mark was there, and made it certain that I was really Caroline Perrett, who was kidnapped from Lepperton, Taranaki, 55 years ago.

My sister, Mrs. Kay, of Lower Hutt, came up last January, and wanted me to go down and stay with her; but I do not like to leave Poroporo, where I have lived so long. My niece, Mrs. Hayward, often comes to see me and the family are overjoyed that I have been restored to them after more than 50 years. And I am content that the mystery of my birth has been solved, and I am no longer a woman without a name. I am getting to be an old woman now, and perhaps it does not make much difference. It seems so incredible to me that I can scarcely grasp it yet. In my mind, however, I am Maori. I think as they think, just as I have always lived their life outwardly. All my interests and my friends are Maori, and my children also. So why should I seek to change my life now?

There is too much romance being made of my life, and many things have been credited to me that are not true. I want to say that those who talk of my memories of my kidnapping are not speaking the truth. It is all a blank to me, and anything said to the contrary is untrue.

I have been misrepresented by some of the papers, who say I married a chieftain. I say quite definitely that is not true. My first husband was a gumdigger, and my second husband is a small farmer.

Was I happy with the Maoris? Well, when I look back over my long life with them, I think I can say yes. Hard work has roughened my body, but it has strengthened me inwardly. I know what trouble is, and I know what it is to fight on and endure in the face of tremendous difficulties. The story I have told *The Sun* is the only authentic story of my life and adventures. Others may write stories, but they are not the truth. I have given *The Sun* as much as I can remember of my life. Details I forget, but the main thread is correct. Working as I did, I had little time to take note of particular events; but if I had the time, perhaps I could tell more of the customs and habits of the Maoris.

But here in Poroporo I think I shall finish my life. I have lived here so long, and with age the desire to change becomes less, until it finally dies out. I have been asked by many of my relatives to go and stay with them, but I cannot bring myself to leave my home and family. And then, again, I might feel out of place among the pakehas, for their ways are not my ways, and it is too late to change my habits now.

HELEN WILSON

Pioneering the Horowhenua

Travelling today through the bare farmlands of New Zealand it is difficult to imagine that much of it was once bushland, cleared by pioneers as late as this century. The Hauraki Plains for example were drained of their wetlands as recently as the 1920's and occasionally, still, piles of tree roots may be seen in the flat fields where farmers are still taking out the stumps of giant kahikatea trees from the peat. Vast forests in the southern North Island were also cleared early this century.

Helen Wilson went to the Horowhenua, the plains around Levin, when bush still covered them, in 1888. Aged 18, Helen had been teaching in Canterbury, when she and her widowed mother were ballotted a twenty-acre block (about eight hectares) for a deposit of four pounds and their promise to make improvements every year. They regarded the fact that their land had a clearing on it as good fortune, for the rest of the Levin settlers had to clear standing bush before they could build.

In her eighties, Helen looked back on her life in three books including a novel called Moonshine. *This account of pioneering on the Levin Block, culminating in an adventurous day out lost in dense bush near Levin, is from* My First Eighty Years, *first published in 1950. The Mr. Wilson mentioned near the end of this extract later became Helen's husband, Charles Kendall Wilson.*

After the ballot was drawn we were taken by the Public Works train to Levin, as the township had been named, and met by a young surveyor detailed to show settlers their sections. The whole place appeared to be a sea of standing bush on both sides of the railway-line. We walked down the line, stepping from sleeper to sleeper, then through some rough bush until we reached a tram-line built by the sawmill which was already operating. We were surprised by the beauty and smooth finish of the track. The rails were sawn timber, nailed to rough bush sleepers, but the whole was heavily ballasted with sawdust - red rimu sawdust, the perfect colour to complement the gigantic fernery through which the tram-line cut a symmetrical tunnel. The damage done in the cutting had long been healed, and the new growth, a soft ferny perfection, filled every cranny. The tall trees, though serving to produce the green mellow half-light, were hidden by a ceiling of undergrowth, principally tree-ferns. There were groves where silver ferns predominated, their fronds, white-backed, intertwined high overhead, making a fretted ceiling. Later we used to call these groves our cathedrals and strike matches under them at night. That day we forgot such sordid things as farming in our delight over this luxuriant causeway, with its smooth, soft sawdust underfoot and the choir of birds overhead. What an approach to our new home! We came to a sunlit break in the tunnel. The surveyor said, with a certain suppressed pride, 'Here is your section.'

We saw what looked like extensive park lands; the turf, short and well-kept, like a bowling-green, was studded with trees - tall, stately, wide-spreading trees and shrubs. Each tree was trimmed at exactly the same height from the ground, with the utmost precision - as level as a ceiling. The whole looked like a well-kept plantation or park. Our ecstatic cries provoked a loud, startled snort, and a sudden stamp of hooves and, before we could speak, a splendid black stallion galloped past, followed, in single file, by about twenty wild horses of various sizes and colours, their picturesque manes and long tails streaming behind.

'These are your lawn mowers,' remarked the surveyor. 'They keep your trees well clipped too.'

I do not remember what either of us said, probably nothing coherent. We asked, of course, whether the horses went with the land, and were told, with a smile, that they were certainly ours if we could catch them. I had, at that time, infinite faith in myself as a tamer of animals and privately determined that I would soon have the whole mob eating out of my hand. How little I understood of the long, relentless war between man and wild things! So, with rapture, we entered upon our inheritance. We paid, if I remember aright, a £4 deposit and the same sum each year with the added provision that we must occupy it and must effect each year certain improvements. This was surely land settlement on easy terms.

My mother and I returned to Wellington well satisfied. Beyond the thrill of its beauty, the clearing on our section gave us the special advantage that we might occupy at once, whereas every other settler on a bush section had to wait till his bush was felled, left to dry and then burnt before he could do as much as walk about his land. This is how it happened that two women were the very first settlers in the Levin Block.

We decided to leave Wellington as soon as we could find anyone to build us a house on the land, for boarding in town was an expense we would be glad to avoid. I will own to a certain secret reluctance. I was a shy, unsophisticated girl, hurried from school to school-teaching in the country. I hardly knew anything of the life of young people my own age. I had seen a glimpse of things in Wellington of which I would fain have learnt more. However, we had come to take up land. We, or rather my mother, interviewed builders, and studied estimates for some days. But it appeared that the boom that was taking place in land had induced a corresponding boom in house-building and though builders were eager to take contracts

A Bush Tramway.

we found none prepared to start work at once. Perhaps they were more scrupulous in those days. I have known modern contractors promise to start half a dozen houses at once.

Our furniture was stored at the sawmill near Levin and we thought we might be more successful in finding a builder on the spot.

We remembered a little cottage built by a Danish workman towards the south of the Levin Block, on a stony clearing. Taking the Public Works train, we went to see whether his wife might be induced to board us. Mrs. Petersen was willing to board us and let us her two front rooms for a moderate sum. I forget what she charged and I fear you would not believe me if I could remember.

We lost no time in moving to these lodgings from which, every day, we could walk up to our section. We bought two billhooks, armed with which, a billy and some sandwiches, we set out every morning to attack the clumps of spikey bush-lawyer, which were the only green things on the section we could bear to exterminate. In an amateurish way we must have done pretty good work. We slashed and hewed the springy piles to pieces, burnt stalks and leaves, sowed grass-seed on the large, round, bare patches we had made and purred with satisfaction to see the down of green blades appear.

I remember that the wild horses made sad havoc of some of our patches of new grass. They rolled in the soft earth, apparently danced and held midnight revels so that they made shallow basins where we had raked the earth smooth and flat. An examination of the clearing showed nine of the primaeval giants of the forest still standing, their clean, stately columns seeming to soar to the skies, and their branches, freed from the struggle for light and air, flung wide and bushy, but still out of proportion to the enormous trunks. They looked like green parasols hoisted on tall masts.

Still more attractive than the giant matai and rimu, because they met the eye without the effort of gazing upwards, were the trees of medium growth - miro and matipo. These, when space had been cleared, had spread like huge weeping willows, and as never leaf or twig was allowed to push downward within reach of a horse's outstretched neck they were trimmed straight as a ceiling, every tree at exactly the same level.

The clearing was apparently circular with a slight but distinct rise in the centre, providing a perfect building-site. The encircling virgin bush had developed a natural edge of ferns and shrubs that protected the bush and gave a finish to the clearing. A house built on that rise would be standing in natural grounds such as a millionaire might envy. How were we to guess that surveyors take no heed of fine building-sites and that the boundary line of the block ran straight through that rise?

Mrs. Petersen proved the kindest and cleanest of landladies but, oh! the fleas! The place fairly heaved with them, inside and out. Men and dogs had camped there and left a legacy beyond control. The strange thing was that neither she nor her husband or son seemed to feel them. One morning when I had caught and killed so many that I felt as gory as a butcher, she said with surprised admiration, 'Haf you r'ally gotten one?' ....We had to get away somehow, even if we had to buy a tent. Then came a decrepit old Swede who said he was a 'push carpenter' and could build us a shed for our goods where we could live until a house was built.

We had learnt by now that timber was no problem. We had already had rough boards and bits of firewood thrown off the tram-line and we knew we only had to ask the trolley driver and we could have as much as we liked. So far we had asked for 'facecuts', the first slices off the boards with the bark adhering, but even the second sappy boards were practically for nothing. I do not remember the exact cost, but I know that four years later, when we built a house, the price of heart of rimu was four shillings and elevenpence per 100ft. and matai flooring the same.

The structure built by the bush carpenter was about 12ft. by 12ft. We purchased nails, hinges, a lock and one window and we sat down on the short cropped lawn to watch the wonder take shape. Presently I exclaimed, 'Why! There's nothing in this building, I see how it is done. If I had a hammer and saw I am sure I could do it', and there and then we decided that as soon as the man had gone we would try our hands at this 'push carpenting'.

On the advice of the builder, the roof, as well as the walls, had been weatherboarded. He had said, without much conviction, that if he made the pitch of the roof high enough and overlapped the boards well it should be watertight. We reasoned to our own satisfaction that one board placed over another *must* throw off water. It seems incredible now that we knew nothing of, or gave no thought to, that blessing of pioneers, corrugated iron. So many things had proved easy that were supposed to be impossible that we trusted to our luck.

Photograph from Helen Wilson's My First Eighty Years *includes her brother H.H. Ostler standing on left.*

We had brought a miscellaneous collection of what we called furniture. We had been careful to pack everything that we thought necessary for a primitive life. We had packed as well as our *lares* and *penates* certain things precious to us because they had been hard to come by and we feared would never be acquired again. Thus, after much hesitation, we had brought a piano. We saw, now that our goods had been brought down, that it would be impossible to store them in the new structure and live in it too. So, after a few days of impossible congestion, when one had to climb over the piano to get into bed, we made ourselves an al fresco dining-room. A splendid matipo, with a spread like the largest weeping willow, grew behind the whare. We strewed sawdust under it as a carpet. Three really valuable carved oak chairs that we had not been able to find it in our hearts to part with we had wickedly put out there, saying we would cover them with sacks if it rained. A small iron table and a colonial oven we had bought in Wellington for the prospective house stood upon two kerosene boxes to form a sideboard....

One day we looked out to see an old Maori man walking casually around our garden. Horrible! What to do? My mother, who had never deigned to show nervousness, strode out to him and said firmly. 'What do you want?'

He smiled benignly, saying, 'I look roun'. You t' widow?'

We both drew a deep breath and wondered what the next move should be, but it soon dawned on us that there was no guile in the old man. Quite a long conversation followed, of which I hope he understood more than we did. At any rate he called the next day, bringing us a large pumpkin. What a treat it was!

It was our custom to work outside, my mother gardening and fencing and digging until lunch time, then, as neither wanted to go in, we took it in turns to prepare the meal. 'In' is a euphemism, for our fire was outside and so was our dining-room. The day after our Maori visitor came my mother cooked pumpkin and made it into a tasty dish with butter, pepper and salt. The next day, when my turn came, butter was off so we dined cheerfully on pumpkin. I might not have remembered that trifle but when writing to my sister in Melbourne we must have made a story of it and she always afterwards referred to that autumn as our pumpkin-and-pepper period.

It was some time after we moved into our whare that rain tested the roof. There was a drip, drip, drip, right on to my mother's bed. She got up, hammered out a sardine tin and, while I held the light, pushed it into the crack and returned to bed triumphant. In about half an hour a drip developed over my bed. There were no more sardine tins so I took a ship's biscuit, prised up the board and pushed it in the crack. There it did the work required until morning....

We had now reached only May of our first autumn, 1889, a particularly beautiful season. Day after day and week after week were so warm and still and sunny that we were tempted to believe we had come to a land of perpetual summer. My mother suggested that, as it was my birthday, we should take a walk to Lake Horowhenua which lay about two miles to the west of us. We crossed the railway and entered the bush beyond it, and found without difficulty a surveyor's line, clearly defined, that was the northern boundary of Levin Block. It was not too bad walking in single file if we lifted out ankle-length skirts to prevent their catching on the supplejacks and small growth that had been cut some six inches from the ground. Presently, from the dim bush shadows, we came out into blazing sunshine on a grassy sand-dune overlooking the lovely lake. It was wonderful to look at the open sky and wide horizon after our enclosed existence in the bush clearing. We enjoyed watching the sun exhibit his brilliant, age-old box of tricks as he set over the low sand-hills. Then we turned to go home. We were amazed to see it had grown dark - unbelievably dark.

However, the tips of the cut supplejacks shone white in the gloom and we thought they would guide us. They did, until we came to a place where a tree had fallen over the line. Coming, we had been able to walk round the head of the tree quite easily and as easily find the line again. We could no longer do so. It was dark, quite dark, and we never found that track again. We were lost.

In a bush settlement there is always considerable talk about 'getting bushed'. We knew that people are apt to walk in circles and get lost in a few acres. From time to time the mill-hands would go pig or cattle hunting and be missing for a night or even two. The train was often asked to whistle loudly and frequently to guide someone who had been away too long. But no soul knew of us having left home, or would dream of enquiring. We might have taken a trip to Wellington for all anyone knew. We began to think our plight serious. We knew there were fifty miles of standing bush between us and Palmerston North. We must avoid going north at all costs.

My mother said, 'We've only got to find the Southern Cross, follow where the Pointers point and we'll come out in the clearing where the Petersen's live.'

But how, through that canopy of leaves, could we hope to see more than one star at a time?

We blundered on. It was incredibly rough going. That part of Levin today looks perfectly flat but it seemed to us that we were continually falling into deep ravines where surface water frightened and wet us. Once we saw a patch of sky showing a few stars. My mother said she recognised them but I doubted it. The train came up and its roar, reverberating through the bush, sounded very near, but my mother thought the sound came from our left and I was sure it came from the right. We discussed the very remote possibility of our new friend Mr. Wilson guessing where we had gone because it was he who had given us the directions by which we found the cut line and who had spoken of the lake as worth seeing from that viewpoint. I was for making ourselves as comfortable as we could and waiting for daylight, but my mother feared her bronchitis, so we blundered on, scratched and torn and not at all sure each yard we fought did not take us further north. At last we came to almost impenetrable undergrowth and no high trees and, after a final fight, we were in the Petersens' clearing and the Southern Cross hung low on the horizon in front of us.

Day was dawning when we reached home.

List of Authors

The stories in this book appear under the names of the authors as given on their books or in library records. This list adds the maiden names or married names of each along with their dates of birth and death, where known. In this way it is hoped those interested in reading further can make connexions with other pioneer records and families of the times.

ELEANOR ADAMS b. 1879(?)
JANE MARIA ATKINSON (née Richmond) 1824-1914
ISABELLA E. AYLMER
LADY MARY ANNE BARKER (née Stewart) 1831-1911
J.M. BUCHANAN
ELIZABETH PRINGLE CALDWELL (née Tait) 1820-1907
CAROLINE CHEVALIER (née Wilkie) d. 1918
ELIZABETH COLENSO (née Fairburn) 1821-1904
RHODA CARLETON COOTE (née Holmes) 1822-1892
SARAH AMELIA COURAGE (née Hopwood) 1845(?)-1901
JANE FINDLAYSON b. 1851
CHARLOTTE GODLEY (née Wynne) 1821-1907
BRIDGET GOODWIN (Little Biddy of the Buller) 1813?-1899
SARAH HARRIS
ELIZABETH HOLMAN (née Morris) 1824-1917
'HOPEFUL' Maggie Campbell (?)
LADY MARY ANN MARTIN (née Parker) d. 1884
SARAH LOUISA MATHEW (née Mathew) 1805-1890
MARIA MORRIS (Mrs. Tahuika)
CAROLINE NGOUNGOU (née Perrett) 1866-1943
AMY PATERSON (née Robinson) b. 1848(?)
ELIZA RACHEL JEAN STACK (née Jones) 1829-1919
MARY TAYLOR 1817-1893
ELLEN TAYLOR 1826-1851
CATHERINE HENRIETTA ELLIOT VALPY (Mrs. Fulton) 1829-1919
'WARATAH' W.S. Hindmarsh
MARIANNE WILLIAMS (née Coldham) 1784-1879
HELEN WILSON (née Ostler) 1870-1957

Sources of these Adventures

Here is a list of published sources from which material has been drawn. Manuscript material is listed further below:

AYLMER, Isabella, *Distant Homes, or, The Graham Family in New Zealand*, Griffin and Farran, London, 1862.

BARKER, Lady Mary Anne, *Station Life in New Zealand*, Macmillan, London, 1870.

BROOME, Lady Mary Anne, *Colonial Memories*, Smith, Elder & Co., London, 1904.

COURAGE, Sarah Amelia, *Lights and Shadows of Colonial Life*, Whitcombe and Tombs Ltd, Christchurch, 1897; second annotated edition, 1976.

GODLEY, Charlotte, *Letters from Early New Zealand by Charlotte Godley 1850-1853*, edited, with notes by John R. Godley, printed for private circulation only 1936; Canterbury Centennial Edition 1951, Whitcombe and Tombs Ltd, Christchurch, 1951.

'HOPEFUL', *Taken In; Being A Sketch of New Zealand Life*, W. H. Allen & Co, London, 1887.

MARTIN, Lady Mary Ann, *Our Maoris*, Society for Promoting Christian Knowledge, London, 1884.

'WARATAH', *Tales of the Golden West*, Whitcombe and Tombs Ltd, 1906.

WILSON, Helen, *My First Eighty Years*, Pauls Book Arcade, Hamilton, 1950.

WOODHOUSE, A. E. ed., *Tales of Pioneer Women*, Whitcombe and Tombs, Auckland, 1940.

The following authors are quoted from diaries, letters or reminiscences held by the Alexander Turnbull Library and reproduced with their permission. The item numbers refer to the Library's cataloguing system:

ELEANOR ADAMS: *The Milford Track*, MS PAPERS 3542.

JANE MARIA ATKINSON: Emily RICHMOND, *Family Letters of the Richmonds and Atkinsons 1824-1914 1824-1862*, qMS RIC.

ELIZABETH PRINGLE CALDWELL: WASHBOURN family, Papers 1850-1960's, MS PAPERS 1771; qMS CAL (typed transcript of Elizabeth Caldwell's reminiscences).

CAROLINE CHEVALIER: *Reminiscences of a journey across the South Island, 1866*, MS PAPERS 352; qMS CHE (typed transcript).

ELIZABETH COLENSO: *Diaries, letterbooks and notebooks, 1862-1895*, MS COL.

RHODA CARLETON COOTE: *Papers, 1853-1867*, MS PAPERS 1248.

JANE FINDLAYSON: *Diary 1876-1877*, MS PAPERS 1678.

SARAH HARRIS: *Letters 1841-1843*, MS PAPERS 3761.

ELIZABETH HOLMAN: *Reminiscences 1897*, MS PAPERS 3881; qMS HOL (typed transcript).

SARAH LOUISA MATHEW: *Extracts from 'Diary' (autobiography) of Mrs. Felton Mathew*, qMS MAT.

MARIA MORRIS: *Reminiscences, 1861-1869*, MS PAPERS 2296.

AMY PATERSON: *A contemporary account of the Tarawera eruption*, MS PAT.

ELIZA RACHEL JEAN STACK: *Jottings from my New Zealand journal, 1858*, MS STA.

MARY TAYLOR: *Letters from New Zealand*, 1848-1858, qMS TAY.

CATHERINE HENRIETTA ELLIOT VALPY: *Autobiography, 1915*, qMS VAL.

MARIANNE WILLIAMS: Henry WILLIAMS, *Extracts from the letters of the Revd. Henry Williams and his wife from their first setting out as missionaries to New Zealand in September 1822 to the end of 1824*, MS WIL.

Further Reading and Useful References

The books listed below contain accounts or references to pioneer life which proved useful in locating original material in archives. Some further books by the authors of this volume are also listed.

A New Earth: Pioneer Women of New Zealand, National Council of Women, Wellington, 1975.

BARKER, Lady Mary Anne, *Station Amusements*, Hunt, London, 1873.

DRUMMOND, Alison, *Married and Gone to New Zealand*, Paul's Book Arcade, Hamilton, 1960.

DRUMMOND, Alison, *At Home in New Zealand: an illustrated history of everyday things before 1865*, B. and J. Paul, Hamilton, 1967.

HARPER, Barbara, *Petticoat Pioneers Book Three*, A.H. and A.W. Reed, Wellington, 1980.

KEENE, Florence, *With Flags Flying*, The author, Whangarei, 1972.

MACDONALD, CHARLOTTE, *A Woman of Good Character*,

MACGREGOR, Miriam, *Petticoat Pioneers*, A.H. and A.W. Reed, Wellington, 1973.

MACGREGOR, Miriam, *Petticoat Pioneers Book Two*, A.H. and A.W. Reed, Wellington, 1975.

MANSON, Cecil and Celia, *Pioneer Parade*, Reed, Wellington, 1966.

MANSON, Cecil and Celia, *I Take Up My Pen*, Pigeon Press, Wellington, 1971.

MEADS, Diana; RAINER, Philip and SANDERSON, Kay, eds., *Women's Words*, Alexander Turnbull Library, 1988.

SARGESON, Patricia A., *Victoria's Furthest Daughters: A bibliography of published sources for the study of Women in New Zealand*, Alexander Turnbull Library with the New Zealand Founders Society, 1984.

SCHOLEFIELD, Guy H. ed., *The Richmond-Atkinson Papers*, Government Printer, Wellington, 1961.

TAYLOR, Mary, *Mary Taylor, Friend of Charlotte Bronte*, edited, with narrative, notes and appendices by Joan Stevens, Auckland University Press, 1972.

WASHBOURN, Enga, *Courage and Camp Ovens: Five Generations at Golden Bay*, Reed, Wellington, 1970.

WILSON, Helen; BARRER, Nina and SPURDLE, Flora, *Brave Days: Pioneer Women of New Zealand*, Reed for the Women's Division of New Zealand Farmers' Union, Dunedin, 1939

A Dictionary of New Zealand Biography in two volumes. Edited by G. H. Scholefield, New Zealand Department of Internal Affairs, Wellington, 1940